Escape

Escape

A TWIN BLISS
RESORT NOVEL

MARGARET ADETIMEHIN

For more information, kindly visit www.margaretadetimehin.com

Cover Illustration and Design by margaretadetimehin.com

Text Layout by margaretadetimehin.com

10 9 8 7 6 5 4 3 2 1

Dear Reader,

Onahi and Lola's story is one I've been wanting to write for the longest time! Something spicy. Something sex education(y). Two people meeting and having chemistry that makes them question their sanity. And there's a lot of sex-stuff in here, winks.

While editing their story, I was given the opportunity to go on my first vacation and on my returning flight; I knew I wanted to Escape, just like Lola, every other day, to somewhere new, doing something exciting and daring.

In this light, I hope you try something different from your norm and take calculated risks. Pamper and indulge yourself and, when possible, those around you.

Thanks a lot for reading Escape! If you are a new reader—new to my books—I hope this encourages you to read my other books and reach out to me via linktr.ee/camaa_pearlwrites. For the promotion of Escape, I did a lot of fun things you can find on margaretadetimehin.com/blog and @twinblissnovels on Instagram.

I am excited to share more sizzling stories in the upcoming Lagos Lovin' series and other collaborations, God willing. Till then keep reading and having a swell time!

XoXO

Margaret Adetimehin

Playlist

Dunnie—Foolish

Simi—Smile For Me

Korede Bello—Romantic

Rotimi—Love Somebody

Russell Dickerson—Yours

Johnny Drille—Romeo & Juliet

DJ Spinall, Fireboy DML—Sere

Shawn Mendes—Stitches

Ed Sheeran—Perfect

Kizz Daniel—Happy

DJ Cuppy—Werk

Jidenna—Bambi

For Wally, and all the girls who dream of traveling the world with the ones their heart beats for.

It's only a matter of time.

Prologue

Gobota Island, 847 AD

HEAT FROM THE WATER BURNT her eyes. Her baby wept, but there was nothing she could do. If only she had listened to Farai when she was pregnant, she wouldn't be going through this now.

"Add more Marula twigs!" She could make out the shape of the aged healer even with steam causing fog in her eyes. She had not wished this for herself, nor her newborn child.

Arriving the island in one piece and dragging her dead husband from the sea, after drifting for days on a log of wood when their shipwrecked and other things she experienced after living with this people should have made her more open to the tradition, but she never believed in magic, sorcery, or witchcraft. Even then, new to the environment, the people

had bathed her with an infusion of leaves and roots from the Marula, dressing her wounds with the leaves.

"It would chase the malevolent spirits from possessing or taking you with him." Those words had been an eye-opener. For she chose to live from then on, even though her beloved husband, who had dreamt of starting afresh in a new world, was gone.

Unlike most widows, she was in an unknown land with overly caring people, with riches she didn't know what to do with. She'd been happily welcomed into the home of the widowed Maame Farai whose daughter, Farai, was happily married with three sons. Farai tried matchmaking her with every eligible man in the village, but she never fell for it.

When Farai invited her to the farms to join the other women celebrating the planting season, they moved from house to house, dancing, singing, making shrill sounds.

"The Marula fruits help us chase the worms away from the field. This is how we thank the Marula tree for favoring us." Farai danced away, then returned with a tall smiling man, who made her blush—it had been a long time since she did.

Later that day, she sat under a Marula tree with other women of marriageable age and newly married ones, alongside an elderly woman, brewing beer for the celebration that week. Maame Farai had begged for her to be part of the women— she didn't understand why.

"Pass the calabash!" one would say, then the others would respond, "Drink! Drink! Ayeeee!"

She had gotten the calabash three times and had drunk from it three times. It was divine. Probably the only good

thing that would make her love the Marula, for she had tasted the green-yellow fruit and found it too tart for her liking.

The flesh between her legs was on fire. She wanted to rub it on something. The calabash was with another woman. The speed at which they were consuming it, she was of the mind there would be nothing left for the festival. Pain and pleasure shot through her system, she needed somewhere to lay down, someone to hold on to.

"What's in this drink?" she shouted at Farai.

Farai giggled, understanding what was happening to her. "You were here from start to finish. You saw everything."

She moaned, but other women were ignorant of what was happening as they sang and danced, although some were experiencing similar symptoms like her. "Just the Marula?"

Farai gave her a wide grin. "Yes."

"I feel funny." She clutched her legs together as mosquitoes from the night came to suck on her blood. She was too sensitive. She could hear everything happening louder than usual. Even her own heartbeat.

"You are ready then. Maame would be glad to hear all her pleading was not in vain."

"Ready for what? What is happening to me?" Her voice shook, scared of the unknown.

"You are under the shades of the Marula tree, you have drunk of her and she has heard your plea."

"What? I made no plea." Her eyes darted up angrily at the murmuring leaves.

Farai ignored her, jumped to her feet, and began dancing. "I can't wait to dance at your wedding."

"W-wait."

At the end of the week, she witnessed her first Annual Marula Festival. She drank more Marula beer in defiance to Farai's words. She enjoyed the drink and really didn't wish for a man in her life, as she was scared of going through loss again. She had also applied the light virgin Marula oil on her skin. She thought nothing about it when a younger woman asked if she was sure to use it. All she cared about was that it made her glow. There, she met a tall smiling man with whom she had deep conversations with. He gave her his Fire Water drink, which made her eyes water so much, she laughed it away with him. The Fire Water was a stronger version of the Marula beer she had drunk nights before.

Beneath the night sky, some distance away from the celebration she whispered, her eyes looking to the ground, "I like you."

"I like you too!" he confessed.

They stared at each other for a while, then began laughing until she got into a coughing fit. True to Farai's words, weeks later, she got married to the tall smiling man.

With him, she opened up about her wealth and they bought a massive portion of land for farming. They built their home in the center of it all and she looked forward to having her own children that would run through their fields.

Two great harvests passed, and she kept seeing her monthly blood.

"Eat the fruit." Maame Farai urged her, "If you want to have the children your heart so desire, eat them and give him a bottle of this," presenting her with a bottle of Marula beer she had personally kept after the recent great harvest, "when he returns."

The last time she ate the fruits was years ago and she didn't like their tart taste. But she had no other choice but to eat them. When she did this time, she realized it had a pleasant sweet-sour taste. Maame Farai's constant visit and plea finally paid off again, two months later, she was pregnant.

The Marula had done enough. She was tired of owing everything to it. When Farai visited few months before the birth of her baby, Farai begged her to drink the infusion from the bark of the male Marula tree.

"If you want a son, I can ask Maame to prepare it for you. Please... so you don't have to be washed on fire, heated by Marula twigs."

"Heated fire? Why would they do that?"

"Calm down. It is only done if the mother births a baby girl."

"Why?"

"So that the baby may be endued with fertility, softness, tenderness and early maturity."

"That is abominable!"

Farai's eyes darkened. "It is our tradition. It is what we know. It is what has kept us and our ancestors."

"I'll let fate decide for me. You are giving too much credit to a mere tree."

"It is not a mere tree; it is the Marula!" Farai needed to let her understand the power of the *mere tree*. "The Marula is the wild golden fruit of Africa—the one sacred tree, with nuts so rich, kings once fought for them. The fruits are so fertile." Farai looked at her pregnant tummy. "It is the marriage tree and the determiner of baby's sex!"

She shook her head in defiance. Farai wondered if wealth sometimes made some people stupid to the powers of nature and her gifts.

"I believe I will birth a son," she said. "If I don't," her eyes lit up with promise, "I would plant a special Marula tree at the entrance to my land."

Farai smiled. "I know how much you don't like this glory ascribed to Marula, and I hope you birth what you believe."

It was Farai herself that added more Marula twigs to the fire, smiling at the proud heiress.

PART ONE

One

Washington DC, USA

Lola

HEY BEAUTIFUL, COMING OUT OR should I come in?

I read the message notification on my phone's screen, then push it to the side, before smiling politely at my colleagues, giving my full attention to Robbie who is speaking.

Oh, snap! I forgot. I completely forgot *our plans*. More like his plan. I pick my phone that has been sitting idle on the table for hours, so the vibration doesn't distract miss goody two-shoes, Thelma.

Escape

I can't go out nor can he come in *here*, cause I'm at work, staring at my husband's face, wondering when we would go home together.

In my wildest dreams.

Thelma begins her explanation for why she chose her strategy. We're supposed to listen, take notes, and give feedback. I'm doing all three with a different approach. The doodle on my notepad looks remarkable—a cat made from number six and its multiples.

Coming out or should I come in?

It's Friday, I should be out for dinner. With Jackson, my date, hoisted on me by Carolanne, my housemate.

My phone vibrates. I glance at the screen—a message from Carolanne. And another one from her. Before I can read it, a new message from Jackson pops up. I give Thelma a wry smile, but she tightens her lips in response.

"Please carry on." I pick my phone. "I'm listening."

Jackson: Where are you beautiful?

I glance up from my phone to find Thelma giving me a stern look.

"Yes... so?" Robert, whom I fondly call Robbie, urges Thelma to continue. Robbie is my work bestie, my work husband, my friend. Ours is a simple but complicated relationship which I'll clarify in a bit.

To tell the truth, I've been looking forward to hooking up with Jackson for some time now. From our truncated chats, we have been able to find a balance and he has expressed his liking of me and his respect for my passion. And I guess I like him too. I guess. This date was supposed to help me place him on my relationship map, but here I am staring at Robbie, wondering why he hasn't hinted we move things further.

At 4:30 PM, I should have messaged Jackson that I would be late or not even make it, but... I have no excuse. When the opportunity to brainstorm with Robert and Thelma came on, I couldn't resist. Thelma is from another team, but occasionally, we collaborate on projects. I brought up an idea to help fast track my promotion, but I couldn't do it alone, so I brought Robbie on board, and... he brought Thelma.

My phone vibrates and I can no longer ignore the full-grown man who has done no wrong. "I'm sorry guys, I need to pick this."

"Please do." Thelma sighs, tapping away on her keyboard. "I'm suggesting we all take a break instead."

"Yeah, and return with fresh ideas," Robbie adds as he stands up, stretching his body—his torso wrapped in a checkered cotton shirt and legs, molded with jean trouser.

As I make my way out of the mini-conference room, Robbie holds my elbow and mutters, "Thanks a lot, for everything." Without waiting to hear my muttered 'it's no biggie', he turns to announce to Thelma, "Anyone needs coffee?"

"Tea please," Thelma smiles up at him and I have to force myself from shaking my head. Yuck. She needs to keep all that drool to herself. Leave my man alone.

My phone vibrates and I hurry out of the room, plugging my earbuds.

"Hello?" I ask pacing the hallway.

11

Escape

"Hey beautiful, how you doing?" Jackson's American accent cuts through the rap music playing in his background. "Was worried sick 'bout you. Why haven't you been responding to my messages?" I scrunch my nose as he blows air into the phone. "Had me thinking the worst. Tell me you're fine."

A wavering smile crosses my face. "I'm okay. You?"

"I'm good. Couldn't find parking close to your apartment so I'm circling your block." Living in Washington DC, parking spaces are like gold in residential areas, especially in the evenings. "Can't wait to see you all dolled up for me. Coming out anytime soon, beautiful?"

"That's the thing."

"Uhn?"

"I'm at work and—"

"Work?" he scoffs.

"Yep."

Robbie passes by me, mug of hot brew in hand, and mouths, *Sorry*, with a grin. Were I not on the phone trying to right a wrong, I would have punched him on the shoulder. "I should have called earlier to—"

"Carolanne says you're home and—Whatever. Stop playing. I can't seem to find a place to park..." his voice trails off.

I wince, waiting for the moment he believes me. "I'm at work Jackson."

"It's Friday, Lola." So, you know how to use my name. No more *beautiful*...

I bite my tongue from telling him, it's pronounced *Law-la,* not *Low-la.* He's got Nigerian parents but has never visited Nigeria. "I know. But we need to finalize on—"

"Fuck that!" I stop pacing, trying to figure out when we got to hundred, we were still on five. "You had me making my first dinner reservation at *Regals* and you're going to do this—"

"I'm sorry."

"To me?"

"So sorry. I didn't know we would be here till past six and from the looks of it, we might be here till God knows when." Not sorry you had to reserve a dinner date, but that I can't be there with you, eating the freshly baked bread. There's just something about the mini pieces of bread served in restaurants. Fluffy cute bread.

His loud breathing fills my speaker and I lean on the wall.

He sighs. "I'm sorry, beautiful." Not as sorry as I am. Heavy breathing comes from him, while I hold mine. "I shouldn't have lost it there. Know what? I'll call to mov—"

"Jackson... Jack?"

"Yeah?"

"Tonight is out of it. Why don't we do it some other time? Bills on me. Work is—I just had to work extra tonight." I squeeze my eyes shut, doing a five to one countdown. When he doesn't reply, I add, "I'm sure you understand." He traveled for business the first time we were to meet.

"Tomorrow?"

"I've got hair and nail appointment." Liar.

"So, what—"

13

"I'll let you know." You'll never know.

"That's fine."

"I'm sorry. So sorry."

"All's well beautiful." Glad you're calm about this now.

"Thanks a lot for understanding."

My bad. I should have called to cancel or tell him I would be late, but I guess everything works out for good. Spending extra time with Robbie... the opportunity of working late into the night with him—even though I have to deal with miss goody two-shoes, Thelma—is not something I'll give up for a first date. *Now I'm a bad picky person.*

Tapping my phone on my trousers, I resume pacing the hallway. I didn't ask or tell him to ask me out on a date. He had assumed Friday would be a good time to hang out, very thoughtful of him, but I didn't confirm or say yes.

I scroll through earlier messages from Carolanne.

Carolanne: Hot date and I didn't know?

Carolanne: Where are you? He's calling, I told him you'll be out in a minute.

Carolanne: Missy? What's up?

I shoot a message to her. **Sowie... Told him I'm at work.**

She responds immediately. **You should have checked in with me! Now he'll think I'm a liar.**

Ah-ah. I type back.

Lola: Is it far from the truth?

I can see her rolling her eyes, muttering how I just wasted this moment with a dream *spec* wherever she is, and this puts a gleam in my eyes. Jiving with Carolanne, with me having the upper hand is rare and always has me feeling light. I walk back into the mini-conference room with a steady and calmer gait.

My phone vibrates.

Carolanne: That's the thank you I get for trying to set you up. I tried reaching you before picking his call, but it's like once you're at that place, your mind completely disconnects from the world.

Now that hurts. Carolanne doesn't seem to understand that all I do, at least for now, is for us. I can't remember the last time she paid the bills—gas, electricity, and water. For a while now, she only pays her part of the rent and I allow this because she's looking for a better job and can't stretch her budget.

I juggle my day job here and my freelance job as The Brand Guru on social media, with plans of starting my own firm. Saving up funds... Working nights, late nights, to ensure paying bills is possible. And yet she's getting angry with me for *standing up* her prospective guy that would probably not propose to me or even offer to buy me a meal if it's not date night.

"Lola?" I glance at Robbie, pasting a smile on my face. *What did he ask me?* "Thoughts?"

"Uh?"

"We need to finalize the colors." He sits on the edge of the table, tapping a sharpie on his thigh. His hard strong thigh. *Focus!* "The sky blue or navy blue?"

"Hmm." Clearing my throat gives me enough time to gather the thoughts I had before seeing Jackson's messages. "A mix of both. The contrast would make it attractive."

Thelma loosely waves a pen at me. "We are already changing the shape of the logo, do we need to change the color too?"

"Yeah. We need to. It's what would make our project stand out. Men would buy into such."

After a brief silence followed by Thelma tapping away on her keyboard, Robbie says, "With what you're suggesting, we would need to collaborate with all internal teams to roll out the changes."

"Not just that," Thelma looks sharply at me. "How do you suppose we can pull this off with the budget we have on ground? You need to consider the cost. The implications."

"That's the interesting part," I beam. As smart as I believe Thelma is, I have to remind her of the loopholes in plans. Shoulders back and my fingertips forming a steeple on the table, I drop the good news. "We don't have a budget."

"Just yet," Robbie adds, dimming my news, just a little bit.

"Yes," I nod at him, "just yet. And this means we can show them what changing their brand icon can do."

"We are talking about the biggest portfolio the company holds. Are you sure you want us to pitch this?" She directs her question to Robbie.

"That's why I brought you in." A little smile plays on the corner of his lips. Robbie is a natural leader. Making everyone see the best in themselves. But if he thinks giving Thelma is the way to go around letting her see she can—

"We are going to need all the help we can get," Thelma mutters under her breath but it is loud enough that Robbie and I catch it.

"This is becoming a campaign," Thelma complains while Robbie returns to sitting and tapping away on his laptop.

"That's what I do." I smile.

Thelma sighs. "I understand your passion for this, but you need to calm down a little. Let's go one step at a time. We shouldn't be focusing on their logo and colors. Let's tweak their landing page instead."

"That's right." God knows their landing page needs complete overhauling.

Robbie looks up from his fevered typing. "But for us to do that, we need to settle on colors and also change the logo."

"Exactly! You always get me, Robbie." I bestow upon him a smile and turn to do the same to Thelma, which might be called a smirk, but she shakes her head at me.

Killjoy.

"If we share with them a quick project, it will cost thousands later to rebrand. After last year's presentation, their Global Communications Director kept hinting that their 50th anniversary needed something different." I quickly type into the shared document I see Robbie has populated. "And this my friend, is magically different."

"So, we focus on convincing the males, since they're more on the board," Robbie says.

"Yes... yes!" I grin at him. "Or... we can—"

"I'm tired," Thelma says in a firm voice.

Escape

"Of the ideas?"

"No. I think we should call it a night. We can think up fresh ideas next... Tuesday. We have more than enough to start with."

A nod from Robbie confirms we are going with miss goody two-shoes wish. I begin shutting down my laptop, gathering my notepad and pens. "I'll set up a poll on Twitter to see what people think of colors—"

"Isn't that giving too much away?" Thelma asks.

"I think it helps in idea generation. Directly from the target market." I zip my laptop bag, ready for escape.

"We haven't gotten the account yet." Her voice is not so firm anymore.

"Like I *said, idea* generation." If miss goody two-shoes doesn't understand that I gather and create splendid ideas from my social media engagement, I don't see any reason to explain to her.

From her jerky movements as she settles her iPad into her bag—bag big enough to fit a two-year-old—I know she has it up to her neck having me on this project. My project.

"Robert," I'm so glad she doesn't call him Robbie, "Please tell miss-know-it-all over there to calm down with all the ideas." She stops struggling with her bag and focuses on me, her eyes going back and forth between Robbie and I. "I get it she... You... have new ideas, but we need to get it organized and not just keep tossing them and posting on social media is so... unprofessional."

There, she said it. I am unprofessional.

And maybe she is correct. I couldn't even cancel on my date for this evening professionally. I stood a good man up.

"And we would," Robbie says to Thelma before looking at me, with a warm smile. "Lola, don't feel bad about what she's saying, I understand you're excited about this project of which I am too. Feel free to tell me everything on your mind and I would make sure that it manifests the same way you pictured it."

"Fine. Thanks Robbie. I'm not bothered, and I understand that I have skills and talents that some people wish they had." Oh snap. I didn't know I had said that out loud.

"Oh... let's not start Lola. Your table is always in a mess. You barely concentrate during meetings. You have everywhere in a mess! Maybe if you have the skill of arranging things after using them, get to meetings on time and concentrate —"

"That's enough." Robbie's voice is final. Thelma keeps quiet, her eyes fixed on me, but I choose to make this my own turn to share my thoughts on the matter.

"Thelma... I respect you. But I won't sit here and listen to you talk to me like that. I never forced you to join this." I point to the table. "You know the potential this project has. And I'm sorry if you don't like my organizational skills. I'm sorry. But I'm working on it. Please cut me some slack."

Robbie looks like his peacemaking skills are out of the window. Thelma fumes, her nose flaring. She tries speaking, but nothing comes forth. Then she spares Robbie a quick glance, before marching out of the room.

Great.

Escape

"I'll speak to her." Robbie rushes, "But please don't take it personal."

I watch as the love of my life runs after Thelma.

****

"WHY DIDN'T YOU TAKE THE trash out?" Carolanne asks as she rummages through the kitchen in our open space living room.

It's been less than three hours since she returned home from wherever she went to spend the night and she won't let me Netflix and chill in peace. Not like watching Sylvia tell Gbemi, Richard's wife, that she is real and exists is comforting but..."Is it smelling?"

The loud bang of the cupboard startles me. Watching *Sylvia* is spooky enough without Carolanne having to bang things. I hit pause, then turn to watch her arrange spices and the likes on the island. "It doesn't have to."

"Then what is it?"

Carolanne considers me worthy enough to be glanced at—she places both palms on the island, leaning into it as she makes her point. "It's easy and simple. It's just for you to tie the bag, pick it up, and walk out of the door, just out there," she points to the door, "and put it in the trash can."

I nod my head, as whatever she is trying to say doesn't make sense at all. She hisses and adds, "Because it is full."

"Ah-ah! I knew you were trying to make sense, but I just didn't know where you were coming from."

She turns and places a pot under running water. "It's not funny. You could at least have tied it, then insert another bag."

"My bad... I had other important things to do. And besides, I didn't even know it was full." I return to watching my movie.

"Other things like?" She finds a spot to sit on the couch and begins pressing her phone.

"Other things." In case she missed it, I tell her. "I'm watching a movie, and this is the revelation part."

She continues like I have said nothing. I feel her eyes on me. "Oh, other things like you not telling Robin—"

"Robbie." I instinctively correct her before thinking. Oh, snap. Here we go.

"Robin or Robbie, whatever his name is, that you are into him and can't wait to fast forward to when he pops the *marry me* question?"

I roll my eyes; I don't even want to get married soon. "How did this turn into the Robbie talk? I thought you were concerned about trash."

"Because what you did yesterday was trashy, and you know it." Her eyes hold mine, but I am the first to break our staring match. "And we both know it's because of Robin."

"Robbie."

"Whatever. Can we place a bet?"

"Not interested. What are you cooking?" I hit play and didn't see her advance until she snatches the remote from me. "What?" I sink into the cushion, staring up at her.

She gives a cocky smile. "Now that got your attention."

"You always had it, you just want to ruin my mood and I won't let you do it."

Ignoring me, she continues, "A bet. You tell Robbie you like him, and I'll never complain about the trash or whatever."

I size her up and her response is a shrug. Is she even supposed to use that as something to barter with? "That doesn't count because I pay most of the bills here."

"Okay, let me switch it up a notch. Tell him and I'll prepare your meal for the next two weeks."

Now that has my attention. Instead of spending time in the kitchen creating meals, I can have my own room- scratch that, house service. My own personal butler. I smile broadly at her. "Whatever I want?"

She crosses her arm, grins, and cocks her head to the side. "Don't push it but yeah, something like that." She says in a sing-song voice.

"You'll also join in helping me flesh out my business plan? Create my website? And... my laundry?"

"Hold it." She waves a hand at me. "Just because I want you to own up to your feelings doesn't mean I'm willing to sell my life to you. I've got things to do."

"You know it's your job to support me."

"Are you in or not?"

"I'm in. But I'll have to start taking food to work or something."

"Why?"

"Because Thelma does that and he's always like 'You're so thoughtful Thelma!' and I—"

"You think he likes food?"

"Which man doesn't?"

"Rubbish. You say he tells you your ideas are great."

"That's work, not... I don't know how to explain it."

"Good. Trash that thought and go as you are."

Easy to say. I've never asked a man out in my whole twenty-six years and I'm not about to start now. Kudos.

"Whatever you do, make sure you don't lose your job, and while you're at it, help me find a job."

Her phone beeps and she hiss.

"What?"

"Bills—Argh." She walks off to the kitchen. "I'll make popcorn."

"I thought you were going to cook."

"Not anymore. Wish I could order in."

"But?"

"Way out of my budget."

"You and your money issues. I have an idea. What if you become a baby mama for a rich guy?" I join her in the kitchen. "Like one of those rich guys you meet during your bartending gigs in those fancy houses and—"

"Nope. Not me. That would work for you. I don't have the looks or time or even know where to start..."

True. She is the exact opposite of herself in public. A complete wallflower. How she manages to hold a job as a freelance bartender working her way through school in computing courses is a complete combination of shock and surprise. I met her on a *Roommate* website as an international student from Nigeria two years ago and we clicked.

"That's true, how's your YouTube channel going?" she asks.

Nice one. Great tactic. Spin it off on me. About YouTube. That is an aspect in my dream world I am trying to create. I currently have close to three thousand subscribers that look up to me for lifestyle tips. Being this close to being monetized, it's like everything I post doesn't make sense. My views have been dropping and it's a crazy algorithm system. I do well helping small businesses on Twitter and Instagram, but for my YouTube brand, it's like it doesn't want to gel.

"I need new content. I'm thinking of switching it up. But I don't know what to do."

"You could film your new romance with Robbin," she chuckles.

I roll my eyes. "Yeah right. Lola to the world. Brand manager and YouTube relationship brouhaha. Perfect. I want to do travel but... it's still a thought. The blog is going strong though."

She laughs. "I also want to do travel but the cost alone. Let's just stick to your lifestyle tips."

"Yeah. Speaking of YouTube and lifestyle content, why don't you prepare jollof rice while I film you?"

Two

Twin Bliss Resort, Gobota

Onahi

TWENTY-SEVEN. BREATHE. TWENTY-EIGHT. Breathe. Twenty-nine. Breathe. Thirty. Fuck!

And it's a wrap, my fifteenth rep of lying leg curls got my hamstrings burning.

As gently as I can, without showing how tired my knees are, I move off the machine and sit on the edge of its bench. My breath comes in short successions and moisture begins to build on my exposed legs and arms.

Escape

Passing a fleeting gaze across the general gym, my mind takes note of how things are running smoothly. The clank of metal hitting metal, the deep breaths of encouragement and determination from other guests with fitness goals mirror my short breath.

My knees will be aching this time tomorrow, but it will be worth it. Leg days are dreadful, but I survive. I'm not a fitness enthusiast, but I believe in keeping my body and mind active which is why I am currently at Twin Bliss, instead of anywhere in the world.

Okay to be sincere, I am not here because I want to, but because I need to. To get my mind off what's eating at me. I keep telling myself it's not the end of the world—although it hurts to see a plan, a goal, a... whatever! A concept of something so promising, go down the drain.

How can you be so dense Nahi? Why didn't you see that coming?

The plans and thoughts we had together blinded me from seeing what was really happening. How is it possible that someone whom you have complete trust in, who knew your next steps, who claimed to understand why everything needs to be the way they are, allowed control be taken away from them and you never noticed on time?

I probably could have saved us, but it's all a matter of ifs and probablys.

No, I don't think so. I—I I'm so confused about what exactly is happening. I'm not putting my mind into it again. From now on I am just going to focus on myself and other important things. Other important things that would get my mind off my recent visitor who made me storm the gym two hours ago.

I pick up my water bottle, phone, and towel, then place my towel on my head to avoid unwanted glances and begin a lazy jog back to my villa. It's peak season and the guests keep trooping in. People, especially ladies have the habit of staring at me, especially when I'm dressed in gym wear—this I've noticed in my two-day stay here. Usually, I exercise at home in my private gym in San Francisco, and whenever I'm in Lagos, Nigeria—same thing.

Home.

Glancing at my phone's screen, like a quick reminder of why I'm here instead of San Francisco, I see my sister's missed call. My sister worries, the other one too. One acts like she doesn't care, while the other shows she cares a lot, me? I'm the sweet spot in-between. It's funny how two people come out from one womb within minutes of each other and display contrasting personalities.

A resort shuttle passes by, bearing new besotted guests and I smile, proud of what my heritage has accomplished with Twin Bliss. I recall my twin sisters and I giving guests tours and telling wild tales that were passed down to us to make money during summer break. Those moments were golden—I made friends and found new terrains to explore during that period.

Now, finding something to get my mind off this unnecessary festering wound that's causing nothing but pain and anguish is the new cool. I should probably invite friends over.

Escape

Fuck! A fool. That's what Anthony wants to make of me. My mind wants to rehash his visit, but I don't want to. He thought I needed clarification, an explanation of sorts. Fuck him and his explanation. My avoiding calls should have spoken volumes but for him to track me down till he found me here... Shit. I was staying away from their lying and deceptive asses but still, they found a way to get to me.

I almost make it to my Villa without going back in time, but my mind is still reeling from the audacity.

"Onahi, I'm sorry," Anthony said, standing with feet spread out, in my spacious office space in the resort's admin building. "But as a friend... your best friend, if I can still—"

"Hey, hey it's enough." My voice curt and direct as I raise my palm to stop him from whatever bullshit he was about to spill out. Best friend? Friend? He never deserved those titles.

I have friends. A lot of them. But they never could keep track of my going and coming. For him, I gave him full access to my life. It's surprising what giving people access to your life can make them do.

Leaning forward, taking deep breaths, I address the elephant in the room in a tight voice. "That I have actually kept my calm, my cool, about what you did, about everything... that should say a lot. But for you, you Anthony, to come in here, feeling like you're clean, clear, and justified for the actions you took—"

"I didn't—"

"I'm not done talking." I didn't offer him a seat when he knocked earlier, and he had the sense not to come any further. I blame Salewa, my interim personal assistant who is eager to please me for letting him get through my door. Doesn't mean I will free her of her duties, but she needs to understand boundaries.

"For all it's worth, I'm sorry." He had the effrontery to look away from me, biting his lips, looking at the stretch of water outside the walls, before returning his gaze back at me.

Stretching my feet forward, I relax on my chair, a hand to my jaw, "You know what? Let's cut all the bullshit." His eyes grew wide. "Why are you here?"

After waiting for several moments, I hiss.

"Tsk, tsk. See Tony." I stand up from my chair and move towards him, his gaze stays on me, calm and unflinching because he knows I won't bite. At least not this time. "I told you things. Things that happened in my relationship, not because I wanted you to put your hands into it and," I toss my hand in the air, a malicious grin on my face, "solve my problems. No. Not that Tony." I stop in front of him, towering slightly above him, arms folded. "But look," I smile, leaning into him, before carrying on in a whisper, "You did that and even made it worse." I end, leaning back, swinging on my heels.

Tony lets out a whooshing breath, his eyes, avoiding contact, and when they do, he says, "I'm so sorry, you know this."

"I know." Blessing him with a sinister smile. "That's why you are standing here." I turn back, walking all the way to my desk. Thoughts of how he made my life completely change in an instant befuddle my senses. I wish I could turn back the hands of time and he could undo everything he did. Besides his meddling in my relationship, for the time he was, he was a great friend.

"You didn't have to do this." I sigh as I sit on the edge of my desk, looking out into the large expanse of crystal blue water.

"But you never had it together..." His voice came in a soft whisper, "I had to help."

"And the help you gave, did it solve the problems? Or make matters worse? Destroying a seven-year friendship?"

"Nahi..." His voice seems closer.

Staring at the gentle ocean settles my troubled mind. It's never going to be the same. The clarity of the whole situation makes me know this, which he has not come to realize. "I know what we did was wrong and it's breaking her. If you would just—"

"I would not take your scraps." There's ice and determination in my voice. "Not in this lifetime. Not in the next. And not ever." I turn my head to face him, my true emotion setting ice over the room. He nods as our eyes meet, before shuffling his feet. He knows his time is up.

Getting up from my desk, I go around the table and let the chair swallow me. I busy myself with tidying my desk. "If you know you still have a bit of that friendship you think you have for me, kindly leave now."

"Nahi, it doesn't have to be like this." My head turns in fast motion to the sound of his voice. The audacity. His voice is pleading but it's a done deal. He made the rules. "You both can work this out. I know what you want her to do—"

"It was never her. It was you. You Anthony. You encouraged my fiancée to call you whenever I'm unavailable. You told her, in front of me, that I am emotionally unavailable, and I smiled, but I never knew you were the therapist...the therapist who would go on to getting her think I am controlling her life and need to—Fuck!" Taking deep controlled breaths, I hold on to the edge of my table. "If you were my friend, you would never have played good cop bad cop in the first place."

"You're just so transactional!" He spits.

Haha. His true emotions are surfacing, and I don't give a damn. What he really wanted to say was how transactional I am. How I make all my relationships count for something and ensure I steer it in a direction that benefits at least one portion of the party. It's a trait I have that has made me who I am today.

"And that's why you remain a poor deadbeat who knows nothing about opportunities and people and the only time he realizes he can make good use of it is when he brainwashes his best friend's fiancée. That's the difference between both of us—I know how to maximize opportunities and bring out the best in people in a way that works for good and not the opposite."

"And you think you can just discard people when they are no longer useful?"

"I did nothing of such."

"She's willing to—"

"You both made a choice!" Taking a deep breath, I spill everything in my guts, my fingers pointing at him. "Tony, enough with the self-righteous indignation. You were just a means to an end, just that you didn't turn out the way I thought you would. You thought I would never find out? Or did you think I didn't know how low you could go? Just get out of here, and I mean TB resort before we fuck this up more than it already is."

The thing with Anthony earlier today was not my best side. I guess I'm still grieving what he did and had to lash out at him since he made himself available. It felt good because I have been avoiding them, but that doesn't mean I want to do it again.

All I want to do is get my mind off the unfolding boring drama called my life. I'm sure my African heritage would be excited. My story can feature in some unrealistic TV show titled, The Aromantic Fiancé.

As I step into my villa, my thoughts have moved on to taking a shower and visiting the casino or club later in the evening. Something to take my mind off things. It's been a while since I let loose. That's the reason I came here, to let go and start afresh. To keep my body and mind active. To have a good time.

Chill. Relax, and think of something else to do while I allow this tidal wave go over.

****

"CAN YOU PLEASE CHECK THAT stuff? It keeps beeping." My female companion whom I met last night hisses, before burrowing deep into the covers. "So annoying."

"I've got it." Before I get off the bed, I pick my briefs from the floor and quickly shove them on as I get off the bed.

Briefs on, I stride towards my workspace, avoiding the condoms on the floor. What the fuck did the bartender add to my drink? My tongue tastes like paper. A glass of water would do magic for me right now. What was I thinking going with what the bartender had specially created for those who dared last night? The curtains billowing from the other side of the room distract me and I redirect my step to sliding shut the glass doors.

Last night was crazy.

I stare at the woman on the bed whose first and last name I can't remember. The one whom I indulged in trying out seventy-seven plus sexual positions last night at her request. I grin, all thoughts of finding out what was in my drink from last night vanishing as my dick starts coming alive.

My computer dings again, and I hasten to turn it off. When I left for the club last night, I apparently left the machine running. It was as though demons chased me out of my villa as my mind kept returning to Anthony's betrayal.

The screen before me shows my search history into a company I am interested in funding. Another ding and a new email pops. I am about to shut down the system to focus on the beauty on my bed when another email follows the previous one and it's on the thread that has been going back and forth between the board of directors and the CEO of Twin Bliss Resort.

It's none of my business how the Resort is being run, all I should focus on should be my returns but as I begin closing tabs, I mistakenly click the next email open. The word

EMBEZZLE catches my attention and I sit on my chair immediately. A morning romp between the sheets or on the patio overlooking the tumultuous ocean can wait.

Using both hands, I lazily rub sleep from my eyes, before taking a deep breath. I can't believe these people don't know how to handle things themselves. Shaking my head, I dig deeper into the emails.

I have been ignoring the back and forth and for them to add me to the mail thread, it must be important. Or a mistake. In summary, it's obvious the resort needs someone to come in and take charge.

I read through the email thread some more. How did they expect this not to turn ugly?

The CEO, Alberto, has been going about the need for change in some stuff or have an investigation carried out but the board is not having it. There are some things outside Alberto's power as a CEO and I understand his frustration at this limitation but the old businessmen on the board of directors—who are more of my uncles and some distant relatives—have good reason to limit the power of CEO.

Really, I shouldn't be concerning myself with this, probably stay aware of what is happening as a major stakeholder, but this looks intriguing, seeing that Alberto is warning the board of directors of imminent embezzlement.

The sheets ruffle behind me. "Baby? Won't you come back to bed?"

My mind goes blank, then slowly comes to. Baby? We only just met last night. Just last night. We had a couple of drinks and did a couple of shots. Nothing much to know about each other. All that was on my mind was to get my mind off the demons eating at me and then she came along. She with her blonde hair and blue eyes. I was already drinking before she came along, getting all friendly and touchy.

To test the waters and her intentions, I asked, "Want to see where I stay?"

"You look like a resort resident." She giggled.

"I am. So?"

"If you were asking if I wanted to get naked with you?" Her eyes roamed my body in beach shorts and a polo shirt, before licking her lower lips. "Yes."

I grin. "I'll request a shuttle."

"Let's not waste time then. More shots before it arrives."

And now I'm her baby? What people make of relationships, glorifying it like it's something sacred. Giving names and titles... Messed up. And no. I'm not from a broken home or that kind of shit. I am from a happy home. My parents love each other, which I want for myself, but with what I've seen and experienced, I don't think I'm cut out for the feathery stuff.

"Baby?"

"Yeah?" I swivel my chair to face the blonde siren on my bed, covered in rumpled sheets.

"Come on... It's cold, come to bed."

"I closed the doors, and turned on the heat a notch, it should get warm shortly. And work is happening. I'm sorry." I turn my chair back to the screen.

Maybe instead of researching the next company that's seeking funding from me, I could actually start looking into this issue at Twin Bliss. I've got about three more weeks according to my calendar to spend here.

"Work?" She whined and from my side view, I can see her sitting up, her head on the headboard as she holds the cover to her chest. "This is a place for people to relax, remember? How come your room has a workspace?"

It comes with the perks of being more than a guest, I'm tempted to say, but I hold my tongue. We aren't anything yet and this... This is another reason why I'm not getting into a relationship anytime soon. Too many questions.

"If you know the right people to ask, you might get it."

She scoffs, "You think I don't know who you are?"

The hair at the back of my neck rises and I turn to face her, eyebrows raised.

She smiles and it is blinding, the sun rising outside has nothing on the brightness of her smile and my heart skips a beat.

What the fuck?

"Hush Prince Ali... I've got your secret covered."

I let out a huge breath, a grin replacing my furrowed brows. "It was never a secret." Or was it?

"Just come back to bed soon, okay?" She bites the bottom of her lips, and her name comes to me. Heather.

She had said her name was Heather from Boston.

I smile at her. Something passed between us and my title of being aromantic might be changing soon as Heather is making me aware of some things my body could do. Like my heart beating faster and me getting scared she might have followed me to my villa as a gold digger.

I never cared before.

But...

"How about you help me with maybe a bottle of water or juice from the fridge? Something to revitalize my energy."

She clears her throat and flops back on the bed, smiling coyishly. "Give me a minute, Prince Ali, I need to sniff your aura, so it can support my journey to getting your supplement."

True to her word, I watch as she sniffs the pillow I laid on minutes ago, before picking her phone from the foot of the bed.

Voodoo shit.

Chuckling, I rub my hand on the back of my neck and turn to face the screen. "I think low-key, you're a nutcase."

Her gasp has me turning my head back to her. "Oh my gosh." She's off the bed, scrambling around for her stuff. "I'm sorry baby, I need to get out of here right now. I have an urgent situation—Needs my attention—Last night was great." She runs to me and lands a promising kiss of things to come on my lips.

"What's—"

She moves like lightning and is already at the door. "See you around and take care!"

37

Escape

"Okay..." I say to an empty room.

What had her running out like that? It's kind of fishy but I trust she'll find a way to locate me if she wants to. I chuckle. She knows who I am, hell, all she needs to do is go to the admin building and ask the right questions.

Ding.

Another message.

I swivel back to my screen. It's no biggie. At least I can worry about real problems without questioning my feelings for a one-night stand.

Several minutes pass and I have no map for the next steps to take. It is something that has to do with the global marketing and accounting team heads. I can't seem to wrap my head around it because the more I stare at the mail threads and documents, the more confusing it gets. I don't know why the board doesn't want to call a meeting. Reaching out to a cousin who's on the board for more insight could be the way forward, but I don't want to answer questions about my fiancée or what is happening with my personal life.

Be that as it may, I'm taking on this project as my new pet. It's a perfect way to get my mind off the current demons chasing me. I am good at what I do and there are more important things to do, than working on things that I have no control over. A vivid example is of people who have no respect whatsoever for boundaries and friendships.

Getting an external eye on this whole potential embezzlement drama might be the best option. Alberto is a good guy; I'll give him that—he has been making the resort look and be better. But well, he's finding it hard to manage this issue on ground and external help should make him focus on making the resort better. No matter how good everything in life is, there's always room to make it better. Everything, even people, always needs fixing.

Definitely making the resort my pet project this vacation.

I shoot an email to Alberto, the CEO, and two other friends, before picking up my phone to order breakfast on the Twin Bliss resort app.

Three

Lola

"CAN'T WAIT TO HAVE THIS done and move on to the next big thingy." It's TGIF and we're hanging out on a rooftop restaurant, waiting for our orders to come out—Robbie's treat after our show down earlier in the week. One of Robbie's features is that he's great at planning. Something I need in my life.

"Oh really..." Thelma picks her glass of iced water and her tongue darts in search of the straw she had specially ordered. Madame doesn't like drinking from public cups—germs and bacteria sharing with strange individuals were not her thing.

"Yeah." I shrug, taking note of a group of smiling professionals getting settled in the bar area. Where we're seated is adjacent to the bar area, with an umbrella shading us from the setting sun. The rate at which this heat keeps smoldering one, to the extent that the loose lightweight jumpsuit I'm putting on is becoming uncomfortable, has me thinking of going somewhere with pools or beaches. Yeah. A beach. Somewhere like Florida for a weekend. Refresh myself and return. But going alone would be boring.

Going with Carolanne is not an option. I like spending time with her, but when I think of beaches these days, with all the Instagram pictures I see on my feed, it's either I go alone or go with bae.

I glance at Robbie, and he is reading something on his phone. Trust him to turn this into another meeting and not a true TGIF.

"Phones please." I tap the table, a big grin on my face.

"You must be kidding me." Thelma turns her attention to me, her brows raised.

"If we took the effort to leave the office to spend time together, we might as well enjoy each other's company."

Robbie swipes his manicured fingers on his phone screen. "One moment, please."

"Waoh." Thelma's eyes follow the server as she arranges our meal on the table, but her next words are for me. "I'll never believe that came from you if I was not here."

"Things happen." A thin smile stretches on my lips, which Robbie notices because he nudges my feet under the table.

Escape

"Wait." I spread an arm across the table in my attempt to stop them from devouring their meal. "I'm sorry." I should have been more subtle.

If looks could kill, Thelma's eyes would have butchered me in pieces.

"So sorry. I just need to take pictures; this meal looks artistic."

"Seriously? Why don't you just take a picture of yours?"

"Nope..." Although we're not the best of buddies, having a picture of her with her mouth wide open as she chews is not something I want to have on my phone.

"Please make it snappy before it gets cold."

She didn't complain or die when the food had not arrived. Such a drama queen. I begin taking pictures, snapping from different angles.

"I get it you don't visit this place often but at least act like you do." Thelma muttered under her breath.

Pausing between what I will term my last shot, if she hadn't spoken. I go for her. "Whether I visit this place regularly or not does not stop the fact that I can take nice pictures wherever, whenever and however I want to." Robbie's feet nudges again. What's his problem? "And it's for my lifestyle blog."

When we were deciding what and where to eat, Lady Thelma opposed going to a restaurant. She didn't want us spending extra money when we could decide to eat at her place. I don't know why she doesn't like living a little. Afterall, it's not every day we eat at restaurants. Now she wants to spoil my shine.

The pictures I took captured the essence of our meal—the steam and variety of colors. When we finally get to eating, the taste of onions explodes in my mouth while the velvety texture of pasta mixed with extra cheese grinds smoothly as I chew them to pieces. I had to add extra hot sauce in my meal because I just had to. My mom's meals have been spicy ever since I can recollect and whenever we travel to Nigeria, it's even way spicier. I miss the bread too. Next to bread, I would eat pasta every other day. Not just anyhow bread, but Agege bread, the ones sold in African stores. This meal needs more salt.

"So...." Thelma begins between bites. "What are the things you'd likely do once we have this project closed?" She has been extraordinarily nice recently.

"There are so many things to do." Stretching to pick the saltshaker in front of Robbie who is now studying the environment more, I shake enough salt to get my taste bud going, then take a bite.

"Hmm... What would you like to do... Like something for fun."

Am I missing something here? Thelma is trying to get to know me or what? Sparing a glance at Robbie who has been notoriously quiet since we got here, I feel outnumbered. He is smiling... is he glad Thelma is making civil discussion outside work? Was this the aim of this outing?

"I'm asking because you're always working—I mean we always discuss work. Something outside work."

Is this good vibe or what? Is this I'm no longer threatened by your ambitions, vibe, or something? Something or someone is making her hold a nice conversation with me. A new dick she complains about me to has advised her to play nice? I catch myself in time before I laugh out loud and smile nicely instead.

I play with a purplish vegetable, before giving it the honor of entering my mouth. "I'll definitely be breathing fresh air. Maybe go to Florida for a weekend. Try nice restaurants like this and vlog my experience."

Actually, left to me, if I make my moves soon, I'll be on a trip with Robbie to somewhere in maybe the Bahamas. Somewhere far away from miss goody two-shoes who knows everything and apparently nothing; except for cooking nice meals and treats. Treats Robbie lusts after.

She doesn't look me in the eyes when she asks, "Speaking of blogs, how's your blog going?"

Oh snap!

Can this lady just allow us to eat in silence and not bring up sensitive talk?

"It's going well. Just need more content to post. You know, these days, I spend time trying to create content for...us."

Oh... my blog that brought me brand deals before I clocked eighteen. Nothing serious or big, but enough to make me realize my passion for branding. I am the queen of branding in Nigeria but based in the US.

Thelma left for home from the restaurant, but I headed to the office with Robbie to get my phone charger. I should upgrade my phone, but it was never part of this year's budget. I know myself though, once I get tired of my battery draining before I even get it charged, I'll walk into the closest phone store and get a new phone, charger, and all.

"Good night Robbie!" Passing his open office, on my way to the elevator.

"Goo-what the?"

Tilting my head into his office space, I tap on his door. His dark brows are furrowed as he scrolls through his laptop.

"Knock, knock. You okay?"

"Hey Lola. Sorry about that." He leans back on his seat, grinning.

What's happening here?

I look down the deserted hallway, almost everyone has retired for the weekend, then proceed cautiously into his office. "I'm coming in...."

"You're always welcome here."

"I know. What's happening?" Placing my bag on his table, I sit my ass to his left side, nothing suggestive, just two work buddies having late night convos. "What was the fuss about?" I smile, tilting my head to the right, studying him.

Robbie covers his mouth with one hand, stares at me, then takes the hand off. The smile that follows has my ovaries working overtime but I'm a big girl, I got this.

"I just got a message from an old friend." His twinkling eyes went back to his laptop screen.

Never have I seen him so excited and at loss for words. "Care to share?"

He shrugs, looking back at me. "Nothing serious." His head shaking tells me otherwise. "We attended an event a while ago and he was fun. Didn't even know he would remember my name or email."

"Small world uhn?"

"Small world." He shakes his head again. "It wasn't anything fancy. I helped him with his project...something like that he was working on." He bites his pink lips, then drums his desk. "Now he wants me to come over to spend some time at this resort, all expense on him."

Resort?

Talk about dreams coming true. Could it be the Bahamas?

"What!" I tap his shoulder, my eyes round with surprise. "Here I am thinking of friends with pools and you have someone inviting you to a resort. All-expense paid. Robbie!"

"Slow down Lola. It's not like that."

"I don't care. I'm not the one with friends that invite them to resorts, all-expense paid." Who knows the kind of resort and where it is located. Probably some run-down stuff in Hawaii or someplace like that.

He scoffs, "You really need a vacation."

"I'm telling you." I want to turn his laptop to confirm the name of the resort and if the offer is open to two people. If I can convince him to go, maybe we go along and I can pop my offer as Carolanne suggested and..."What's the name of this resort?"

"Twin Bliss Resort, Gobota Island." He smiles, covering his mouth with both hands as he processes the offer.

"Hmm...You've got friends! Robbie, show me the way..."

"Me?"

"Uh-un. Can I see?" Yep. I need to see for myself what the fuss is all about.

He turns his desktop screen and I stare in wonder at the modern futuristic design mixed with a dose of mother Africa. The blue waters call out to me and their tagline reads, *'Come getaway from life's hassles.'* It doesn't look like Hawaii, but it looks like a ton of money. I swallow as I take in the beauty.

Thank you, Jesus. This came at the right time. Once this project is underway, Robbie and I can look into this together. Pending if it's still valid.

"Where is Gobota Island?" Lol. What the heck is Gobota?

He chuckles, "No idea. Doesn't sound like a real place."

"Heck. It looks unreal." What have I been thinking? I bring out my phone and do a quick Google search to find that it's somewhere in Eastern Africa. It's been around for a while and one-night costs over two thousand dollars, inclusive of other services. "Urm...it does exist and it's like one of the special and most expensive undiscovered resorts in the world."

Robbie has moved on to other things. He's checking something else in his mail while I rattle on about the wonders I keep discovering in my search.

"Are you kidding me?" I scroll through the available amenities and activities—dinning under the stars, cycling across town, snorkeling and other grouped activities. "I haven't heard about this place dude. Who on earth handles their marketing? I live for good expensive stuff and I haven't heard of this?" All shades of my professionalism gone since work is over, Thelma is gone and Robbie is back to being *my* friend.

Urm...actually, I am rebranding my online image. I used to post content on affordable things to do, DIY and all, but now..... This girl is coming in hot! I'm signing deals with top brands. Hot brands! Expensive shit! And visiting a resort like this will be a great way to kick it off. If Robbie has me as his girlfriend or something, it will definitely boost views. Oh... Carolanne is rubbing off on me. But vlogging my relationship with Robbie isn't such a bad idea. This could be our first official date. Hashtag interracial couple.

"You should roll more within my circle. You know... be intentional with friends."

"Whatever. At least I'm not the guy who chases after the girl who brings food to him every other day. Tell me if that's friendship."

"Is someone jealous?"

Me? Jealous? For what I already have? "Hell no. You and I have history no amount of food can take away."

"Good. I like that we're clear on that. You know you're my day one."

"How did we go from discussing the world's best hidden secret to discussing Thelma?"

He looks at his screen then sighs. "I can't accept this offer."

"Why?" I will like to pursue the Thelma discussion, but him rejecting this resort offer is impossible. Not on my watch.

"We have this thing going on for us. Your promotion and that of Thelma's to handle a new team is also tied to this project. Leaving everything and going for a vacation is off the table right now."

"I see. I get you." I wasn't thinking of work when he showed me that stuff. See why Robbie and I blend perfectly? He's my opposite. The balance I need.

"And this offer is fishy. Rich people that aren't your close pals will not just randomly ask you to come around. We've not communicated in years. I wish I had the time to find out why, but I'll prefer sleeping dogs to continue snoring. Once we're done initiating this project, sure thing."

"You get it. See why I love working with you? You're so dedicated." I place my hand on his and he tightens his hold on mine. "I need to read up on this though." I wave my phone in his face. "I'll make it my weekend getaway. If I can't go there just yet, I'll study more about it."

He raises his brow, and I extract my hand from his.

Picking myself and my bag off his table, I add, "I saw some articles on the myths and legend tied to the place. It makes it kind of unique... and mysterious. But I think it's all part of the marketing and package that comes with... you know... having money to afford such an expensive place. I want to understand the allure. What he sent to you is different from what's online."

"I could send you the email if you're interested."

"Please forward the email. I was thinking of a spot to vacation and... I'll just check it out. It looks... interesting. The type of place I would like to visit for... influencer purposes."

"Lola the Brand Guru!"

Escape

Giving him my signature lip-zipping wink, I sashay out of his office.

Four

Onahi

I THOUGHT THEY KNEW AND understood me. This is the fourth time the same number is calling today and I am tempted to pick and curse, but I won't let it get there. The option of turning off my phone is becoming juicier.

I'm not trying to run away from my reality, no, I'm not. In fact, I'm acting more responsible than I have been in the past two years by getting interested in the resorts' activities. Now is not just the right time. I bet there will never be a right time to pick that call.

Why can't they just leave me alone?

The phone stops ringing.

Escape

It rings again and I ignore it, focusing on my computer screen. Heather's image flashes in my mind's eye. "I need to get all this aggression off my chest."

True to her word two days ago, she returned and has been returning ever since. We have this unspoken agreement of not asking too much, but just enjoying each other's company at night in my villa.

An email pops on my screen and it's from Alberto, the CEO.

> ...with my position as the CEO, I believe this is affecting the internal team and will later affect external communications. My hands are tied but need your permission to move this decision forward.

I thought this matter had cooled down, but from the look of things, this is only the beginning. The members of the board are so old that it's hard to get anything across. Left to me, I'll take out some old heads and replace them with fresh heads. We need fresh eyes on and for the resort.

Speaking to my cousins to follow through with re-organizing the board might take a while. As forward thinking as most Akachis are, some Akachis pride themselves in doing things the old-fashioned way. I love old fashioned things, not their ways.

With Alberto struggling to get the board to understand his stance and myself having nothing serious doing, having the ball rolling for future change sounds intriguing. I wanted to start this before, but this thing with Heather takes my energy and I spend my days reading and researching the next company I want to buy.

This is what I should be doing. Living a life of leisure. Dousing out fires people created themselves. My ancestors went through all the stress for me not to. Restless, I scroll through Instagram. An image of Lucas Opeyemi fills my screen and it details his latest accomplishment.

He is yet to respond to an email I sent earlier, so I call him before my surprise gift to him and his wife becomes a no-show surprise gift to me. We haven't spoken in years, but our friendship was neither here nor there. Fun guy with great acting skills. Nollywood's best.

"Do I need a bird to deliver my message to you?"

"The money bag himself," Lucas laughs.

I snort. "Have you checked your email recently?"

"You should know I am not glued to my phone, I hardly even check my mails."

"With your status, don't you know how important emails are?"

"Man, you are not the boss of me."

I shake my head at that.

"Remind me who the celebrity is again?"

I smile. "Anyways man. I sent you an anniversary package. Check your email for full details."'

"Hmm... is this a peace offering? Are you trying to make me forgive you for not keeping in touch?"

"You're the one always busy and you know, I've got to keep things running. Been seeing the news and wanted you and your woman to come on a holiday. I've been here for a while, and it would be a great opportunity to catch up."

He tries to pry information about the women on the resort, but I hang up. He's as dramatic as they come. I've done my part for romance, and I hope his wife, Barbara enjoys her stay here.

My phone rings and without thinking, I pick.

"Are you still there?" Eni—short for Ahieni—my sister. And by there, she means the resort.

"Hey sis, what's up? How you doing?"

"Stop acting nice. It doesn't fit you."

A guffaw burst from my chest. "What do you want?"

"Nothing."

"Hmm..."

"Have you spoken with her?"

"No."

"Perfect. She doesn't deserve you. None of them do. They don't deserve us."

Oh Lord. Eni, and her dramatics.

"Anyways, I just want to let you know that I got the money. And I believe this is going to work."

"You see, I told you."

"Hey... it worked doesn't mean that you're always right."

"Not everyone has a big brother to help them make their problems go away."

"Big brother? Nahi, give me a break."

"I bought out your shares to absolve you of all family duties, so you can travel the world and start up your beloved foundation for child brides in West Africa."

"And in the same breath, giving you over 70% of Lurane Capital Group's portfolio and over 50% of the Twin Bliss Resort's shares. Thank you brada. Thanks for your kind acts."

It's actually it's almost 50% of Twin Bliss Resort's shares as I do not have hers locked to me. But I can easily sway her to my side when it's time for meetings "But who is free from family duty now?"

"Like I said, thank you."

Ahieni is weird. I'm her brother and the only one allowed to say this. Last year, she got out of her four-year long relationship and started attending a group. More like a cult. There, she got this vision that she was living a life of gluttony and selfishness.

She later confided in me that she was going to sell her shares to the highest bidder so she could live a selfless life and I know a couple of people who would like nothing more than to be a part of the group and the resort.

Instead, I bought her out, with the promise that once she is done with her pilgrimage, we can always negotiate having her funds back. What she doesn't know however is that I didn't buy or sell out anything, I only set up an agreement to send a fixed amount quarterly, had all email updates and mails sent to her sent to me instead. When she realizes she's going through a phase, she would have me to thank later.

"Like I said, big brother duties. Okay. I've got a call I've been waiting for on hold. Gotta go. Be good. Love you. Bye."

I disconnect the call to connect with Williams, my cousin. My handpicked replacement on the board. We've been buddies for a while, so if there's anyone that can help me get into the mind of the board members, their plans, and views, it would be Williams.

"Hey man, what's up?"

"I'm good. I'm good."

"Want to bring me up to speed with what's going on with the board? And why do I keep getting these emails flying back and forth between the CEO and the board of directors."

"Man... Are you sure you want to get into this?"

"Dude, if I'm asking, then I obviously want to get into it."

"Okay man, since you asked. This is not factual yet. There's a lot going on. A whole lot. There's a scandal waiting to happen. Sex. And money. Alberto had an affair with the Comms Manager, and she threatened to leak some evidence. Alberto, scared to get his wife's family pissed, is siphoning funds from the banks as insurance. And he had a fall out with the Head of Accounting who saw some discrepancies—"

"Know what? I'm not following. Can you send me an email? Of what needs to be done? This sounds like a movie script or something."

"I know, yeah. Some board members don't want to look into it because Alberto is giving results. The Resort is flourishing than before. He's got everything under control. While some are concerned. Now Alberto went ahead to threaten the lady because he's on the good books of most board members and when she said she won't leave, but will instead show evidence of their affair he went ahead to say things about her in an email to the board members."

"Williams..." I take a deep breath. "Can you please simplify this and tell me what needs to be done? Where can I come in? Sounds like fun."

He laughs. "Whatever man...I don't think you should butt your head into this. We can solve this on our own."

"When have you guys solved anything without my help? Even when I was still a new fish to the water you all needed my help. So, you're welcome. Thank me later."

"Yeah. You have that skill."

"I just wanted to know if you can help me get your board members together so we can discuss what the heck is happening on this resort? Why is someone not resigning or getting fired? I'm damn tired of seeing these emails flying back and forth when you guys can organize a meeting to sort this out."

"Calm down man. Calm down. The thing is man you can plan all you want but life has a way of making things fall into place at the right time. Now is just not the right time to schedule meetings because all board members are in different locations and finding a Hospitality Manager, Comms Manager and a CEO... Think of the relocation and all that. We can't move things too fast but know this. We are working underground. A committee has been set up without Alberto's knowledge."

"Alberto must not get wind of this." On second thoughts. "Other investors too." It's not about the money for me, it's about keeping face. If other investors back out, I am capable of convincing some people, because I can't pump from my end.

"Def. The recruiting agency is still working on this without any headway. Trust me. We've got this covered. Enjoy your vacation, okay? I heard you're back in the marriage mart."

"Yeah...that."

"You'll be fine man. Take your time and find you the right woman."

"Thanks man." Never said I was looking.

"It happens even to the best of us."

"Urm... Williams, can we go back to being investor and director?"

"You know this is illegal right?"

"Fuck that."

He gives a deep belly laugh. "Bye man."

"Thank you."

"Yeah, you owe me."

"You bet."

Five

Lola

WOULD I BE A BAD PERSON if I use the code in the email to register? Robbie is... Why am I calling him Robbie? Robert. It is Robert!

He doesn't know this good lady he has lost would not pine and cry for him. I just want to take something that will make me forget all these thoughts warring in my head. Become numb to the betrayal. Is the promotion worth it? I can't believe I didn't see it. Didn't notice it.

Still can't believe my eyes. I can't believe I've been deceiving myself, while he strung me along. *You know you're my day one.* Good riddance. I don't even want biracial kids anymore.

"Lola common. He was never yours to begin with."

"But I liked him. I'm sure he knew 'cause... we clicked. We just... clicked." I snort, then sniffle. I don't like him anymore. He is in the past. What did I even see in him? He rarely talks. Just... "I liked him." I resume staring at the screen, hot tears rushing down my cheeks. "I should have listened to your advice and told him already."

"That wouldn't have changed a thing. Maybe complicated it."

"I can't believe I was so nice to help him plan Thelma's surprise birthday party from scratch and then he goes ahead to propose to her! In front of me!"

Carolanne giggles and I glare at her. Whose side are you on?

"It's not funny..." I blow my nose into the tissue paper she shoves in my face. "You don't know how it feels. How hard it is to find a man that understands you. And doesn't feel small because of your knowledge."

She tilts her head to the side. "I'm sorry." She moves in to hug me, still cackling like a witch and I struggle to get her off me. "Sorry now."

"And he's a good man. A good man."

She moves me from side to side and I keep bawling.

"I'm going to do it."

Carol pauses in her mockery of consolation to stare at me. "Do what?" Her eyes wide in concern. "Please don't have me calling social services or whatever it is they are called, here. I bind and cast all forms of suicidal thoughts in your head." Getting up from the couch, she picks her phone, her legs twitching as she fiddles with the device. "In fact, I'm calling your mother. What's all this?"

From deep within me, it starts like a cough, then I begin cackling, just like she had been doing moments ago. She tosses her phone, reaching out to hold me as I fall off the cushion, to the floor. Laughing so hard.

"Lola?" She shakes me. "Lola?" She shakes me so hard my teeth clatters.

I pull out of her grasp, getting up, and wiping tears off my eyes. "You're a foolish girl. You thought I was considering suicide?"

She shrugs, looking at me from the floor. "Is that not what they do there?"

"Everywhere, not just here."

Carolanne drags herself back up the cushion and I sit beside her. "So, what did you mean by, 'I'm going to do it'?"

Letting out a heavy breath, I lean back on the couch. "Let's say I have a ticket to paradise."

"You know you still sound like someone preparing to meet their maker, right?"

"Shut up. I'm not dying anytime soon."

"Then speak like a sane person."

"I'll be right back." I sniffle as I head to my room to get my laptop.

Escape

This is a bad idea. A completely bad idea. But it's been over a week since he shared it with me. He said he wasn't going to use it. We are supposed to present the project next week but at this point, I care less. Thelma has successfully changed everything to suit her and I hardly see myself in the mix.

"Here." I sit back on the cushion, handing Carolanne my laptop. Playing on the screen is an introductory video to the *Twin Bliss Hotel and Resort*.

"Wow! This is true paradise," she mutters as she watches, sighing and *ah-ing* as the playback continues. "A night for over two grand?! Who visits a place like this?"

Let's drop the bombshell shall we? "I have a ticket for a two-week stay."

Her head swivels to me. "You what?"

I laugh, then squeeze my eyes shut. "I have a ticket for a two-week stay." Opening my eyes.

"Shut up!" She glances at the screen, then back at me. "How come? I sleep with you so I should know all these things."

"Please don't post that on social media. You sleep with me? The heck you sleep with me."

"Girrrl stop. Stop, stop jor. Tell me. How come? You got a raise? A company retreat? A reasonable company will not pay that for mere staff." She clears her throat. "No offense to you."

"None taken. Please." I stretch my hand to her. "The remote." All traces of tears gone. I just want to watch a sappy movie, go to bed, and sleep. I might even call in sick tomorrow. There's nothing much to do on Fridays anyway.

"Tell me now." She hands me the remote. "How did you get it? Two weeks! That's... Lola." She glares at me.

"Robert."

She leans back dramatically, furrowing her brows. "Let me get this straight. Robin. Sorry, Robert gave you a ticket to this place so you can start an affair while his fiancée is... I'm not getting this."

Laughing at her confusion, I retrieve my laptop and place it to the side. "No. No. No. You got it all wrong. A friend invited him. Don't ask me. I don't know who. And he needs to use it before the month runs out. He said he's not sure he would make it. So... he forwarded the email to me since I was as curious as you are. And... I'm considering using it."

"And work?"

I raise a brow, so work?

She stares at me then back at the screen. "Is it for two?" The machines in her head begins whirring.

"Why?"

"This is a once in a lifetime opportunity."

I shrug.

"The people you meet in places like this. That business idea you're thinking of, you'll find an investor ready and waiting. And this Robbie guy, he would be a shadow to the men you'll find there."

"Nice insight, but who goes on a vacation alone?"

"That's true oh." Her shoulders droop, the machines whirring in her head coming to a complete stop. I hit play on the video again. What if I go? What's the worst that can happen?

"Wait."

What is it now?

"You're going alone. So, there's a high chance someone will be there alone too. You can meet your baby daddy and live happily ever after!"

"Hold it. I came up with the baby daddy thing for you." I correct her.

"For us." She says. "You can start, and I'll follow."

I hiss, shaking my head. "Thanks a lot. But pharmacists rarely take the pills they prescribe."

"What do we do now?" She sighs.

"We watch TV. There's ice cream? We have that too."

I select a rom-com movie and in no time, I'm giggling.

"Oops."

I turn to Carolanne who currently has my laptop with her. "What is it?"

"Urm... check this out." She turns my laptop to me.

If she has messed with my laptop, it will not be funny. I move to check what she has done, and my web browser is on the Twin Bliss resort page.

Thanks for accepting your gift certificate.
You got 100% off for your scheduled staycation!
Please present this gift certificate with an ID when you register at the cashier.

Your scheduled staycation? "What have you done?" I glance at her, then back at the laptop, struggling to comprehend.

"I only wanted to test if the code was working or attached to a specific email address. I didn't know it was going to go through."

"Shit. Shit. Shit." I remove the laptop from her lap and scramble around the website, looking for a way to cancel.

"I don't think you can do anything about it."

"Oh Carol." I lean back on the chair, biting my bottom lip.

"Well... You already said you were going to do it. So... Just do it."

I glare at her, then resume my search to cancel the reservation.

"Think of it as a gift to yourself."

"What dates did you pick?" Maybe I could present it to Robert as a wedding gift, proposal gift—whatever.

"Sunday?"

Staring daggers at her, my heart races a mile per second. "Sunday? This Sunday?"

She shrugs half-heartedly. "Next. I was only testing. I didn't know it was going to go..."

Letting out a deep breath, I close my eyes. What to do... What to do....

****

Escape

"I CAN'T GET A DIRECT flight?" The call is on loudspeaker and Carolanne is pacing my bedroom carpet.

"I'm sorry ma'am, there are only interconnecting flights to the location."

"I don't—"

Carolanne snatches the phone from me. "We'll take it." She announces.

I tap her lap, and she mouths an ouch.

"Okay ma'am. I can make payments for you on this call, after which all the information you'll need will..." What the heck am I doing? Why am I agreeing to this? Carolanne asks for my credit card, and I hand her my wallet.

"Thank you very much," Carolanne says to the operator.

"Is there anything else I can help you with today?"

Carolanne replies, "That would be all, thank you." Then disconnects the call moments later.

What have we done? I take quick shallow breaths as it feels like my skin will come off my body. This is so not happening right now. Who would I say I am when I get there? I'm supposed to present an ID, won't that be traceable? I'm so not spending two weeks. One week and the end.

"It's fine." Carolanne's calm voice reaches me before her arm comes around me in reassurance. "Just think of all the things you'll be doing. You can get the Solo Traveler's Handbook by Jessica Ufuoma, it's going to boost your confidence."

"Carolanne...." I say with gritted teeth, "you're not helping."

"Jokes apart. It's an eBook, so no fears about delivery. And... your flight is tomorrow; we need to pack."

"I've got to go into work tomorrow."

"Who says you can't take half day off? Tell them you need to take the two weeks off immediately."

"For?"

"For mental health issues."

"Pfft."

"No one would stop you. You have to be in the right frame of mind to deliver the best result. This is America. I'm sure they would even make it paid leave."

"How do you know these things?"

She shrugs. "I've got friends." Sitting on my bed, we stare at each other in the mirror. "You're a smart talent, Nigeria's Lola the Brand Guru. Since you're smart but not street smart, I am here to help you."

I smile, then frown. "And the project?"

She turns to face me. "They would do it themselves." Then holds my hand reassuringly. "Stop worrying about nothing." She waves an arm as she continues whimsically, "Think of the men... The crazy things you can do. No one would likely know you." She pauses to stare at me. "Then the baby daddy. A baby daddy that can afford a two-grand-per-night resort. Now that's goals."

"Yuck."

Six

Onahi

BLISS. THAT'S WHAT THE RESORT promises and that's what I'm getting. Relaxing on the chaise by the pool outside my villa while sipping a Gin and Tonic Cocktail made by the island's best, scores all the points.

Shit. I forgot my phone.

Stepping in from the evening sun into the welcoming coolness of the villa, I pick my phone and as I return back to the pool, I spot Heather walking down my path, her expression sour. It's been over two days since our last fuck-fest.

"What's wrong?" I ask as she draws close.

She looks at me funny, stares at me for a while, then smiles. "I was heading back to my reality. And although I know we don't have anything special going on, I wanted to let you know I was leaving."

I take a sip of my drink, feeling indifferent. I thought she had left already, but it's nice she's taking it upon herself to inform me. "Thanks for letting me know."

"Can we talk?"

I hope she's not about to play the I'm pregnant card or worst of all, I'm in love with you card. There are some things I'm not prepared for, hence why I prepare beforehand for them. I used a condom every time I as much go near her. "Sure, let's go inside."

"I need to say some things and I think it's best I do it out here." She looks at the door to my villa, longing written over her face as she swallows. "You know what would happen if we go in there." She smiles as her gaze returns to mine.

"Hmm. Do I?"

Shaking lewd thoughts from her head she continues, "So...." Gesturing towards the chaise, and I follow her lead.

A goodbye fuck wouldn't be a bad idea, something to hold me down for the remaining days I have left.

"My time with you has been memorable. I've learnt a lot, tried a lot and... you..."

"I get it." I give a small laugh. "I'm a good fuck."

She smiles. "I know this might come to you as a shock but I have actually been in a committed relationship for the past four years."

I snort and she places her hand on mine.

"He cheated on me and a month later, I jumped ship when he proposed marriage."

I laugh, pulling out my hand and excuse myself for being insensitive.

"It's alright. And I'm sorry I had to put you in this position."

"You should be. Should I be thankful your Texan oil magnate father didn't come searching for me too?"

"Stop it, Nahi. I know you're hurt, but—"

"I'm not. Actually, far from it. It's just..."

I'm fucking transactional. I spent the last two weeks fucking a woman screaming my name from sundown to sun-up. She took her time, sharing bits and pieces of her life and it's only the fact that her father is a Texan oil magnate I can vividly recollect. Just because I didn't want to commit to her. But look at the bright picture, if I had decided to commit to her, I'll be in a fucked-up situation right now—my emotions in a twist. Alas, it all works out for good.

"So, what changed?" I ask her.

"I know this might sound crazy, but I-I saw a lady two nights ago, by the beach. I saw her. Dressed in a sequined red dinner gown. She told me...she told me everything good will come and I should have no fear about his loyalty."

Heather had drunk-called me that night. She didn't make it over because she wanted to sleep it in and since then, she became a no-show.

"Were you guys drinking together?"

She lets out an exasperated sigh. "You don't get it, do you? I don't think she's human. When I went on the tour, one of the guys said some spirits are connected to this resort, and they sometimes appear to people who are confused about love."

Bullshit. That's a tale my sisters and I fine-tuned during our holidays here, acting as tour guides. Now it's being peddled to our guests for extra tips. Stuff lonely rich people will happily buy into. For someone who is actually a son of the soil, a direct descendant, it is weird when people talk about these things like they're real. If these things are real, they should have happened to me. I should have had an encounter. A foreigner visits and all of a sudden, they're having encounters with ghosts.

"Are you sure I shouldn't take you to the clinic?" I smile. "I've not seen you in days and now this."

Her eyes twinkle. "I know you don't believe me, but I really wanted you to know that you are special and will find love someday. Thanks a lot for everything."

I am not looking for love, but thanks, I think to myself as I watch her walk away.

Earlier in the week, while relaxing on this same spot, I had gotten a call from Jay after watching Ahmed's failed proposal on Twitter. Ahmed was my dorm buddy in Cornell, while Jay, short for Janelle, was his childhood friend who later joined us in college and grew on me in time.

She giggled when I told her I had been expecting her call. "I saw the news. You and Ahmed, huh?"

"Yeah?"

Escape

"I take it he didn't tell you he'll propose tonight."

She sighed, confirming my initial thoughts. Ahmed is a friend, but a sneaky one. And when it came to women, the few times we'd hung out, he was never interested—making excuses and all. After the booze, he disappears for the night. Lord knows what he's got planned for Janelle, because I've never in my whole life seen a flicker of romance between them. I'm not the only aromantic or transactional individual in the world after all.

"Are you okay, though?"

"I'm fine now."

"So... Did he get you to say yes? I know Ahmed has a way with words and can sell snow to an Eskimo." A crafty and tricky individual. I keep him close because having him far would be worse and he's got great business acumen.

She laughed. "Yes, he did. Ahmed and I will get married."

"Congratulations, Jay."

We spoke for over an hour, bantering and scheduling the perfect day for her arrival at Twin Bliss. Ahmed had called before her, asking for a favor—that I make space available for her. It's peak season and most villas, booked.

"Okay dear, I'll circle back with Ahmed with details for your scheduled rides from the airport."

"Don't worry. You can send them to me."

"You sure? 'Cause I don't want you forgetting to add this to your visual daily planner. You still use it right?"

She laughed. "I'm autistic, not dumb."

"I know. Just wanted to make sure you have that at the back of your mind when you get the email. Even though I know Ahmed will pester my life to know the whereabouts of his special fiancée."

"Thank you, Onahi. You're special too."

I'm special. True. With the patience of a snail and the speed of a tiger.

PART TWO

Seven

Lola

"YOU'LL NEED TO BOARD A ride to the dock before you get to this resort ma'am."

After spending thirty almost-miserable hours to get here—this includes two lengthy stop overs, sightseeing Paris on a low budget during the eleven hours stopover and maintaining a sense of calm during my twelve-hour flight from Paris to Gobota, as my clumsy seat mate kept letting his meal fly out of his plate—the last thing I need right now is to take another means of transportation to my final destination. I want to lay on a proper bed and sleep away these feelings of betrayal making my chest heavy.

Escape

If I can find someone that will take my bags so I can cry in peace, I would do so in a heartbeat, till I fall asleep. The thought of sleeping in this lounge, although more grandeur than that of Paris or even Atlanta, makes my skin crawl.

I need a bath. I had a quick shower for twenty euros at the Paris layover before heading into town with no prior plans. If I had planned ahead, I would have probably enjoyed touring the city of love. But I was grumpy all through my first high speed train ride and ended up at *The Louvre* which turned out to be fun but a lot of walking. After complaining about sitting for hours from Atlanta to Paris, I couldn't stand three hours of walking and regretted taking my bath before heading out.

Your ride has arrived.

Finally!

How does one get out of this place? Where do the rides park and wait?

It didn't take long to figure it all out. Thanks to the map of the shared riding service I had been advised to download by one of the attendants. Pulling my suitcase and hand luggage I begin trudging to the visualized location.

Looking up, I spot the first exit sign. Is this the one that leads to the private parking? Or the park and ride? Why must everything be so organized? I opt for the exit sign. It will give me a better chance of spotting the silver ride waiting for me.

My phone keeps buzzing and I struggle to get it out of my back pocket—it could be a message from the driver cancelling. That's when I'll leave this suitcase here, fall on the floor and start crying, till help comes. I hopped on the plane to be free of stress and worry, not compound it.

Oh snap!

It's only an engagement on the last picture I shared of myself in Paris. The pamphlets from the lounge suggested connecting to their free Wi-Fi. I did, and was expecting messages pouring in from above and beyond, but after waiting a few, nothing came in. Only two apps worked. I requested a ride, the wait in-between confirming my ride, I decided to share a snippet of my time in Paris. Paris, the city of love. Pulling my suitcase and hand luggage, with my bag hanging sweetly on my elbow, I begin scrolling through the comment section.

Who is he? Tell us the secret—He? These people must be joking? You guys are in for a full ride. So, I can't visit a place on my own? I can't spend time with myself? I chuckle. Just wait till you see me in my villa and I upload a YouTube video telling you of my experience. Social media trolls who think they know everything happening in my life just because I share some things online, have a thing or two coming.

I thought you were in America—And so? How is it your business if I am in or out of America? Your duty is to like, comment and share.

Looking up, a frown marring my angelic face, it takes me less than fifteen seconds to realize I have duped myself of time by using the first exit door, instead of the next. Tshewww. Nonsense.

Where is this ride now? Closing my social app, I open the itinerary I saved off the internet. Am I in the right place? Where do I go from here? Oh Lord, have mercy. Am I lost in a land where no one knows who the heck I am? I haven't even gotten a message from any familiar person, only strangers and

Escape

I can't even seem to find an internet connection that will work for all my apps. Urgh. This is grating on my nerves right now.

"Need a hand?" A deep masculine voice asks.

I scrutinize the owner of the voice who turns out to be a silver fox—he looks young and has a completely shaved smooth, shiny head that mirrored the wall he was leaning on. And a grey beard, rich grey beard. It looks so fluffy, I'm tempted to touch it and sigh.

Imagine if he bends his head, offering it as a mirror, I'll see an exhausted replica of me. I hold back a laugh, smiling instead. "No, thanks."

In return he spares me a wry smile.

Walking further, I pause to send a message to my driver, but the message on my screen has me tempted to scream. The guy cancelled on me!

Arrgghhh!

I will break this phone now! I was so close! I just needed to confirm which spot he was because there are loads of exits a-a-and.

Trying to book another ride is useless as the app keeps telling me I'll have to wait fifteen minutes to be connected to another ride.

Tears threaten to fall off my eyes as I look around. I can do this. What the heck? Why am I letting a little resort on an unmarked island get to me?

"Hi. Need help?"

Blinking a couple of times before giving the strange man my attention, I paste a sly smile on and turn to face him with raised brows. The first guy was trying to help and I ignored him, maybe it's not so bad to ignore people on your abrupt trip to a 7-star resort.

Unlike the silver fox who subtly tried to help, this one is brash. Taking matters into his hand. He's got neat cornrows on, with a diamond stud in one ear. He looks good, but, I'm not buying.

He rushes on, "You looked lost, in need of rescuing. And here I am." He smiles. "To the rescue."

Cheesy but I am buying it. I need all the help I can get. His smile is slow, as he takes the handle of my suitcase to rest them on his knee. "So where are you headed?"

Did I mention brash?

Someone is in superman mode today. My inner girl laughs, clapping her hand, with her lips pursed. "That's so thoughtful of you. But I've got this covered." I grin, trying to reclaim my luggage. "I've survived thirty hours, what's another hour? That's if I know how to get to where I'm headed to." I mumble the last statement under my breath.

"Is it your first time here?" He squints under the harsh sun, and I nod cautiously.

Did the Solo Traveler's Handbook talk about meeting strangers? Nice looking, brash strangers?

"My name's Nonso by the way. Forgive my manners."

Oh. A Nigerian-American, 'cause his accent doesn't sound forced. His Igbo accent is slight, but I can tell he is well traveled.

"Lola."

"Nice name. Lola... Like the jeans by the way." His gaze flickers over me.

Okay... Add cocky to the brash.

"I'm headed to the Twin Bliss resort, you?"

The choristers in my head begin singing hallelujah until his voice breaks through again.

"So, you mentioned you'd spent thirty hours on air?"

"Yeah. Yeah, all the way from Maryland, USA. And funny, I'm headed to Twin Bliss as well."

"What a coincidence."

He leers at me, but my mind tags it to be the regular reaction most men have when they encounter me. I need all the help I can get. I spent some unbudgeted funds in Paris and need to start cutting costs.

"I'm from Lagos, but I spend a lot of time in New York, so close to Maryland." He grins like a schoolboy. "I assume you are new to the resort?"

We begin a leisure walk towards the area marked Park and Ride. Why didn't I notice it when I got here?

"Yes, first time." I say with all the cheer I can muster. "And it's so...beautiful here. I could barely tear my eyes off the view from the flight. Can't wait to see the resort firsthand."

He chuckles and I smile. "I have to agree. It's one of the best on the Island."

"There are others?" I ask, raising my brow in disbelief. I've done my research, but anything to get this guy moving with the help he's offering.

"Small motels and guest houses."

"You're kidding right?" I fake a surprised face. Like everyone doesn't know there are always small hotels close to big ones for spies and broke ass people.

He chuckles, and I'm glad he feels like he's educating me. What I need from him is to figure out how to get to the resort and find a bed that has my name on it—make that Robbie's name.

"Well, I'm kind of a regular here, so it's only natural that I know the place."

We come to a stop, and I watch as people hop into rides, in twos and in groups.

"Booked your ride?"

The rate at which I'm smiling, I might need something for my cheekbones later. "Not yet. My driver cancelled on me while I was figuring out this maze."

"Oh." His look changes in an instant and it looks sincere. "I'm sorry about that. Did you use the Ona app?"

"I have no idea what the name is, but I know it's not Ona."

"Give me a moment." He pulls out his phone and begins swiping, his brow creasing a couple of times.

I let out a sigh, taking in the sight around me. Nobody seems to be in a hurry.

"There," his voice jolts me back to him. "Your ride should be here in two minutes."

"That was fast."

He shrugs. "The idea of creating business on this island was to ease customers. So, it shouldn't be stressful for a pretty lady like you to get a ride."

"I know, right."

"And before you find out and think I'm trying something," he brushes his hand through his braided cornrows, "I'm Chinonso Kalu."

I stare at him clueless. Is the name drop supposed to be important?

"Lola. Lola Dade."

He smiles and I smile back.

Something fishy is happening and I don't know what it is. And thinking about it, he and the first guy who tried to help might be from the same area in eastern Nigeria because of the shape of their heads.

"Kamil is here."

"Uhn?"

He shakes his head. "Your ride." Smiling. "Kamil is your driver."

"Oh, thank you."

We find my ride, a black SUV with the perfect leg room—unlike the economy flight where my knees almost buckled—and arrange my luggage within. Turning to appreciate his kind gesture, I stretch my hand for a handshake.

"If you ever need a ride here, the Ona app is your best bet."

Okay... please leave my hands before this ride leaves with my luggage in it. It won't be funny this time around.

"I'll like to see more of you on the resort. And for starters, on the resort, I'll suggest you try out the *Eclipse Bar*. They always have something going on. You'll have a good time."

Can I go now? "Sure, sure. Thank you Nonso."

He lets go of my hand and I finally get to relax my back on something, even though it's still moving.

What's so special about Ona app? While the driver waits in line behind other cars as we move in a slow crawl out of the parking lot, I scan through the internet in search of Ona. The first news I see is an interview of the man whom I just left at the parking lot, and what his experience has been like since selling Ona for millions of dollars and becoming a venture capitalist.

A venture capitalist!

I scramble to look at the man who looked so young, in need of company, but he is no longer standing where I left him. What was I expecting?

Relaxing back on my seat. I take a deep breath, closing my eyes as we begin moving in a fast and steady pace.

I'm not taking any conversation for granted anymore. As much as I'm here to enjoy the ambience, I need an investor.

"Ma'am?"

Why didn't I notice Kamil was Indian?

"Uhn?" I sit up, looking around. I need to be more conscious of my environment and the people in it. I keep getting lost in one maze or the other in my thoughts.

"We're here," he says, smiling.

"Thank you."

Escape

Looking out the window, I spot the name, Twin Bliss, scattered on multiple boats and yachts on the bluest waters I have ever seen in person. Which will I be getting on?

"Are you sure this is the only way to get on the island?" I ask no one in particular. The water looks good. Good enough to drink, but not enough to drown in. When I die, I want it to be on a bed, with my grandkids around me.

As though sensing my agitation, Kamil smiles through the rear-view mirror. "Twin Bliss offers the best service. You can either get there by water or air. And personally, I believe this experience is way better than taking a flight."

"Hmm..." I am here, so I bet I have to deal with it. I look out the window again as other guests alight their rides in high spirits, at least I'll have bodies to latch on to if we ever come close to drowning.

The thought of pulling my suitcase across the white sands makes me weak all over again. "Uhn, Kamil? Can you please help with my luggage?"

"It will be taken care of. Please wait in the car till we pull up."

A pleasant, uniformed man in black and gold approaches the car. Kamil winds his window down, and they exchange pleasantries. He winds the window back up and smiles at me. "He'll help you get your luggage on the boat."

"Thank you!"

Pulling my sneakers off my feet, I toss them into my handbag, then pull out my purple neon sunglasses—I bought multiple colors, just for the fun of it.

When Kamil parks properly, I thank him once more, and he wishes me the best of luck. Hands free of luggage and only my handbag to be bothered with, I begin a leisure walk to the dock, taking calculated strides across the white sand.

A helicopter whirr overhead. That could have been me if I had taken my time to plan this trip, but I'm not dipping into my savings when I can enjoy this stolen moment. Haha!

Colorful flowers of different species wrapped a coffee brown trellis wall on the path to the building and leads to a large expanse of water with a transparent footpath that makes the idea of walking on water a reality. By the time I arrive at the admin building, I am rethinking dipping into my savings to return for a longer stay. Besides the giant tree that looked out of place by the entrance of the resort, the landscaping and design are on par!

The admin building itself is glass-walled, bright with natural light, reflecting the villas and occasional glimpse of the ocean in the distance, making them look like paintings. The relaxing ambience of the space is heightened by jazz music and a high ceiling, holding low hanging lanterns, and illuminated flowerpots. I can only imagine what this space looks like at night.

Although busy with murmurs of 'how can I help you today' 'thank yous' and 'you're welcome,' there's a sense of calm with what I can only describe as the soothing scent of the ocean's mist mixed with the strong musty, spicy fragrance of vanilla, clove, and cinnamon.

After registering, the cheerful front desk assistant tells me to download the resort's app to get one-click access to resort facilities, like butler service, shuttles, meals and more! In no time, I am in a shuttle, heading to my private villa.

Escape

"Welcome to the Addis Ababa villa, Miss Lola. I am Biftu, your butler. My job is to see that your stay here is memorable."

Biftu, who should be in her late twenties, is adorned in a black suit with gold tie. She smiles, presenting me with a bucket of champagne. She takes me on a tour around what will be my room and living space for the six days, sharing more information than my mind can take. My head is currently stuck on appreciating the thoughtful and intentional design that makes Twin Bliss a brand that speaks for itself.

"...there's a telephone directory, a brochure with activities and Wi-Fi password on the coffee table over there. I hope everything is to your satisfaction?"

"Yes, please." I grin at her, and she excuses herself from my villa, the door gently closing behind her.

The room, glass-walled on one side with neutral colors and a mini-bar, overlooks a private terrace with sun loungers, a table and two chairs. The natural lighting from the glass can be controlled from the resort's app as it is a smart window. In front of my villa is a private garden and a porch swing with stand. And the view! Gosh. There are some cards on the table with ads on marula this, marula that, ignoring them, I sieve through until I find what I am looking for.

Connecting the Wi-Fi password placed on the table, the first person I video call is Carolanne—gushing about the view and resort activities—when I hear a knock on the door.

"You have a visitor already?"

"Shut up." I glare at her. In our conversation, I had shared my interaction with the Nonso guy as well as a woman I had met claiming to be an actor's wife. "Probably room service or my butler."

"Go 'n' check it out. You won't find out who's there if you keep staring."

Opening the door, a well-built man in a black and gold uniform, which I've associated with the resort, smiles at me. "Apologies for the tardiness ma'am. Your luggage has arrived."

Luggage? I raise a brow at him.

Noticing my puzzlement, he moves to the side to reveal my hand luggage and suitcase on his luggage cart.

Wow!

"Thank you." I wave him off, shutting the door. He had helped secure the suitcase in my room, telling me to beckon my butler when I was ready to settle in, using the app.

"You won't believe it, I completely forgot I had a suitcase." I chuckle as I resume my conversation with Carolanne.

"That place must really be a thing."

"Babe... words can't describe the elegance." Staring at my suitcase, a thought pops in my mind. "You know what? Why don't you go to sleep, even though I know you won't."

"You didn't think about that before you called?"

"I didn't know I am now eight hours ahead of you. Whatever. I need to take my bath, get some sleep and be ready for tonight's activities at *Eclipse Bar*."

"Yasss girl! Maybe you'll find your baby daddy. The Nonso guy."

"Shush! I'm not looking for anything serious."

"Who's talking serious stuff here? I'm talking about having fun." Her eyes twinkle and I nod in agreement.

"I deserve some fun." I start off slow and low. "Yeah. I'll do that."

"You do deserve fun. And I'm proud you made the right decision."

Chuckling, I reprimand her, "I stole someone's ticket. And I might be an impostor. But..." I shrug, my voice firmer. "I deserve some fun!"

Eight

Onahi

"WELCOME TO PARADISE, JAY." I smile into my phone, anticipating the moment we get to see each other in person. It's been a while since we hung out. Having her over should be fun. Since Ahmed won't be making his grand entrance anytime soon, we'll probably spend lots of time together exploring the island, catching up.

She gasps in awe, her expression priceless and brutally honest through the screen of my phone. "Is there a better word than paradise? This is seventh heaven, Onahi. I honestly feel like I just died and went to heaven, like I'm walking through the pearly gates."

Escape

I chuckle. "That makes me Angel Gabriel then. It's so good to see you."

"Good to see you too." She grins.

"Have you called Ahmed?"

Her brows furrow as her brain processes my question.

"Because he has been on my neck about your arrival."

"Oh him," she sighs. "You know he worries a lot. I'll call him as soon as I end this call. But first, I need to take in this view. This is where you've been hiding all these years?"

"Not really, I rarely spend time here." I really don't want to talk about my goings and comings when I promised Ahmed to help her settle in. "Oh Jay, have you checked in?"

She confirms she hasn't, so I give her pointers on how to go about it.

"See you at *Eclipse Casino* tonight?" That's the spot young vibrant guests prefer compared to *Gobota Specials*.

"Urm-I..."

"When you're done settling in and rested, that is."

"Sure!" She giggles. Her mind works with the speed of light, but literally processes words.

"I'll see that this trip is memorable for you, Jay. Call me when you're settled."

Ending the call, a message pops on my screen. It's from Femi. A Hollywood friend of mine who needs help in sealing a movie sponsorship deal with Duncan Dugo, Bodo's big boy and investor.

Femi: I'm here. Meet me at Gobota Specials.

Femi: Drinks on you.

I smile as I drop my phone on the table. My guys are arriving. This is a long-needed vacation even though I have gone ahead to mix work in it but all in all, I can foresee a great happy ending.

On cue, the telephone rings.

"Good morning sir," Salewa says brightly over the phone. "I hope you are having a wonderful time with us?"

If I take out all my personal baggage, with the service being provided, I believe I am. And she is doing a great job managing my schedule, while making me feel like a customer at home and at ease.

"I am."

"I'm glad."

Her infectious personality has me smiling, forgetting her mistake with Anthony.

"You told me to notify you once the reserved Addis Ababa pavilion has been taken."

"It has?"

"Yes sir."

"Great! He came alone?"

"One moment sir." Buttons click and she's back on the line. "Urm... it's a she, sir."

"A she?"

"Yes sir."

Escape

"Okay. Thank you Salewa. Have them send me the name she used during registration."

"That's not all." Her voice takes on a tinge of excitement and awe. "Lucas Opeyemi just checked in."

My sister's face pops up on my mobile phone as it vibrates, and I send the call to voicemail. I'll return her call once I'm done playing host. My voicemail box must be filled by now, seeing the amount of calls I've been rejecting.

"Thank you Salewa. Urm... I'll be stepping out for the rest of the day, keep my calendar—"

"Light. I know sir." She smiles over the phone. "I'm glad your friends are showing up. Maybe you'll loosen up a bit."

The guts of this young lady to say that to me. Speaking over the phone must be a courage booster because the Salewa I know only focuses on her job. In some ways, it shows she cares for my wellbeing, which is... nice. I smile. "I'm loosened up."

"No sir. Not that type of loosening up sir. You should mingle with friends and enjoy what you sell."

"Nice one Salewa."

"You're welcome, sir."

It's been an interesting couple of weeks. With familiar faces on ground, I'm so sure it might get wild.

Pulling out a brush from my drawer to set my hair right, I let out a long breath, pick up my sunshades, then head down to the lobby, game face on. It's barely past noon but the sun here takes no prisoners.

The elevator opens and the first person my gaze lands on is Lucas Opeyemi—Nollywood's finest—followed by the phones pointed at him. Fans. Always on him, like flies to shit. Even in a sophisticated resort like this. He has an adorable light skinned plus sized lady hovering around him as they discuss animatedly with the concierge. Occasionally he ogles the lady but masks it with feigned irritation.

Barbara must not be aware of this.

Honestly Lucas needs to get his act together and act like a married man. When I sent the tickets, I specifically told him it was for his anniversary. This—I don't support. But as a bro, there are some codes we are bound by till the other bro gets wise.

Sauntering towards them, it takes less than thirty seconds for Lucas to turn his bored eyes in my direction which automatically lights up.

"My Manchi!" he hails.

I grin as I take him in a hug, cordially slapping each other's back. "It's good to see you man."

Lucas grins as we ease out of the hug.

"How long has it been, twenty years?" It's not been that long. I attended his wedding ceremony in Lagos, Nigeria about eight years ago. But what type of friend would I be to Lucas if I can't be a little dramatic? I grin, sizing him up. "You disappeared without a trace fam," And we shake hands.

"Me? Disappeared? I'm on your screen man. Everywhere." He laughs, pumping his hands in mine. "Just accept you're a pro at shutting friends out. You enjoy working like a jackal."

"Says the movie star that hardly stays out of the screen. I tried following up on your progress, my guy, I lost count."

"Or you got carried away with business deals." He winks and we laugh, our laughter bouncing off the walls.

I've missed Lucas and his ways. He has a way with words that only smart people can match with. It has helped all through his career as the few movies of his I've seen, he does justice to the roles—nailing the characters; hook, line, and sinker.

While we catch up on his trip to the resort, the light skin plus sized lady drapes herself around him, arms on his elbows, while her head rests on his shoulder. They must really be a thing because the smile she displays doesn't sing side chic or the type of women Lucas has mentioned he prefers.

Lucas goes silent, his expression tending towards irritation and frustration. "Oh, uhm..." he begins, placing his hand over hers. It looked as though he wanted to pull them off him, but decided against it, letting it rest there. "This is my wife, Muyiwa."

Wife? I thought Barbara was his recent wife? How and when did he get married and I didn't know about it?

Smiling warmly at Muyiwa, I take her hand and place a kiss on them. Her palm is soft and warm. They smell like they were dipped in some expensive fragrance oil.

"You're a true beauty. I am so glad to have you here."

Muyiwa's cheeks turn a bright shade of pink as she grins. Her eyes sparkle as she leans into Lucas who is not having it.

She, on the other hand, is indifferent to Lucas' obvious cringe as she replies, "And I appreciate your kindness. Coming here... It means so much to me... To us."

And I can see it in her eyes. Except she is an actress like her husband, I believe she wants time alone with her husband and she is getting it.

"The pleasure is mine, ma'am."

"Sweetheart, sweetheart..." Lucas begins, obviously irritated by her show of excitement. "I think you should go with this gentleman that has been waiting for us while I catch up with my good friend here."

Muyiwa gifts me another smile, then turns to narrow her eyes at Lucas before strutting off.

She is a beauty. A thick beauty that promises no-dull-days.

"Okay," Lucas' voice breaks my attention from his departing wife, and I shake my head. "Spill."

What is wrong with Lucas? Why is he hot and cold with her? One minute he looks like he will fuck her right here, the next, he wants to shake her off him. I'm tempted to talk about it, but I've been keeping Femi waiting for too long.

"Let's join one of my guys by the beach." I begin walking and Lucas follows my lead. "His name is Femi. A nice guy. I am sure you've not met, and you would be most interested in meeting him."

When Lucas only grunts in response, taking in the view as we get into a shuttle, I add, "He is a world class movie producer."

Good. I can see curious antennas rising in his head.

Escape

****

"BUSINESS MUST BE REALLY GOOD, my guy. Show me the way now." Lucas stretches his head out of the shuttle as he ogles a group of ladies clad in swim wear. "Guy..." He shakes his leg as he turns to me, "See this ripe—Oh God," he swallows. "See daughters of Eve strutting about and you say you don't have one to yourself."

I smile. "This just happens to be a beautiful place that appeals to beautiful people."

"Don't patronize me, Onahi. Tell me." He waggles his brows. "Have you?"

Have I slept with any of the ladies? "Yes."

"I knew it! Spill it man."

From the side mirror, the shuttle driver's expression relays one that will happily do without knowing what two grown men do in private, but since it's been a while I expressed myself to a peer, I indulge Lucas.

"It was a one-night stand that turned into one-too-many nights." That's the best description I can give.

"I knew there was no way you'll stay here without getting into action... with these pretty little things I've been seeing from the airport. Manchi!"

Lucas. I have missed him. Maybe my plans with Jay might change as this guy is obviously not here for his anniversary.

"Good pussy?" He asks.

"Hmm... was good. And somewhat kinky. C'mon man, you're married."

Lucas eyes me.

"We shouldn't be having this type of discussion."

"I'm married, not dead."

"That's true. What happened to Barbara? When did you and Muyiwa..." I gesticulate with my hands coming together as a sign of marriage.

"Manchi man. It's a long story."

"Mehn, you must be sick or psycho. How is it possible your anniversary with Barbara falls on the same period with Muyiwa."

"Good pussy." We chuckle. "At least it was good. I can't wait to be rid of her."

Rid of her? What the fuck is wrong with Lucas? That lady looked loyal. He literally wanted to fuck her in the reception area. There was something weird going on there. "What's wrong with her?"

"Didn't you see her? Isn't she... too much? Too much to bear?"

"I didn't see that. She looked pretty to me. You like your women fleshy if memory serves me right." Although Muyiwa is on the extra thick side, she looks fab.

"Well, I guess I've grown an appetite for, you know, other things." A skinny lady walking a dog steals his attention and they exchange a smile, before he returns it to me, his expression now neutral. "She's messing with my reputation and you and I both know that my acting skill is all I've got. I won't let her sabotage that. I need my space."

I nod my head as his words sink in. Everyone with their cross to bear. "Want to know what I think?"

"What?"

"You need Jesus, man."

"Says the guy who enjoyed drunken orgies."

"I was young and crazy about pussy."

"Oh... then see me as young and crazy about pussy."

Chuckling, we alight the shuttle and I put on my sunshades.

We walk the rest of the way to *Gobota Specials* overlooking the blue sea. Cane chairs are arranged under thatched shades, protecting guests from the harsh midday sun. The ocean is calm with gentle waves, spotting boats on its horizon; a perfect view for longtime friends to relax and catch up over bottles of whatever's available. The cool breeze from the gentle waves acts as mediator between the humid air and hot beach sand.

Lucas compliments the changes he has seen in the resort, and I graciously accept the praise as I scan the perimeter for Femi.

"Akachi?"

I whip my head around to find an old, familiar face. A big grin spread across my face, as Femi stands up to shake then hug me. It's been a while.

"Femi." I smile as I withdraw. "Meet my friend Lucas. Lucas, Femi."

Both mumble their greetings as we settle down on the round table. There's a fourth unique and unfamiliar face and I smile at him.

His skin is charcoal black with a glow I can't describe, while his eyes, behind nerd glasses, are an arresting grey—an image I will not forget.

"My bad," Femi begins, "meet Rasheed. Rasheed, Onahi and…"

"Lucas," Lucas spits out his name. Probably pissed Femi didn't catch it or fawn over him. Petty.

Femi and his companion had already started with water and grapes placed on the table, and as we settle down on cane chairs, a server appears, takes our orders, then leaves with a bow.

"Welcome to my turf," I say.

"It's nice." Rasheed smiles and I blink a couple of times as his peculiar pair of eyes unsettle me. They look too cute to be on a man. It would be rude to ask if they were contact lenses.

"What brings you here?" Lucas directs his question to Femi.

Bloody opportunist. I'm sure he just remembered whom I told him Femi is and is now acting his way into the guy's space.

Femi smiles, leaning back, an elbow resting on the chair's arm. "Business. You?"

"Pleasure."

"That's one thing I hope to eventually get out of this trip. But business first."

Escape

"Very important," I say.

"I'm glad you're around," Femi says to me, "heard Bodo's big boy can be difficult to pin down."

Duncan Dugo is a fish. Born and bred in Bodo, not so far away from Gobota Island. News reaching me is that the old man almost died recently. He has tried on many occasions to be a chummy friend, but we just don't click. The day he had the guts to propose I sell my shares of Twin Bliss to him, I drew the line.

"I don't think you should worry about that. You've worked with the likes of—" A phone rings and it turns out to be Lucas'.

He declines the call, then prods me to continue, "He has worked with the likes of?"

"Yeah," I catch my thoughts. "The likes of Tyler Perry, Shonda—" Lucas' phone rings again. "Want to pick that?"

"It's fine. It's Muyiwa. She won't stop till I turn my phone off."

"Then pick the bloody call."

"I'll silence it." Lucas swipes multiple times on his phone, then places it face down just as our orders arrive.

Oh, Lucas.

He stares curiously at Rasheed who chose to drink a non-alcoholic beverage. "It's not too early to drink alcohol, you know. It's almost three. With these meat and roasted plantain, I don't think that drink will do justice to your taste buds."

"I don't drink."

"That's strange. A man that doesn't drink." Lucas says between bites of goat meat. "How many women are you keeping?"

Rasheed grins, shaking his head as he picks at the buffet on the table. "Not me."

"Not everyone is like you Lucas." I chew on a roasted plantain as I turn to study Rasheed. "You're married?" He looks young but old enough to be off the market.

"Nah... I'm not up for commitments but..." He shrugs, a mischievous twinkle in his eyes.

"Ehen!" Lucas grins. "That's what I'm talking about! Femi are you married?"

"Yes."

"And on a scale of one to five, how likely will you do it again in your second life? With five being never."

"Lucas, what the hell man?" I ask.

"No, oh. Let Mr. Femi answer." Lucas takes a gulp from his bottle. "We are having fun and trying to get you inexperienced ones to know what you're going in for, should in case you decide to be dumb about the situation. So, Femi..."

Femi looks uncomfortable as three pairs of eyes zone in on him, waiting for his answer. The little I know of him and what is on the back of every book he has written is that he is happily married with kids. Aren't all authors happily married?

"Say 3.6?"

"Ah! Femi!" Lucas stretches his hands out to shake Femi, but Femi waves it off with a shy smile, taking a swig of his beer instead. "See my guy there." Lucas says to Rasheed and me, "He knows what I'm talking about. Women are God's best gift to men but having them in your space two-four-seven is man's greatest punishment."

Rasheed scoffs.

"There's nothing I've not given my wives. Nothing. The best house. Cars. Everything! But they want me to be at their beck and call."

"Lucas, calm down."

"I'm calm," he swallows. "It's like she wants to spoil my shine. My freedom. Every time, complaining about what I didn't do with her. Always trying to infuse herself into my space. Then keeping quiet, giving me silent treatment. I don't know which is worse, the complaint or the silent treatment. Anyways, I'm divorcing her after this trip and that's final."

It's obvious Lucas is talking about his Muyiwa and not women in general. Whatever is happening in their marriage is really biting at him and instead of communicating with her, he's lamenting over a drink with guys.

"Speaking of cars," Rasheed begins, intentionally steering the conversation off women. "Who chose the shuttles and carts for the resort?"

Furrowing my brows, I recall the meetings I was involved in for the rebranding of the resort. "I think I had a say in it."

Rasheed purses his lips as he gives a tight-lipped smile. "It's a nice collection."

"Thanks man. You're into cars?"

"Into Tech... and cars."

"Oh…" Lucas says and I turn to him thinking he is awed by Rasheed's revelation but the rude prick is leering at a lone lady who just walked past.

My mind goes back to the info Salewa shared with me earlier, about the lady who checked into the Addis Ababa villa. Did she come alone? Is she Robert's girlfriend? What does she look like?

Nine

Lola

WALTZING INTO THE *ECLIPSE BAR* in a short black dress, after napping all afternoon, I smile as heads turn. *Nonso boo, please show yourself.* The *Eclipse* boasts of a nightclub, bar, casino, and other forms of entertainment. With so much to do, I could do a lot of crazy stuff and no one in my real world will ever find out.

I make my way to one of the bars, taking in the activities on the casino floor. Occasional coins dropping, followed by squeals of victory and grunts of frustration came from guests on the casino floor. *It's casino night baby. I'm putting all my cards on the table. Try a game of luck and see what it gets me.*

Ignoring the allure of the casino, I make my way to the bar, the array of bottles displayed on the rack calling my attention.

Every part of the bar area my eyes scan has occupied stools and the bartenders have their hands full responding to orders, mixing drinks while holding courteous conversations.

"Hello," a familiar masculine voice I heard at the airport says over the cool background music.

Retracting my gaze from the array of bottles, my gaze falls on the silver fox.

"Sorry, my bad." He chuckles. "I saw you at the airstrip earlier today."

Yeah. It is the guy from the airport.

I smile, shaking his outstretched hands as he introduces himself as Duncan, then looks around like he's expecting company before offering me a stool. I sit gingerly on the stool. It's so sweet of him to offer help even though I had rejected his offer at the airport.

"If you don't mind, can I gist with you for a bit?" He asks.

This guy must be a guardian angel or something. The white beard gives him away as one. Even though I don't know what to discuss with him, I'm curious to see how this pans out.

"I make good company," he pushes.

Since I know no one here and I'm yet to sight Nonso, I give him a shot. After all, Nonso had only mentioned that I'll have a good time here and wanted to see more of me on the resort. Nothing more. Better a bird at hand than one in the bush.

I smile at Duncan. "Sure. I guess." Let's get this party started!

We talk about work, his and mine. He visits the United States from time to time. Has a couple of investments here and there. In summary, he's a big boy from this locale. *Hmm... I must be using the right perfume or something.* He asks for my phone number and why not? I give him mine in exchange for his. I will not sleep on this offer. Nonso was a one-time opportunity, even a venture capitalist at that. No. My Nigerian ancestors will not let me sleep well if I miss another opportunity again.

The bartender finally makes it to us and I order what he is having—single malt Scotch whiskey.

Duncan's eyes take on a faraway look and it irritates me that I decided to give him my time, and he chooses to zone out on me. "So, you want to try this smart lady with a game of poker."

"Yes. Yes, I'd love to."

Good. Looking to the bartender who's sorting our drink, I turn to raise a brow at Duncan. "Can we proceed to the tables?" Smiling, I add, "Once we're done with the drinks though."

He clears his throat. "Sure." Tilting his head to the side, sizing me and the challenge I present. "But don't you want to go somewhere quiet where, you know, where we can talk and I can get to know you better?"

What is he insinuating? Nah... He's not my type. I don't dig old men. If I want to do crazy stuff with a stranger, him, nope. Nonso, hell yeah! When I daydream, it's for a baby daddy, not a sugar daddy.

"I don't want to do that tonight. Tonight, I just want to try my beginner's luck with a game of poker."

He relaxes back on his stool, and I feel a twinge of pity for him. Poor Zaddy thinking he could get a taste of this. He looks like he delivers pants down, but I don't fancy him. The bartender chooses this time to place a decanter and two shot glasses between us.

"What's on your mind?" I ask as Duncan takes his time doling out our drinks, such a gentleman, bidding his time. Touché.

He hands me a shot. "I'm wondering how Lola finds Twin Bliss Resort." Then he takes a swig of his drink, his eyes on me, then smacks his lips.

I take a sip of mine. Malty, tastes like caramel. "Not bad."

"It's one of the finest whiskeys and quite expensive too."

To answer his earlier question, "I find Twin Bliss very..." How do I describe it without sounding unexposed? "It's just beautiful. I'm glad I brought my trusty tripod to capture the scenery and memories."

I take a gulp of my drink, and he cautions me. We speak about my photography, and I clear the air, stating it is for my lifestyle blog.

"So, you're from Bodo. I actually thought you were from the eastern side of Nigeria. What is it about the Marula tree?" I wave my free hand. "Been hearing a lot about it."

Escape

He leans in conspiratorially, winking and I lean in to get dibs on the sacred bit of information he is about to share. "Have you read the brochure?"

Nonsense, I chuckle, slapping him playfully on his shoulder. "You made me think you were going to say something sensible."

He throws back his head, letting out a deep laugh. He later calms down and I smile. "Well, all of it is in the brochure. It's quite important to our people and the resort in particular. That's why they have that giant one planted close to the entrance."

Oh, I see. I have not taken my time to tour my room properly, hence why I haven't read the brochure. After hanging up on Carolanne, I arranged my stuff, took a much-needed shower, then napped as planned.

"Interesting," I mutter, rubbing my palms together.

"Indeed," he says, closing his eyes.

Enough of the merry go round. The whiskey is already getting to my light head, but I didn't come out for small talk, I came to have fun. "So, are we playing?"

He opens his eyes, and his breathing changes, low and shaky, then he blinks.

"Hey, you good?" Leaning into him, I peer at his face that had gone pale for a moment. Had he seen a ghost? "It looked like you blanked out for a bit."

"Yeah." He swallows, offering a wobbly smile. "Yes, and no. I think we can play. My personal favorite is blackjack and poker. Extra points if it's naked poker but I stake it for others as well."

"Blackjack sounds like fun. I'm not trying naked poker any time soon. And even at—"

"You know what?" I was saying something, that's what. "I had a long day and I feel a bit drained. I'll have to take something to ease me into the night." He smiles.

"Hmm, something." I nod, taking the final sip of my drink.

The goat! He wants to have a wild night like myself. Just because I didn't accept his advance, he wants to drug me. Why haven't I gotten up from this stool? It's not like he's the only guy on this resort. My mind flashes back to how I felt upon realizing Robbie's betrayal and my wish to take something to numb me. What would it hurt to try it tonight? An opportunity to know what getting high feels like.

Duncan leans in, whispering in a conspiratorial tone, "It's a secret."

"What is it?" I pout, deciding to play along. What has the big boy got on him?

He grins, a strange look on his face. "Well, aren't you the curious cat?"

Hah! He thinks I'm an innocent goody two-shoes. "Spill it."

"It's a pill." A pill? Not cocaine? Are you kidding me?

"Helps me, relax. Feel things." He moistens his lips, his eyes twinkling mischievously.

I indulge him with a smile. "Tell me."

And he smiles back, pulling out a prescription bottle from his pocket, eyes darting left and right before slipping a pill into my waiting palm.

What on earth is this? This man isn't joking and must be bat shit crazy. I spare him a quick glance before returning it.

"What does it do?"

"I already said; It relaxes me." He places the pill on his tongue and swallows. "Do you want to try?" Stretching another pill to me.

How did he do that? That was fast. Must be a regular at smuggling pills out of his prescription bottle. Before I can make up my mind, he places the pill, which from the club's light looks either purple or blue, in his mouth, then sips his drink.

He laughs and I raise my brow—what's funny?

"For an extra kick." He shrugs. "It's not so bad."

Okay, I can do this. If he is taking it, as old as he looks, nothing bad can come of it, right? I open my palm and he places a pill on it. He's not even telling me the name. How do I know what I'm consuming?

"You're supposed to ingest it," he says.

And I realize I've been staring at the pill for the longest time.

Party pooper.

He winks at me. What the hell? I am already on an island with a stolen ticket, what other crazy thing can't I do? I toss the pill, take a sip, then clear my throat with a cough.

We discuss some more, about the peculiarities of the resort and how its strong history and services makes it stand apart from other neighboring resorts.

Oh snap. My eyes.

I close and open them to look at the people on the casino floor, they seem to be moving off-beat. Oops. It's me, not them. They are not dancing.

The music is louder than before, and I want to dance.

It's working! Oh my gosh! It's working! I shake my head, giggling. I can feel everything. Everything! My senses are in enhanced mode.

"Okay... I think I'm feeling it. Is there a place one can dance here?" I begin nodding to the tropical beat coming from the speakers.

Duncan smirks before taking my hand that lays on my thigh, he strokes it then before letting his fingers crawl to my thigh and I freeze.

"Excuse me, Duncan. I'm-I'm not comfortable with this." He continues in his exploration, and I grasp his hand till he winces in pain. But he's not having it.

Shit.

What have I gotten myself into? Getting chummy with someone who just took three of what's pumping in my system. Lord knows how many he's had before we met.

"Let's get—" He begins, trying to shake my hand off, but I hold still. He turns white. "Camilla?!" Then squints to someone on the floor, before taking his hands off me like he has been scalded.

Camilla? That's a woman. Who is Camilla? Whoever she is, she just saved me from this old pervert.

"Erm, Lola. I have to go."

Go? Good riddance. But not before I give him my mind.

Before I can voice my irritation, a deep baritone voice says, "Duncan."

I raise my head and my gaze lands on the owner of the voice who is towering over us in our seated state. Lips drawn tight as he looks down at Duncan.

"Onahi."

There's tension in the air as both men regard each other— Duncan acting like a cornered rat, the dark biracial stranger looking even hotter with his lips curled. What does he look like smiling? Hmm. New challenge.

Dropping my whiskey on the counter, I smile at him, noticing both buttons on his polo shirt are unbuttoned, giving me a glimpse of his thin neck chain and hairless chest. I like that.

"Onahi..." I sing.

Duncan mutters something, tapping Onahi on his shoulder, before excusing himself. Perfect. Thank you for giving us our space! Let's hope Mr. Onahi here likes whiskey.

"Are you okay?" Onahi leans close, speaking over the loud afro music.

"Never been better." I smile, then nod at Duncan's empty stool. "Wanna join me?"

"You sure?"

I smirk, "I dare you."

He smiles; it's lopsided and divine. Can we leave this place and take a walk on the beach? Where I rub my chest on your chest. And you're only few inches taller than me, so we would be rubbing in all the right places. *Oh, so perfect. Not Nonso, but will do.*

Ten

Onahi

DEFINITELY THE LADY WHO LODGED into Robert's room. "What are you having?"

"Whiskey." She smiles, her eyes bright with excitement. "Heard it's the finest."

"Nice." My gaze observing how the black dress molds her slim body, stopping somewhere around her thigh, displaying legs for days. Long, trim athletic legs.

"You want some?"

Hmm? I raise my eyes to hers, confirming she caught me staring. She bites her lips, pink lips begging to be kissed and I contemplate her double-barreled question. "I'll place an order."

"No, you shouldn't." She pouts, leaning into me. "You can share mine." Then adjusts herself with a smirk, her eyes raking my frame.

I smile, shrugging. "If that's what the lady wants, then—"

"Who are you to say no?" She belches.

Giggling, she covers her mouth. "I'm sorry," she chortles, then places a hand on my thigh. "What were you going to say?"

My knee jerks in response to her touch, but she is too far gone to notice my reaction. Her hand remains there, burning a hole through my naked thigh.

"I was going to say, I'll go along with that. But yeah." I grin. "Who am I to say no?"

Jay and I were having an enjoyable time earlier on a table not far away. We had ordered our drink, when a call from Ahmed came through and she had to excuse herself to continue her conversation. I waited for her return, after all, she was to be my vacation buddy. While waiting, I spotted the guy I had seen hanging around her during arrival cast a furtive glance in my direction, before following in her wake. Dude must think he is sharp or something. Looked responsible though. I trust Jay would shake him off if she isn't interested.

Wanting her to have a good time, since she confessed to returning to Nigeria a few days ago, then came the drama with Ahmed's proposal, I left her with her new friend whom I acknowledged with a nod. After which, I stepped out to tell the bouncers to keep an eye on the new friend. While outside,

Escape

I confirmed Robert had not arrived, then returned to find the mysterious lady who had taken up residence in his villa, fighting Duncan off her. Good thing she had it under control—I would have stepped in to set Duncan straight.

"Hi..." she says grinning, stretching her other long dainty hand to me. "I'm Lola Dade, nice to meet you."

What are you playing at missy? That's not the name on your ID. I decide to play along, accepting her hand. "Onahi."

"Yeah, I got that. I like it. Sounds Nigerian, but you don't look Nigerian."

I shrug. "It's a complicated genealogy." She scratches my palm with her index finger and a jolt of sexual energy travels from my palm down to my crotch. Lightning fast. What the fuck?! I pull my hand from hers and a frown creases her brows.

Nodding towards the decanter that's got just an inch of whiskey left in it, I ask, "How many of that have you had?"

She takes her other hand from my thigh, looks at the decanter, then grins at me. "Not much. Two? I'm not usually like this. But tonight, I tried something new. It's dope."

Sighing, she runs her fingers on my thigh again. God help me—she can't keep her hands to herself. The hair on my skin rises. My butt tightens as pleasure courses through my veins. Okay. This was not what I expected when I heard someone had taken up residence at Robert's. She could be his girlfriend, sister or worst of all, fiancée. Those legs... With the things I want to do with her, with them, Robert would cease speaking with me for life. It's thrilling frolicking with another man's woman, all a game, until it happens to you. I've never intentionally done so and will not start now.

"Are you here alone?"

"Of course!" Her fingers, which I've started enjoying, cease their ministration. They tread to the edge of my shorts, then back to my naked thigh.

Clearing my throat, I try again. "Are you here with someone? Waiting for anyone? Boyfriend? Husband?"

She begins laughing, her lithe frame shaking from the pleasure of expressing joy. Her cleavage vibrating in unison. It is so sexy—I imagine her riding me, her body shaking and bucking the way it is now. Goddamnit Nahi!

She pauses, clearing her throat, then resumes vibrating with laughter. What's so funny about the situation?

She wipes a tear from her eyes, giggling. "I'm sorry." Raising a hand to stall me, she bends her head and begins laughing again.

I smile. A tease. Laughing at my expense, but all's fair in love and war. What the fuck? All's fair in love and war? When did I start spouting poetry?

"I'm so, so, sorry." She waves her hand dismissively. "Because of Duncan?"

"No." Thoughts of him never crossed my mind. "I'm speaking both on and off the resort."

"I'm as single as can be. Both on and off the resort." She gets herself together—folding her arms, with a look, daring me to continue.

The revelation doesn't make the situation any better, but at least, she's not connected with Robert. Who the fuck then was she? An ex? His sister? I don't know much about his family life, but she's too dark skinned to be related to Robert by blood. Maybe a distant cousin. One by marriage? Or an adopted sister.

"And you?" She nods to me.

I raise a brow.

"Are you single?" Her neatly trimmed brows rising to a unique angle.

"To stupor. And ready to mingle."

"Why me?"

This is a complete what I ordered versus what I got situation. She was throwing herself at me moments ago, now she's playing prim.

"I don't know."

"Hmm..."

"Actually... I saw you earlier, when you arrived." Via the security cameras. "Your first time here?"

"Oh. Is there a badge one gets for being a regular?"

"No. Not that. Anyways, I hope you're enjoying your stay."

Her gaze skims my frame and an idea pops in my head—I want her to do that to me naked.

"I am." Her tongue flickers as she moistens her lips, causing a shiver to run down my spine. The way she goes from an adrenaline pumped teenager to a sultry seductress is poof! Mind-boggling.

"What can I do to make your stay more enjoyable?" My dick twitches, ready for action.

Cocking her head to the side, she lowers her lashes and begins humming.

What the fuck?

This is my cue to leave this bat-shit crazy lady, but she had mentioned she took something earlier. Leaning closer, I close the distance between us, placing one palm on her cheek. "Are you sure you are... okay?"

Her eyes fly open, and she smiles. She has the cutest hazel pupils surrounded by a darker iris. "The music... Johnny Drille." She hums then begins singing along. "You are my love... would you be my Juliet and I will be your Romeo, my love..."

Her eyes twinkling with mischief as she gets off her stool, she offers her hand. "Be my Juliet and I will be your Romeo..." Pulling me to my feet, she wraps her arms around my waist. "My love... oh my love. Would you be my Juliet and I will be your Romeo..." She fits perfectly in my arms. While I am getting used to having her in my embrace, she pulls apart, and I feel empty, then returns to hug me, still singing. "My love... my love."

What was that?

I follow her lead like a robot, not sure if this is normal. There are few people on the dance floor as it is not time for hard clubbing. Just matured couples enjoying the solemn music and occasional shouts from the casino floor.

"I've been wanting to dance all evening." She says when the music changes.

"I'm glad you're doing that now."

"Okay, that was a lie."

"What?"

She giggles, tapping my chest. "Not a lie, lie." Her hand remains on my chest, and she begins tracing wriggly lines. "You don't like lies do you?"

"Who does?"

"Well, dancing is the second thing I've been wanting to do all evening. The first is actually to try my beginner's luck at the casino."

"Your first time?"

"I'm actually a champion online. Duh."

"How long will you be on the resort?"

"Six days? Seven? I don't know." She giggles, dancing away, then returns in a flash. "All I want to do is have fun. I've got a secret." Her eyes twinkling.

Finally, I get to know why she's in Robert's villa.

She pulls down my ear and whispers, her voice charging electrolytes in my body. "This is an escape from my real world, and I want to do it all." She licks my ear and I pull back, a wide grin in place. *Bring it on.*

"I'm offering my services to be your personal guide throughout your stay." What did I just say? I've got Jay I'm supposed to be spending time with.

She grins. "I accept your services."

Eleven

Lola

THIS GUY IS HOT! SOMEBODY save me! The stuff Duncan gave to me is not helping matters. *Why the heck did I swallow the pill again?* But oh... it feels so, so good. Letting loose. Just being. Just living. No thoughts for what others think.

Since it is going to be my first in person game, Onahi advises me to play blackjack and from there we could upgrade to Poker. We join a table playing blackjack with a minimum bet of $20. Onahi encourages me to place a bet of $25. The dealer deals our cards. First, I get an Ace and next time he deals the rounds, I get a Jack. The dealer's card sums up to eighteen.

Escape

"Yours is the highest," Onahi whispers to me.

"Blackjack!" I scream, embracing my chips.

"Beginner's luck." I hear someone on the lines murmur, but I don't care. Tonight, is going down in history—I won my first game in a real casino. I'm a certified gambler, bitches!

While other players decide whether to hit, stay or double down. I order my first bottle of water.

Four games later, I have ordered two more bottles of water and gone to the restroom thrice. My throat is parched, and I've been speaking out of turn. Thank you, Duncan.

In between my trips, Onahi plays for me, and I could see the frustration on the other players face, but they never mention it. This sums up my playing at a casino in real life. I lost thrice and won twice.

"You know what?"

"What?" Onahi responds.

"This is not working for me. It's not turning out like I imagined it will."

"I'll fund it."

"No. No. It's not that, why don't we try one last thing I've been thinking of since I saw you."

The tip of his ears goes dark, and I hold back a giggle. It's a treat watching his skin color react when he is not comfortable.

The dealer begins dealing cards and Onahi whispers to me what to say if I truly want to leave.

"Surrender."

"We're out." Onahi pulls me along, while I snag a bottle of water from the table. Impatient, he decides we use the stairs instead of the elevator and I happily tag along.

"Where are we going?" I ask as the cool sea breeze brush against my skin.

"We're about to try what you've been thinking of."

"Oh that." Pulling my hand from his, I pause, staring up into the night sky. Bliss. I close my eyes, hugging myself. "A late-night walk on the beach?" I whisper.

His exasperated breath proves my thoughts are not in alignment with his.

"If that's what you want."

"Of course."

Walking the rest of the way to the beach, we secure a hammock hung between two palm trees. I get comfy in it, while he stands on the sand, arms crossed, looking lost.

"Wanna join me?"

"Are you sure?"

"C'mon." I motion for him to join me and he sits on the edge. "C'mon. Let's get comfy."

He scoffs, then does as I say, like he's indulging a petulant child. Our legs kiss as the hammock swings, causing my pussy to spasm. I want more.

"That wasn't so hard." I sigh, breathing in his manly scent. "Your arms," he glances at them, as if asking what's happening to them. "Put them around me."

"That's something you've been thinking of doing?"

Escape

I sigh, smiling. "I think of a lot of things. And yes. I've been thinking of your arms around me." I sigh again when we are settled. "Now we can stare at the sky, with the ocean just some feet away. What better combination of man and nature can you think of?"

The soothing beach wave serves as background music to our moment together and there's a chill in the air. Goosebumps rise on my skin, and I snuggle closer, his heat warming me up. We stay like this forever, gently tossed by the wind on the hammock.

With the pill wearing off, I rest my head on his chest, playing with the buttons on his polo. Our legs now subtly getting tangled. I decide to ask questions I should have asked earlier. "So... what brings you to the resort?"

"I spend a lot of time here," his baritone vibrates through my core.

We are so close; all I need to do is turn my head and our lips will meet.

"It's a nice place to relax and hang out with friends."

Raising my head to search his face, I ask, "You're here with friends?"

He gives a low laugh, before his arm applies pressure on my back to get me resting on his chest again. "No, I'm not. It's complicated."

"Hmm."

"I've got friends vacationing here. But we're not here *together*. I came here on my own."

"That's nice." My throat still feels parched, so I find a way to unscrew my bottled water and take a sip. I'm never taking pills from strangers. Never. Bodo big boy or not.

"Feeling better?"

"Yes, thank you."

"So, are you here alone?"

"You've asked that before."

"You were high."

"You could have left."

"I didn't."

Detangling myself from his warmth, I stare at his face, made bright beneath the clear lit sky. "Why are you here? With me."

He sits up, holding my hand. His lips set in a strained smile, as he caresses my fingers. "You confuse me."

"That doesn't sound good."

He sighs, a myriad of emotions crossing his face, as though he wasn't sure of the answer himself. "Are you sure you're here alone?"

I raise my arms up in a shrug. He is asking too many questions. I see the heat in his eyes from time to time, but it evades me. What would those questioning lips taste like? Would they make me glad I came here? Would they make my toes curl in delight? Why doesn't he just give in to the heat?

"I'm going to kiss you." He closes the distance between us, brushing his lips over mine.

Escape

Every thought of what he would taste like wash away from my mind as I savor the real deal. His lips are softer than they look. Perfect for kissing. My confused body and mind have found what they have been looking for. He is not Robbie, but Onahi. He is not Robbie, but Onahi. I give a little sigh, putting my arms around his neck, drawing him closer. I need to feel his heart beating in sync with mine. I might not be a pro in bed, but I know how to kiss. I've been practicing since I was in kindergarten. If he is not a good kisser, I will leave his sorry ass for the others. Even that bald-headed Duncan.

I tug on his bottom lip with my teeth, coaxing his mouth to part and when he responds, I swoop in for the kill. He groans his pleasure and I giggle as his arm tightens around my body, telling me he is into it. Great. It is the first time I'll be taking the lead while kissing and I don't know if it's the sea or the drug that's wearing off that has me froward. Whatever. I like it! Curling my toe in delight.

He is a good kisser. Knowing when to stop and when to continue. His tongue gently caresses mine, and I moan in response. Hours, days, years... time flies before he reluctantly pulls his lips away from mine.

Okay daddy... What's it going to be now?

He signs for me to get my feet off the edge and completely lay within the hammock before he lays besides me and resumes kissing. He flicks his tongue against mine, then takes full control, like my turn was over and it's his turn. He thrust his, I tease with mine, playing and giggling in-between.

"This is my first," he says between kisses, his bare leg rubbing against mine.

"Your first what?" I chase his tongue with mine, smiling.

"First time kissing a giggling girl."

I giggle again. "I'm not a girl."

A girl wouldn't be getting aroused or wondering if she could pull his shorts off to admire his growing erection pressing against her. Nor would her nipples be hardening from desire. His effect on me is stronger than the drug I had imbibed earlier.

Twelve

Onahi

"WHY IS IT SO HARD to unzip this short?" Lola mutters in frustration, pulling her intoxicating lips from mine, her focus completely on my shorts. "I want to fuck you so bad." She pouts like a spoilt child.

I chuckle, moving my body slower than normal as I help with the task of unzipping my shorts. I need her lips back on mine. The taste of her lips has ruined me, and I need more than we are doing right now. Whiskey will never taste the same again. "Are you always this impatient? And demanding?" I ask as the zip finally goes down.

She gives a sigh of appreciation. Then frowns, tilting her head to the side, the moon forming a halo around it. An angel. An angel about to be fucked. "When I'm not getting what I need, yes. It's been two years since I last had sex. I've been celibate, waiting for the right man. Lucky you."

Lucky me, indeed.

She reaches for my dick, then pauses. Frowning, she tilts her head to the side, the moon forming a halo around it. An angel. An angel about to be fucked.

"You have boxers on?"

"That shouldn't be a problem. Come back here."

She moans as I resume kissing her. I pull away from her mouth, moving towards her ears, licking and blow air on it. She arches her back, pushing into me and my dick jerks in gratitude. "Fuck," I groan.

Giggling, she continues the motion as I thrust my tongue inside her ear.

"Oh god." She cries. "Yes..." she whimpers.

Better.

Returning my lips back to hers, my hands begin exploring her skin. She shudders when I brush her exposed thigh, murmuring something I don't get. My finger, the explorer, goes underneath her dress, till it finds her panties. It is soaked. Soaked, begging to be taken.

Good. She is ready. But I need to make this good for both of us.

"I can't wait." She says, swiftly rolling us skillfully till she is on top, like she makes out on a hammock every day. It isn't until I feel the cool breeze on my dick quickly replaced by her warm pussy, did I understand what she meant.

Closing my eyes, I savor her warmth. It feels... different. She grinds her waist in a slow rhythm, sighing in appreciation. Biting my lips, my toes flex and I struggle to hold back my sigh of pleasure.

"You're so..." She begins but doesn't end.

My thoughts are on her vaginal walls breathing life into my dick. With each slow thrust, my dick expands and stretches. Fuck... I see lightening when she changes the motion, grinding from a different angle.

"Let's go sit over there." Someone laughs and another. "Yeah, there's a swing there."

Oh fuck. I push Lola off me as footsteps draw closer.

"No..." Lola cries softly. "What is wrong with you?"

Exactly! What the fuck is wrong with me? Acting like I'm pussy starved. Scrambling off the hammock, I adjust my boxers, zip my shorts, and adjust my shirt. "I'm sorry. But I've got business to attend to." Not my best, but all I can cook up in the moment.

Scanning the shoreline, I find the tourists who must have spoken move further away. The night wind had carried their voices to me. What the fuck?! Some random retard must have been hearing us go at it from a distance—all the giggling, moaning and—fuck!

Lola follows suit, as she gets off the hammock, her eyes blazing with anger. This does not look good.

"I'm going home." She takes off her low-heeled sandals, stomps in one direction, pauses, turns to her left, pauses, then turns to face me, eyes still blazing. "Where is the way to my villa?!"

I catch up with her, hold her hands and peer into her eyes. Thanks to those passersby, I returned to my senses. I stopped for her sake and Robert's. For my sake too—she mentioned being high on something and that will be me taking advantage of her condition even though she was more than willing. "I'm sorry about that. It wasn't—"

"Spare me." Dropping her hands like they are hot, I mutter some curse words under my breath. "Where's the way to the *Eclipse*? So, I can trace my way back."

The *Eclipse* is behind her. Right there. The first direction she had chosen to take. "Over there," I point.

With no thank you or any form of gratitude, she begins moving towards the *Eclipse*.

"Why don't you order a shuttle?" I call out.

Without looking back, she gives me the middle finger as she staggers away.

Haven't I learnt my lesson from Heather? From Flora? From women in general? How did she come into my life, in less than twenty-four hours and have me questioning my intentions? I didn't do anything bad. I rescued us from embarrassment.

Once I find out how she's connected to Robert, we'll probably not see, ever again. She had mentioned being on the resort for six days, but the place is big enough for us to never—shit.

Escape

Fuck. Fuck. Fuck. I begin racing towards her as she crumbles to the floor.

"Are you okay?" I kneel beside her, my arm going around her.

"My ankle..." she cries. This time around it's in pain, not in anger or pleasure. "Get your hands off me!"

Tsk. Tsk. Tsk.

"I promise, I'm only here to help. Can you sit up by yourself?"

She grunts in response, sitting up as directed. I move to touch the ankle and she confirms it is feeling better, she only stepped on those tiny prickly dry fruits that fall from the palm trees. I'm tempted to massage her legs, just for the pleasure of it, but common sense takes over.

"Let me order a shuttle—"

"I'll walk."

"Why?"

She sighs. "I thought I was feeling better, but I don't feel good." She mutters something about taking that idiot's prescription pill without asking for the name. "I believe walking will help me... You know... Reduce the effect? I feel like I'm floating right now. Very light."

"And you don't want to tell me what you took? I can take you to the clinic."

"I'll be fine."

"I'll only let you walk if you agree I accompany you."

She hisses, her shoulders drooping, before covering her face with both hands. "Really?"

I remove lint from her dress' shoulder. "Yeah."

She pulls her hand down her face, her voice sounding funny. "I will hate myself tomorrow. You've seen me at my worst."

I shrug.

Her hands drop and she adds, "We'll probably not see ourselves ever again."

"I hope so too."

The corners of her eye glistens with tears. "I'm sorry… I didn't mean it that way."

The fuck I didn't mean it that way. Why is she so emotional and irrational?

"You've got important business you need to attend to," she sniffles, "I'll find my way home."

"I don't—" Shit. I had mentioned that earlier. "You're more important right now. And…" I would never have admitted this if everything was normal. If she wasn't so dramatic and emotional. "I was actually enjoying your company."

She smiles. "Everyone does."

"I'm sincerely sorry." I pick up her sandals, rise to my feet, then stretch a hand to her. "I know a shortcut. Shall we begin?"

It's going to be a long walk, but since I can't convince her, I'll let the distance do it.

Escape

"So... what do you do for a living?" I ask, falling in step beside her.

"I make heartbroken women believe partying is the best way to mend a broken heart."

"A club manager?"

"Nope. Let's try again." She plucks a leaf from the shrub on the side, cutting it off in bits as she speaks. "I make sure everything Twin Bliss says in digital and print media rhyme with the service they offer."

"Communications manager?"

She brings her thumb and forefinger together. "This close. I'm a brand manager." She smiles brightly. "The Brand Guru. That's what my followers call me."

I give a wry smile, with all the drama and stunt she has pulled this evening, I didn't see that coming. "Now I understand why you decided to go off the hook tonight."

She purses her tempting lips. "You do?"

"Yeah. You dropped hints here and there. Your real world. First time this. First time that."

"Yeah." She nods. "That's me."

"So, you've been holding back in your real world, uhn?"

"Not holding back, holding back. Just..." She shrugs, her attention carried away by a firefly. Her countenance relaxes as her eyes tracks its every movement, till it flies far from sight.

"We have a lot of that here."

"That's lovely. I only get to see them when I visit Nigeria."

"Visit Nigeria?" It felt so natural speaking with her that I didn't bother confirming where she had travelled in from.

"Yeah. I moved to the United States with my parents when I was eight. I visit Nigeria every year. My parents returned permanently to Nigeria two years ago."

"That's... patriotic."

"You bet. I miss the food and all. The resort's menu was part of the reason I didn't think twice when packing my bags. Although they say they're world-class, they don't offer Nigerian local dishes like *amala, efo riro...* Just imagine a resort that offers not just French, Italian, Indian, Western cuisines but other cuisines like African, German with chefs from all parts of the world." She laughs at herself, then scrunches her nose. "I'm blabbing. Enough of me. Over to you. Why does your name sound West-African-ish? Wait. Let me guess. You're a missionary kid?"

Missionary style, yes, I like that, not kid. I smile. "Wrong. I have family here, in Nigeria too, although most of us are now based in the United States."

"The home of the brave. And what do you do?"

"A couple of businesses here and there."

"Right. That explains why you're here on vacation. Only rich people say things like that. Couple of businesses here and there."

I chuckle.

"I didn't say that." She zips her mouth animatedly and I chuckle even harder.

Escape

If I don't check it, Lola will be wearing on me. An owl hoots in the distance and Lola tilts her head up.

"This place is… I could swear I met Lucas Opeyemi's wife, the Nollywood guy, on this resort today. But I was too busy settling in I didn't bother to double check."

How did the conversation switch to sighting Lucas? Was she a fan girl? Or worse, has she had something to do with him? That would be a total turn off. With everything that has happened in my world, I wouldn't be shocked, just turned off.

"You like him?"

"Like him?" Her forehead furrows. "Nope. The guy is an industry slut. I don't roll with brands like that. I've not seen his movies, but his scandal makes news every other time I visit Nigeria. His wife seemed friendly. A little dramatic, but friendly. Now that I'm looking at resuming my YouTube vlog, maybe I'll be able to capture some drama on this resort. Or maybe I'll try watch a movie of his while I'm here."

I clear my throat.

"Wait. Are you jealous?"

"What?" My eyes widen. "Lucas is a friend." I scoff. Her response is to suck her mouth, till it makes hollows on her cheek. She can suck on my dick like that if—I shake the thought away, continuing my lecture. "Since you're a brand manager, there are better things to capture and be done on the resort than waiting for drama to unfold."

She shrugs, her action causing her perky breasts to bob. Focus.

"Friends don't make those type of comments, *Lucas isn't worth your time*."

Here we go. "That's not what I said, and you know it. Have you read the brochure? You'll find a lot more to vlog on than Lucas." Shit. I had to go and mention his name again.

"You're the thousandth person mentioning that. I'll check. Although I prefer spontaneity. I'm more of an impulsive person. I love doing stuff just for the fun of it, in the moment. Yeah. And I don't like getting on water."

The brave lady has got some fears. "A phobia?"

"You wish. It's just me not wanting to die in a watery grave."

"I love water. The ocean."

"Happy for you. If I had known getting to this resort involved taking a boat, I would never have gotten on the flight in the first place. But now that I'm here, I'm open, and will not fight what fate throws my way."

We walk by the *Sweet Morning Restaurant*, and it looks like a ghost town. The chairs on the decks made to lean on the table. The poolside entertaining the few couples who dare. When the day breaks, everything will be back to normal, with more guests trooping in and out.

"Oh..." Lola squeals, "My place is over there. Behind that one." She points to one of the Addis Ababa pavilions with private gardens that's within walking distance of my Cairo villa. Not every lodging is a villa, but to make guests happy, the staff of the resort calls every lodging a villa.

"Finally." I say as I stop by her doorstep.

"Does your offer to be my personal resort guide still stand?"

Oh. I said that. The things I've said and done since meeting Lola are just so... "I have a friend I'm supposed to—"

"Don't worry. I just wanted to confirm."

"Yeah."

"So... Goodnight?"

"Yeah. It's been a long day."

"I can only imagine."

"Yeah."

She stares at me, and I stare back. Breaking eye contact, I offer her sandals.

"Want to come in?" She smiles brightly, the moonlight causing her eyelashes to look fuller.

Although my time with her will be the highlight of my day—not the time catching up with my guys or hanging out with Jay—spending the night will most likely be the worst decision. She's still high or tipsy on what she took and might regret it. Let's not forget Robert in the mix.

"Some other time." If Robert swears you're not his woman.

Her expressions turn sour.

"You would thank me tomorrow."

She bites her bottom lips as she contemplates my response, gets into her villa, and shuts the door.

It takes a lot for me not to knock. To beg her to let me in. Sometimes you meet some people, and your souls align. A different type of different. A breath of fresh air. One you don't mind sniffing every time. And when you meet people like that, contrary to popular opinion, it's best to take it slow.

The chirping sounds of crickets and night's insects follow me to my villa. It's best I call Robert, so I understand better what's going on. Maybe he sent her to help me. But that's not possible. He doesn't know why I sent him the invite in the first place.

Thirteen

Lola

OH GOD. MY TUMMY. WHAT did I eat last night? I scramble to sit up in bed but a sharp pain from my abdomen makes me thrust myself back on my pillows.

Oh snap. Last night.

My mind plays everything in reverse motion stopping where Duncan gave me the pill. Why did I make that crazy decision without thinking it through? I thought about it, but I don't think I thought it through.

Well decisions like that makes life fun. More interesting. I hope I don't bump into him or the guy I was mooning over last night. Most of our conversation is muted in my brain, it will be embarrassing meeting him again. What's his name again? He was so cute and, oh no! I can't remember his name. *Somebody shoot me.* I should have just stayed put at the bar or played a game while I waited for my Nonso. Did he get there before or after I left with the other guy?

Blackjack!

Oh snap. Did we change my chips for cash at the cashier's booth?

My tummy rumbles again. I can eat an elephant right now. A full-grown elephant.

"You're awake," a familiar voice which grows louder as it gets closer says. Uh-oh. "Good morning, Miss Lola. It's a beautiful Monday morning."

Oh... It's smiling Biftu. The female butler from yesterday.

I blink a couple of times. "I didn't summon you." Sitting up on my bed as she opens the frilly white curtains.

She stands by the window, holding her hands in a prim posture. "You requested morning duties during your registration."

I didn't know what I was signing up for, I was just excited to have a personal butler to attend to my every need.

"How long have you been here?"

"Over an hour."

An hour? She could have killed me in my sleep if she wanted to and she wasn't even the one that woke me up. On cue, my tummy growls and Biftu breaks into a giggle but stops immediately.

"I'm sorry ma—"

"It's fine." Pushing myself off the plush king size, till my legs touch the hardwood floor. "I'm famished." Looking down my frame, I'm still in my dress from last night which saves me the stress of having to cover my nakedness from her.

"You're up in time for breakfast at the *Sweet Morning Restaurant*. Although they close in an hour's time."

I pick up my phone which I had left charging on the nightstand before zoning out, scrolling through Instagram.

"Your bath is ready, and I've arranged your suitcase into the drawers and closet. But I don't know what to do with that. Should I place it in the bathroom or here?"

I raise my head to find her pointing to my bedroom bestie, Zeus, resting comfortably on the blanket chest. "Oh that. It's a vibrator. You can keep it inside the chest." Returning to scroll through my phone—there's nothing interesting on the gram.

"Thanks, Biftu. And breakfast?" I toss my phone on the bed, contemplating my walk to the bathroom.

"I could order in your meal through—"

I grunt. "Don't worry, just tell me where it is."

"It's right there on the map." She points towards the brochure that has a detachable map on my bedstand. "It's about three minutes' walk from here, right beside the ocean."

Lucky me. Right beside the food house.

"Any meal you'd like to recommend?" I ask, stepping into the bathroom, then returning to the room to pick up my phone.

"If we were home in Ethiopia." Her eyes take on a look of nostalgia., "I'll have suggested you nibble on some *ga'at*."

"What's that?" They sure have diverse hands on the resort.

"Oh, they don't serve that here on the menu, but you can request it. It's a porridge formed in the shape of a volcano with a spicy butter sauce in the middle and a yogurt mixture poured around the sides."

I lick my lips as the image forms in my head, then walk back into the bathroom. "That sounds rich and yummy. You had me at butter."

Awwn... I trail my fingers in the warm water with dried lavender petals afloat. She really did prepare a bath. It looks inviting but today's not a luxurious kinda bath day. I want to wash off the grime from yesterday's adventure, look fresh and relaxed while I have breakfast by the ocean.

"What do you like?" She calls out.

"Anything with bread?" I begin brushing my teeth, while straining my ears to listen to her voice. I look good. Nothing like the night I had.

"Hmm... You could have the signature Arabian breakfast. It comes with fresh bread. It's in the signature meals section if you're self-serving and also on the menu." I thank her, then move on to start bathing.

Scrubbing off all memories of last night, I step out of the bathroom wrapped in a towel and Biftu is still in the room where I had left her.

"Should I—do you...?"

She is unfazed. "Do you need help dressing?"

What is this? Is this some English movie or regency romance? She wants to help me dress? This is where I draw the line.

"Thanks a lot, Biftu, but I'll carry on from here. You can go to the terrace or water the gardens. Just give me a moment." I grin and she nods, stepping out.

"You can come in now," I call out to her, and she steps in.

"Is this what you're wearing for the day?" She stares at me in wonder. Her eyes admiring my legs.

I turn around to give her a better view of my Ankara styled romper that stops on my thigh. "You like it?"

"It's beautiful."

"Thank you."

"But you'll need more oil for those legs. They shouldn't be looking ashy." She moves to pick up a bottle I had received from the front desk while checking in.

"What's in that?"

"The marula oil. It's lightweight and has a mild fragrance. You won't even notice you have it on, and it shines all day."

I shrug, indulging her as she takes her time massaging it into my legs while I scroll through my phone.

"Are you signed up for any activity?"

"Not that I know of." I respond looking down at her neatly braided cornrows.

"There's a lot of activities." She stands up, screwing the cap of the bottle back on, while I move to pick my purse from the couch. "You could order in your breakfast and—"

"There's no need. I need the exercise. I'll figure out what I want to do as the day goes."

Biftu smiles.

"Thanks a lot, Biftu. And please no more morning service or duties." I grin, stepping out of my villa.

****

ADORNED WITH A FASHIONABLE WAIST pouch, a 75cl flask on my hip, neon sunshades—today it's blue—and my fashionable digital camera on my neck, it takes me less than three minutes to get to the *Sweet Morning Restaurant* using the map on the resort's app as a guide.

I guess I'm not the only one that had a wild night. The restaurant is quite busy for a place that's about to close.

I'll place an order then while I peruse what I can engage myself with things to do today. I've got almost five more days and I need to fill it up with eventful activities.

Right before the restaurant is a lagoon pool laid with blue tiles. The effect is ephemeral. Scattered around the pool are chaise lounges, shrub pots and colorful flowerpots adorned with bright tropical flowers. Palm trees act as shade for guests who prefer sitting close to the chaise lounges. For a place as prestigious as this, the restaurant looks like a marketplace. It's hard to find a place to sit and most people are either waving goodbyes or just lingering on their tables, chatting. A server passes with a trolley laden with meals, and I swallow. I can't wait.

Heading over to the self-service section, I look out for the signature meals as suggested by Biftu. They've got Belgian waffles, red velvet pancakes, Nutella crepes, Arabic breakfast—finally, some bread!

I fill up my tray with more than enough warm bread, butter, omelet, chicken, homemade yogurt, and some fresh fruits. I end up placing an order for freshly squeezed tropical juice. Cold, no ice. Satisfied with my self-made Arabian breakfast, I begin hunting an empty table.

I spot a man, nose buried in a book, phones splurged on the table, with three coveted empty chairs as companions.

"Hello…" I shuffle my feet in discomfort while waiting for him to respond. "Hello?"

"Hello, good morning." He turns his head to me, and I gasp.

I never saw it coming. His eyes lock with mine. Eyes so captivating, they draw me into their depths. They look so old, older than the man, filled with deep knowledge.

Tilting my head to the side, I return his smile. Where do they get the men in this resort from? There's always something unique and different about them.

"Good morning. I'm sorry for ruining your morning routine but I would like to sit down and have breakfast. Are you expecting company?" I nod at the empty chairs.

"It's fine, have a seat. Have a seat."

You don't have to say it twice.

I sigh as the bread melts in my mouth, the texture consistent, the aroma making me disregard my reading companion as I mix it up with other things in my tray. Satiated and almost full, I take a long drink of the creamy rich yogurt drink and decide to make small talk—to network. He looks familiar but I can't place him.

"It's a wonderful day to be alive, isn't it?

He nods his head, his eyes still on his book. How does he expect us to be on the same table and not keep company? Not happening... If he wanted to read, he should have had breakfast, returned to his villa, or visited a Library. I don't think all mighty Twin Bliss resort can boast of that.

"I'm Lola Dade." I grin.

He shuts his book, then finally spares me his attention. "Femi Bakare." His lips, set in a tight line.

That's more like it. "So, what brings you here?" His name and voice sound like someone I should know. But I pay no mind to it.

He shakes his head like he's about to indulge a testy child. "Can I read my book in peace?"

I offer a lazy smile. "I'm trying to make friends while enjoying breakfast by the ocean. I came here alone, and it gets boring sometimes." Not a fat chance. It has been extra eventful so far, but he doesn't have to know.

"Fair enough."

"How long have you been here?"

"I got in a couple of days ago. You?"

"Yesterday." A smiling server arrives with my juice, settling the perspiring jar on the table. I nod my thanks, rearranging my breakfast. "I got in yesterday morning."

Escape

"Your first time?"

"Yes, it is. And you?"

"Same."

"You know," I use my fork to play with my left-over omelet. "I came here on a whim."

"Single?" What's with the men on this resort asking if a lady is single?

I give him a tight smile. "Sure. No surprise kids. No responsibilities. Single to stupor. No pets as well. You?"

He raises his left hand. It's devoid of a ring.

Okay Mister. I wasn't coming on to you for a proposal or whatever. I was only trying to be civil, make civil conversation. Both of us being single does not mean I'll hop into a bed with you.

Dropping his book on the table, he scans our surroundings, then zooms in on me. "Do you have plans for today?"

"Sure." He nods slowly, prodding me to continue and I smile. "The plan was to get my tummy sorted out." My fork clatters on my dish and I resign from picking it up as he keeps staring at me, expecting more. Relaxing into my seat, folding my arms, I give up. "I really don't have a plan for today." I should have listened to Biftu and planned something.

"So, I'm guessing you've not had the tour."

It's my turn to nod my head slowly.

"You should try it out. It would be fun, and you'll learn a lot about the island and of course the resort."

Dude is trying to get me out of his hair. Must really love books, academics, and boring stuff. I lean forward to ask, "Will you be joining me?" It doesn't hurt to try my flirting skills now and again, since I did a pretty bad job last night.

"No. No, not at all. You just seem young and look like someone that might enjoy what the island has to offer."

How old are you buddy? I'm twenty-six. Not young, young. And I'm here to enjoy all the island has to offer. My gaze falls on a tall man standing close to an unconcerned seated lady having breakfast, from this distance, I can feel the tension between them.

"Excuse me," I return my attention to Femi who is closing his book and picking up his phone gadgets on the table. "I have to leave now. See you around."

With his back turned to me, his power stride putting more distance between us as he navigates the pool area, my brain clicks. Femi Bakare. The guy who wrote and directed *The Stranger*. The Hollywood-Nollywood movie that won awards and was also very controversial because the lead character had to kill a child to save her husband.

The people you meet on vacation.

Shaking the feeling of losing another likely baby daddy as Carolanne has classified them, I scroll through the resort's app to find more on taking a tour. If I wanted a private tour guide, I should have booked in advance. Since I haven't done that, I have to join a group at the *Park & Mall* area, like a bunch of school kids. How many of us are spontaneous? I'm about to find out.

I roll two pieces of my left-over bread and an apple into my waist pouch, fill up my flask with cold freshly squeezed juice and begin my walk to the *Park & Mall* area. Peacocks I didn't notice yesterday prance about with their colorful feathers glinting in the sun. I should have worn a hat, but I didn't plan to go on a tour. By the time I get to my destination, I'm sure my breakfast will be completely metabolized.

Stopping over at my villa and resting was a possibility I thought of before leaving the restaurant. I even forgot my tripod as well, but I don't want to miss the next available tour that should begin in the next twenty minutes. After that, another hour. And there is nothing else I want to do right now than to travel back in time to see what makes this place tick and how the brand started.

I've got limited time here. God only knows how soon Robert and every other person from work will find me out for the fraud I am. Lost and gone from their world. How soon will they find me? Best to enjoy what I can while I can.

Fourteen

Onahi

WHY IS A SMART, PROMISING woman pretending to be someone she's not? Why is she taking up residence at Robert's villa? She came off as one who would never do something like that—she talks too much to be a thief or an imposter. But these days, one must be really careful. People claim to be who they're not.

Fuck.

She had me acting out of character. I only came to her out of curiosity—to know her better, hear her story and find out if Robert had sent her. But things went down south. She manipulated me so easily into her web.

Escape

Lola...

She is fun though. Has a zest for life I haven't witnessed in a long time. A breath of fresh air and something different. So responsive and adventurous. I'm tempted to take out my twitching dick, use the memory of her reactions on the beach to find some release, so this foul mood would go away, but anyone could walk in here.

Shits messed up.

I had to talk myself out of a lot of things last night. First was to stop myself from going back to her villa to finish what we started on the hammock.

Next was to go take a shower, to wash off all her essence from me, then head back out to find a good lay for the night—it was a few minutes shy of two in the morning and the nighttime activities would be bubbly—there was a high chance of finding a willing companion.

The final, which I eventually failed at, was talking myself out of taking matters into my hands during my cold shower. All I could think of, and smell was her. Her laughter. Her smile. Her curious voice. And most of all, the stolen kisses we shared under the starlit sky. I shot my load in record time, but still went to bed semi-hard, just thinking about her and the many things we could do together.

Waking up later than I normally do had me jolting out of bed, taking a run, then heading over to the admin building. With all the engagement I had yesterday, I left my laptop there and it's a Monday, so why not come in to see what's happening. I need to fire up a mail to Robert. Just to confirm.

I love partnerships. Fuck. I enjoy them. But I hate sharing what should be mine alone. I don't expect all the flowery and rosy stuff, but to know the other person is loyal to me and me alone, that's all I care about. It had never happened to me until Flora's betrayal, then Heather's omission. Fuck. I won't let this happen to me a third time. But having a solo partner as I get older makes more sense.

I've kept my name from blogs and social drama, now is not the time to start wrecking a name I have covertly managed. My father taught me better. Speaking of fathers.

"Hello Dad."

"Onahi," Dad grins into the lens of his phone and I smile back. There's background noise that confirms he's outdoors.

"How's Italy?" That was the current stop they shared on the family's messenger group. He and mom were quick to relinquish the companies to us as we came of age so they could travel the world together. In five years, they've visited 120 cities but keep returning to Italy. They claim they would have fully settled there but for dad's love for his Igbo roots, they spend at least three months in Nigeria.

"It's fine over here." He switches the camera to face his rear and it captures the face of people eating, making small talk, and drinking wine. "Your mom succeeded in dragging me over to Florence to taste wine."

"That sounds fun."

"Not when I have to hold up her head over a toilet bowl later at night."

"Who's that?" Mom says in the background and dad confirms it's me. He turns the camera lens to his left and mom's ageless face comes into focus. Her tanned white skin is flush from excitement. She's holding a glass of wine and the rolling hills of vinery forms a charming landscape behind her. "Don't mind your father. I allowed him eat all the pizza he could in Naples the last time. It's my turn now." She turns to dad behind the camera, her voice low and conspiratorial, "And you promised not to snitch."

Those two, they are like love birds. It's shocking to friends who know my family that I'm their biological offspring. Probably what Flora was expecting when she agreed to be my wife, but I just don't find it easy to be romantic. If that's a thing. To me, it's time spent away from making strategic plans.

"I heard you mom. Don't forget you're getting old. Your doctor said to stop—"

"Stop it right there." She returns to focus, pointing her wine glass to the camera lens. "I know what the doctor said, and we pay them a lot to say those rubbish to us. Ask your dad. I'm taking it one at a time."

"She means she's taking one wine glass after the other." Dad laughs, switching the camera to himself.

"Whatever. Don't worry," Mom stands beside Dad now. "I'll get him. But how are you Nahi? How's your vacation going?"

Rubbing a hand through my hair, I let out a sigh. "It's fine." Then I smile, remembering some friends and acquaintances are around to keep me entertained. "I just found out Lucas Opeyemi is married to another woman."

Mom's forehead creases in confusion, then her eyes go round. "The Nollywood actor? He has two wives?"

"No. No. No. I didn't mean it that way." I laugh. "He divorced the former and got married to another."

"The Muyiwa lady?"

"Oh. You know her?"

Mom smiles. "She's a character."

"That's her favorite hobby now" Dad adds, "reading all the gossip blogs and catching up on Nollywood movies."

"I've done all the work. It's time to enjoy. Besides, it helps me understand your dad better. What about you?" Mom asks.

"Me what?" I hope it's not what I think she's asking.

She shrugs. "Any new girl?"

"You know that's not how I roll."

"Tsk. Tsk. Don't worry. You'll find your match soon enough. Just don't chase her away."

"Mom..." I scoff.

"I hope you're praying and reading your Bible."

I grunt in response.

"It's alright. We're praying for you." She smiles, wrinkles gathering around her eyes. Her heart is the purest heart I know and having her and dad as models for love, family and faith is the best a child could ever wish for. It's all about duty and commitment.

"Thank you, Mom."

"Alright. Take care love. I'm going back to the wines."

Escape

"You'll be fine son."

"Thanks Dad."

"Okay son. I need to—"

"Before you go sir, can you please help me with the board? I have an idea I'd like to present to them, and I need a second pair of eyes."

"Sure." He nods his head slowly. "Is there a deadline?"

"No. Just... Take your time. When you're done in Florence."

Ending the call, I send Robert a mail asking about the guest he sent to the resort ahead of himself. Then a new email from Williams pops on my screen. Enclosed in it are spreadsheets which I begin reviewing painstakingly.

There are double entries in this spreadsheet. Hmm... Interesting.

What is she doing right now? Has she had breakfast? Is she getting acquainted with other guests? What does she like about the resort?

Oh, this summation on the sheet isn't adding up.

That black dress on her was fire. Blackjack? How much did she amass? We didn't cash out our wins from the cashier.

Fuck!

I can't concentrate. Leaning back on my chair, I glance up at the ceiling. Taking deep calculated breaths, I envision her kneeling before me, giggling, struggling to unzip my pants, her mouth sucking on my dick. I close my eyes and I see her falling but can't help her.

"Get your hands off me!"

I jerk up in my seat.

I need to take a walk, find out where she is. What is she doing to me? She didn't even give me a real last name. Why didn't she tell me her real last name? I need to find that out.

That's the best excuse I can come up with to go in search of her.

Fifteen

Lola

I'M NOT THE ONLY SPONTANEOUS individual on this resort—several individuals hurried to the spot after I got there. And it isn't glaring, but I see the *couple thingy* going on—I didn't get the memo. Self-pity almost clouded my judgement, but I shake it off, when I spot a woman with her kids.

Filming our experience on my digital camera as the shuttle takes us on the short trip to the historic ruins, I take in, through my camera lens, the beauty of the island.

We arrive the ruins and the charming image of two chickens courting, the male running after the female, has most people on the tour laughing. The sight and being in the company of these individuals I know nothing about causes me to relax. I smile in remembrance of last night's escapade—the male chicken chasing the female—that was so reverse of my experience.

Uh-oh. Snap!

Last night. I blink multiple times as my act on the beach flashes a couple of times in my head. Wincing as more images I've not thought of from last night, hit me from all angles.

A complete stranger. I made out with a frigging stranger. The arm holding my digital camera weakens, and I stop recording. The tour guide, who introduces himself as Amahle, keeps going on and on, and there are occasional *ohs* and *ahs* from the audience, but my mind is no longer here.

W-we moved from the bar to the casino floor—I can remember that vividly—then outdoors, to the beach, the hammock, and oh Lord. I make the sign of the cross as my ears go red. Did I really cry? Squeezing my eyes shut to recollect the fleeting images, but they are so buried and out of reach.

I didn't just make out, I had sex with him. Christ! My mouth was in his mouth, and his hands were all over my body. I know he told me his name, but I can't recollect it. I shudder thinking of any chance we have meeting each other. I hope he has left the resort and it was just a one-time thing. He had mentioned something about being here for a while. Had he?

Oh Lord. Did I really struggle to get his zipper off or it's my mind working in overdrive?

"Oh." I jump as someone bumps me from behind.

Escape

"I'm sorry," a masculine voice says, but not before I notice him checking me out. Last night's drama is enough to last me a lifetime, so I ignore him and resume filming. *Gosh*. I don't think I can survive the attention I'm getting from men on this resort.

Bits and pieces of Amahle's stories flows in and out of my subconscious. I nod more than I listen to him, as my attention is on the most revered Marula tree. The tree's trunk is sturdy and thick with age. Some spoiled fruits ceremoniously gather round its veiny root. Apparently, we're in time for harvest but are not permitted to touch except given. I don't even want to try it.

"... Marula has been an important commodity since 800BC. The tree can live for several hundreds of years." He pats the trunk of the tree. "This one is several hundred years old." Then tilts his head to the side as he scrutinizes it. "And it would live for more years."

"Merchants from around the world came in their numbers to purchase products made with Marula." He winks as he adds, "It sometimes makes animals go crazy."

There is a collective gasp of shock and awe as others begin garnering interest in the tree.

"If you've seen the Beautiful People documentary by James Uys, you'll understand what I'm talking about."

"Oh, I saw a clip on YouTube about animals going drunk on Marula. It was quite hilarious." A couple more interested people join, murmuring their agreement. "Does that mean marula makes people crazy?"

"Not at all. The animals in that movie ate the overripe marula fruit which can be quite alcoholic. But the ripe fruit can even be given to kids as juice." He raises a fruit and begins demonstrating how to eat it. "You bite off this part, and there... see the juice?" He sucks on the fruit, letting out an open-mouthed sigh.

"For those who haven't tasted it, it tastes like ripe pear. And it's sweeter than passion fruit." He tosses the seed into his mouth, sucks on it then spits it out. "Now that's how to eat your marula fruit. Make sure you don't eat the skin. It's not bad, but you don't just want to eat that, the goal is the juicy insides."

"And speaking about people and marula, I know most of you have been waiting for this... and might have heard that the marula is mythical and powerful."

Here we go.

"Did you notice the marula tree at the entrance to the resort?" He does not wait for his captivated audience to respond. "It was planted many years before the resort was conceptualized. Why? Because the founding mother of the resort never believed in the mythical legend of the marula."

Marketing, branding, storytelling. I'm here for this.

A lady in the audience asks, "So you're trying to say the marula has spiritual powers?" Her concentration on Amahle's next words is evident that she truly is in need of spiritual powers.

"You see, I myself can't give you a definitive answer. The thing with the marula is that you cannot tell what really happens when you take it. It works and sometimes it doesn't."

Escape

A murmur goes through the audience.

"But fret not. Only good things happen when the marula is involved."

"Please let us know the type of things that happen." A man hugs his female companion close. "So, we don't get blindsided by the madams." The female companion hits his chest lightly and others burst into laughter.

Amahle smiles. "Like I said, nothing bad. Just good. Men get more action between the sheets. Women become fertile. It even has love working potions. And it is believed that if you make a love wish beneath a marula tree, it will happen. Even women become fertile by just associating with the marula. The founding mother's story is one that tells of such tale." He proceeds to tell the story of the founding mother, we, his audience, remain captivated.

The lady before me folds her arms, her children flanking her side, as she murmurs so low, but I catch it. "You see you are God's gift to me. You heard the lady had to go through fire and make sacrifices to have a child. I bring you to places like this so you can understand the beauty of life. For you to know I really love you and that you're special."

"But mommy, this doesn't mean you are guilt free from not having enough time to attend my practice or the fact that dad has never attended my games."

"You understand I have to work honey. Your father and I have to do things to put food on the table and afford this lifestyle—"

I'm done listening to their family drama and history. I walk away from the group, pointing my camera to the fallen fruits.

I'll title this video, *touring the estates*. Nope. That's not a good title. I need to think of something more captivating. *The legend of the marula you never knew*. Hmm, that's more like it. Get viewers curious. What's Lola the Brand Guru up to?

"Hello everyone," I turn to Amahle's voice. "Yes," He rubs his palm together. "I'm sorry but I forgot to tell you all, you are supposed to make a wish under the marula for whatever you want. And I promise you it will come to pass. If you really want it. Unfortunately, the marula does not concern itself with riches and wealth, it's merely concerned with love, life, fertility, beauty and happiness."

What's the use of making a wish when there is no money involved? Fertility? I don't want a child right now. It's so stressful being a parent. *Then the baby daddy. A baby daddy that can afford a two-grand-per-night resort. Now that's goals.* Well, I don't mind having a rich guy to myself before the end of this runaway getaway. Just that when my mom finds out, hmm, big disappointment.

"So, if you all can just gather around here... Just come under the shade of the tree and make a wish, who knows? Something magical could happen in your love life."

Ladies—single and otherwise—rush beneath the tree to make their wish, mumbling inaudibly. One of them goes as far as hugging the tree. The men are slow, dragging their feet but not left out of the drama.

Oh wow. I turn on my camera to record subtly. The owners of this place must be having regular field days each time guests go on tour. Scam. I can't waste my time wishing for what I don't understand. It's not logical. Imagine standing under a tree, making a wish, and it actually comes to pass. My parents didn't migrate to the United States for me to remain fetish.

As if on cue, my phone rings. Mommy's calling. An understanding relationship, like what my mom has with my dad, is what I aspire to have. Not with a random John, but with Robert. If indeed the marula really grants wishes, then I want Robert to come down to this resort and apologize to me, so things can go smoothly.

"Hello Mommy."

"Hello my dear. How have you been? I tried reaching you yesterday and it was impossible! I finally reached Carol and she told me you travelled."

Oh, Carolanne and her big mouth.

"Yes Mommy, I travelled."

"Ah. And you didn't tell me. What if something had happened on your way there?"

Not here please. Mommy no. "Mommy?"

"Ehn?"

I ask her in Yoruba, "Can you hear me?"

"Lola, I can hear you loud and clear. You know your sisters look up to you. You can't decide to gallivant the world without informing me first. You'll start making them think they can do as they please without consulting with me first."

The curse of being the first child. "I'm sorry Mommy." I've got three sisters and an overprotective mom.

"Hmm... it's okay now." Then she adds in Yoruba, "When you have kids, you will understand better."

I roll my eyes when she excitedly asks where I am and if I went alone.

"Twin Bliss resort... Just me, Mommy." I hold back a smile when I notice the lady who had asked about the spiritual capabilities of marula making loud vows—looking silly with her eyes closed—like we're at a retreat, before turning my back to the crowd.

"That's good." She sighs. "You really needed a break. Please send me pictures—Lola!"

Pulling the phone from my ear at her squeal, I gingerly place it back on my ear, my heart beating double time. "Mommy what's wrong?"

"One night? Over two thousand?"

She's on her laptop. Letting out a sigh of relief, my heart begins returning to a steady pace. "Yep."

"Lola. Who is funding this trip? You would not make all that money you do to spend on one night like this. Is this a company retreat? Ahan! It's too much."

"Mommy, I got it covered."

"If I hear you're there with a man, it will not be funny o." She adds in Yoruba, "But wait, what are they giving you for that kind of price?"

"It's actually lovely here mommy, you'll love it."

"Eh en. I don't like it. You're yet to buy your house and you're splurging money like this on vacation. Vacation you can do in one hotel in Florida there," same thing I thought too, I laugh, "or even come home to Nigeria."

Escape

"It's fine mommy, I've been racking up some points over the years, so I used it here." That explanation calms her down and she moves on to ask me why I haven't posted on Instagram.

"Mommy... I need to craft the right caption. Don't worry, I'll send you pictures soon. I'm making YouTube Vlogs too."

"Better." She hesitates, "Any interesting men over there?"

Hold up. Someone has stolen my mommy's identity. When did she become invested in my relationship life?

"Common... get off your high horse Omolola. It's about time. I'm not bothering or pushing you to go into a relationship or anything of the sorts. But in a place like that, if you find a good man, it's not bad to, you know, brush him up and keep him."

OMG.

It begins as a quiet chuckle and escalates to a deep belly laugh has me nearly doubling over. *Hello? If you kidnapped my mom or done something with her, please return her back to me.*

Mommy's voice in Yoruba reaches out to me as I try so hard to get myself together. "Did I say anything bad?"

Wiping off tears from my eyes and waving concerned onlookers away, I respond to her. "Nope. You didn't."

If only she had seen me brushing up on a man last night. No. More like rubbing off on a stranger last night. I swallow, then let out slow breaths as forgotten frames from last night piece up together in my mind.

"Good."

"Don't worry Mommy, if I find a Prince Charming, you'll be one of the first people to know."

"I had to put that one out there. I don't know how you got to this resort, but I'm real proud of you. And I don't mind sending something for your upkeep."

"Thanks Mommy. This big girl can cover her bills herself."

"Okay o."

"Yeah. But keep the money for me oh."

"Okay love. Take care. I need to go. I have a team meeting in five minutes."

"Okay Mommy. I love you."

"I love you too my dear. And don't forget, if you find a good man, brush him and keep him."

Sixteen

Onahi

IT'S BARELY ONE AND MY body is ready to give in. After the futile walk I took earlier in the day, I returned to my desk with a clearer head. Only to be reminded that I was yet to have breakfast, now brunch. Left to me, I would have ordered lunch from *Gobota Specials* online, but my curious mind is still on the prowl, hoping and wishing to find the siren from last night without having to go knocking on her door like a stalker.

Impatient to wait for a server to bring my meal, I join the flowing traffic of guests serving their meals themselves. Moving on to the table that has bowls of pasta, a scuffle ensues beside me, and I ignore it, until a digital camera falls by my foot. In reflex, I bend to pick it and I come face to face with her. Blood pumps straight to my dick and it twitches to life.

Fuck. This needs to stop.

She squints her eyes at me, and I know when she puts two and two together.

"Hi." She smiles brightly.

"Hello." We both rise up and I brush a hand across my nose. She scrutinizes the camera, checking for breaks and what-have-yous. Her face scrunches up in a frown and I ask, "How's it?" I gesture towards her camera.

She looks up briefly. "It's fine. The battery's dead."

I nod. "About last night—"

She looks about, then at me, a fake smile splaying on her lips. "It never happened." She taps her head, raising her shoulders in the process. "I can't remember na-da."

I smile in return. If she chooses to play it that way, then, I better follow her lead.

With lack of what to say, an awkward silence loom over us. For some strange reason, I don't want us to move on like strangers. Even though I know Robert's response might change things for me, I want to get to know her more. She is... different... interesting.

"Creating content already." I smile, gesturing at the camera.

Shrugging, she hangs the camera on her neck, nibbling on her bottom lips as she observes the buffet. "It comes with the job. More like a hobby. Captured some cool shots during my tour. Made couple of videos too. Personal thingy." Her voice is light with an undertone that says otherwise.

"I see. Grabbing lunch?" I pick up a long stainless-steel tong going for the spaghetti.

She gives a small laugh. "Obviously. That's why I'm here."

"Good."

Now this is awkward. Something. I need to say something to ease the awkwardness of this situation. "Care to join my table?"

She considers it for a moment. "There's no—"

"I insist."

Her lips are pursed.

Kissable lips. Naturally pink and entic—What the fuck has gotten into me? Let her go. "Please?"

"Okay." She shrugs. "I'll need to fill up my tray, you don't need to wait up."

"I will." In case you change your mind.

Waiting for her gave me the opportunity to assess her physically. I never got the chance to fully do so last night. Her legs, one of the first things I noticed about her last night, seem to go on for days. From the romper she has on, it shows she knows their abilities and happily flaunts them. Her breast is in the B-cup category, but that's something I can work with and that ass... Perfectly curved, sporty and... There she goes, stretching further to pick something off the buffet, highlighting the heart shape. Does it feel as soft and it looks?

I need to stop this. She could be Robert's girl.

Settling down to eat, I look up from my tray, to find her scrambling with her waist pouch. She mumbles something I don't catch and continues her frenzied search. She brings out her phone, then sighs in disappointment.

Alarmed, I drop my cutlery, leaning forward. "What's the matter?"

She looks up at me in dismay.

Please let her not be missing something.

"I forgot to take a picture."

Seriously?

"Or even record a video. And my batteries are dead." She draws her lower lip between her teeth and my dick twitches again.

Adjusting on my seat, I suggest, "You can always do that some other time." Then resume eating.

"I wanted to capture every moment." She hisses, dropping her phone by her camera.

"Like I said, you can always do that later. Maybe after your next itinerary."

"I don't have anything planned," her voice is monotonous. "These times in between are, well, important."

"I recall I promised to be your guide."

She lashes out at me, her voice sharp and direct. "You have a friend, remember?"

Okay. She does remember discussions from last night. "Doesn't mean I can't get your phone number and send you some important things to do before you leave here."

"Nope. Thanks for the offer, but I'll pass."

Looking away from my meal to the ocean, I murmur loudly, "Let it be known that I offered my services and the lady refused."

Shaking her head, she smiles as she toys with her meal. "Like that's not a ploy to get my number."

"There's that for me. And for you, you get a list of important things to do."

"Thanks for the offer, but the brochure and app are doing a fantastic job. And let's not forget my butler too. Did you get one?"

"One what?"

"Butler."

The perfect customer for the resort. So, she enjoys being attended to. I can attend to some needs she doesn't know she has. "I make do without them. Only when necessary."

"Surprising." She sips from her flask, her roving eyes on me, like she's trying to figure me out as well. Well, two can play this game.

"So... What did you like about the tour?"

"It was hilarious." Swallowing a chunk of meat she had been chewing on. "Watching people throw their home training away just because they are in search of..." She pauses dramatic, her fork in the air, "*the one*."

I smile. "You don't believe in love?"

"Me? I do! I love the concept behind the marula tree. Gosh. I'm the Queen of happily ever *afters*. But that one, the one they were trying to sell to me during the tour. Nope. I can do better. What's your story?" she asks, digging into her meal.

"Me?"

"Yeah. Did you come here looking for *the one*?"

"Not me. Like I said, I'm vacationing."

She taps my arm casually, grinning widely. "Me too. I like that."

"Yeah. Queen of happily ever *afters*. That's an interesting title."

She clucks her tongue at me, then shrugs. "It's not easy finding happily ever after. I choose to be my own happily ever after. Hence," she sizes me up, "If I see what I like, I get it. Live in the moment."

"You shouldn't settle for less."

"Ah!" She laughs. "That's where you're getting it wrong. I'll never settle for less. And I'm actually not settling for anything because I'm not in the market. I just want to have fun. Sue me." She shrugs.

My dick strains within its confines, excited at her affirmation. Okay boy. Calm down. She's single. She confirmed it with a high head and now with a clear head. I let out a breath of air. Glad I have not committed adultery, fornication, or whatever it is it's called. I can't remember the difference between the two. All I need now is Robert confirming she's not some bitter ex. And why the fuck is it taking him too long to respond to his mails?

"And the pictures? Videos? The ones you'll post on social media, isn't that attention seeking?" That came out wrong, but she replies without giving a thought to how I presented my logic.

"Attention seeking? Nope. I just love doing it. It's fun. It's a way of life. I've been blogging since I was what? Ten? I used it to settle into living in the States. And ever since, I've evolved. You know." She shrugs. "Having to influence the thoughts of people and getting them to do what you want them to do. Having them to think a certain way about you or a product."

I might as well have given her a dildo to ride on. "Isn't that manipulative?"

She sucks in a breath, like I have insulted her. Lines appear between her brows as she dictates to me. "I don't believe it's manipulative. If you don't see marketing, trying to get you to use a new product as manipulative, then sharing bits about my life on social media is not being manipulative."

"Products. Marketing. Ads. That's about getting people to buy into a product that adds value to their lives. How does sharing what you eat, drink or wear on social media add value to others?"

She gasps. "Excuse me? I don't know what you're trying to achieve with this conversation and how we got talking about this, but if you're trying to tell me that I am doing too much talking about my life on social media, I think this is where this conversation ends. You can't tell me what or what not to do."

"Please don't take it personally." I slightly raise both hands up as a sign of peace. "I'm not opposed to posting on social media. I just want to know more, you know, understand someone like you. Say we start hanging out, will you upload videos and pictures of us online? Will you tell them what we did or didn't?"

"I don't know why I'm still having this discussion." she rolls her eyes heavenward.

"Please." I give a half-smile. "Help this socially inept guy."

That soothes her ruffled feathers. She gulps her drink, then turns flashing eyes to mine, plastering a fake smile. Fuck no. I have struck a nerve.

"Nice shot there." She continues, her voice low, edgy, "All you need to understand is that I enjoy taking pictures and sharing them on social media. I can't speak for others. And if we hang out, and you end up in a frame, don't worry, I'll edit you out or ask your permission before posting."

"To what end? What are you trying to gain with that?"

The corners of her eyes crinkle in frustration.

"I'm only asking because you said you enjoy influencing people's decision online."

"Yes. That's why I found my calling in marketing. Brand marketing. Emphasis on the brand."

This is me pushing it. "So, what I'm deducing is that you either enjoy manipulating people into deciding and making decisions that would have them happy and glad they did? Or you just enjoy the power you possess at giving people options of doing things you want them to do and making them think they want to do that."

"Wait. What are you trying to get out of this conversation?" she asks, her head bobbing. "You are not trying to understand anything. Your only concern is the fact that you may probably appear on my blog, and who knows what secret you're trying to hide or who exactly you are." Pushing her tray forward, she leans in. "If this is some sort of interview before the main thing, thing is, I don't give a damn, or care about who you are. I'm not going to turn myself on and off just because we are experiencing something we can't deny."

She takes one final gulp of her drink. "Thanks for ruining my wonderful afternoon." Then stands up.

I make to rise with her. "I can—"

"It's alright." She stalls me with a placating smile. "Just stay away from me. We don't want pictures of you flooding the internet now, do we?" She says in that bubbly attitude of hers, wandering far away, out of reach. Her tight ass going tick, tock, tick, tock.

She stalls for a group to pass, looks back at me, then continues her march to wherever she's headed.

How did that go? Uhn? What the fuck is wrong with me? Barely two weeks ago, I had Heather eating from my fingers. And now, I can't control a conversation with a lady. I am losing my charm it seems.

My phone beeps. Great. At least this would save me from replaying last night's scene at her door. She has so much against me already. I scan my email, jumping to the interesting part.

Omolola Arogundade is an associate in my firm. A good friend and very good at what she does. As for her whereabouts, she took an impromptu leave and has been out of my reach.

Please call me whenever, I'm concerned about her.

Regards,

Robert Edward.

Dialing the number attached to the email, my heart thuds loudly in my chest.

"Hey, Robert, been a while. How are you doing?"

"I'm good fam. So, what were you saying about Lola? She's been AWOL at work. How do you know her?"

I lean back into my seat, taking a deep breath, "She's right here. Lodged in the villa I reserved for you."

"Oh, my goodness. I can't believe Lola would go that low."

"Go that low? What do you mean?"

"I'm sorry man. I actually forwarded her the email, just for her to take a look. And she decided to, well, take a well needed vacation in my name. There's a lot going on at work."

"It's alright. I'm actually enjoying her company here. Way better than having you around."

"Yeah right."

"So, you say she's pretty good at the marketing and branding stuff?"

"The best. Her head is a rare goldmine in this industry." He pauses. "Are you looking for something?"

"No. Not at all. I just wanted to find out why she was taking your space and not you. And I didn't want to go after your woman or have you hear I'm not treating your sister well."

"Onahi..." Robert laughs, and I smile in response as he doesn't confirm my earlier suspicions. Amazing. We're all clear.

"Any good friend of yours becomes a good friend of mine. I'll make sure she enjoys her stay."

"Thanks man."

"It's my pleasure."

"Oh, and when you can, please let her know we miss her and to pick my calls."

"Sure, I'll try."

Seventeen

Lola

"ALL THIS WITHIN TWENTY-FOUR hours of arriving the resort?"

I shrug, closing the door to the terrace.

"*Gurlllll*, you're having a swell time."

"No, I'm not. Besides the good food, tour and meeting some interesting... people, there's no swell time anything." I pout.

"You can't tell me nothing. You're having fun and that's that."

"I don't even know what to do tonight." Dragging my feet to the bed, I fall limply on it. "No one to hang out with. No one to disturb. I'm a living expression of Akon's *Lonely*."

"What about your butler lady? Ask her for things to do."

Slapping my palm to my face, I groan. "That's the problem. There's a lot to be done. There's just too much. I can't bring myself to make a choice."

"I see."

She's not seeing anything. Even though I read and ingested the Solo Traveler's Handbook, it's not easy implementing what I read. There's the harlequin night's dinner I would love to try, but there's no Robbie to try that with. There's the helicopter tour of the island, but no one to experience it with. There's also the—

"Lola?"

"Hmm?"

"Why don't you start from the bar you went to last night?"

"To disgrace myself again?" I clear my throat, then swallow, changing positions. "Thank you, I'm not interested."

"Serious babe. From there you can, you know... figure things out from there."

"Hmm-mmh."

"Come on. You said you made some money there the other night. Go and demand your money and win some more cash. You can't spend all that unbudgeted fund and return here broke."

Now she knows its unbudgeted, after *mistakenly* activating the gift card—I'm not buying that anymore.

"And if I lose the money?"

"You can't. Just don't try anything stupid again, like taking pills from strangers."

Closing my eyes shut, I scrunch up my face. "That was a once in a lifetime mistake. Don't make me regret telling you."

"If you don't tell me, who will you tell?"

"Shut up."

"So, what's the plan? Hiding like a chicken indoors, or owning the night?"

"Carol..." I cry, and she giggles.

"See you sounding like a baby. And you want to become a baby mama."

"Nope. Not me. You!"

"I've told you. But doesn't the idea play in your head sometimes?"

"With the number of times you've resounded it. It does. And yes, it sounds like the easy way out, but nope, I'm not taking it."

****

CONTRARY TO MY FEARS, I'M making new friends on the floor tonight. And maybe some enemies? They're not enemies, enemies. It's just that I've won some friends' money tonight and they're not so happy I won over their money. The Queen of happily ever *afters*, has now added a title to her ever-growing list; Queen of Blackjack!

I've made enough money to book a villa for three nights and I think that's enough luck for one night. Cashing out at the cashier and entering my account information to transfer my funds, I resist the urge to get more chips, then make my way to the restroom.

Done with my business, I step back on to the floor, my gaze going to the bar section. PTSD from last night telling me to ignore, move out and go to bed. But it's only just few minutes past midnight. I'm no Cinderella. I'm going to take a walk to my villa, but not before rehydrating my body system.

Making my way to the bar, I motion to the female bartender over the loud music. "Can I get water in a plastic cup, please?"

"Sure. One of those nights uhn?"

"Yeah." I force a tired smile her way. "And please add some lemons."

For just water and lemons, it takes the bartender a while to return with my order. She spins a shot to me and hands me my requested plastic cupped water. What's happening here?

"It's from the gentleman over there." She nods to the opposite direction, grinning at me.

Gentleman over where? My brain reminds me of my last experience, Carolanne's warning, but I ignore the voices in my head. Surveying the area, the bartender had nodded to, my gaze lands on him! Blackjack! I smile, reeling from my superstar wins and now meeting with the braided New Yorker, who is now rocking a full afro. What a night. We meet again. Hello Nonso.

I sip my water, shyly drooping my eyelids as he walks over, a shot of drink in his hand.

"You seem to become prettier with each passing second."

My ears go pink at his remark. "We've only just met," I shrug. "Once?"

"Yeah. But it feels like I've known you for eternity."

"Nice try."

He smiles and we stare at each other for a while. "Want to sit and have a drink?"

"Urm, I'm not drinking tonight." That was what I used in playing my new friends on the casino floor. They thought I was ordering lemon cocktail, when instead, I was ordering water and lemon.

"Too bad. I was hoping we could chat over a couple of shots."

Haha! Been there. Did that. Last night is so not repeating itself. Not on my watch.

I turn to the exit, then back at him. "I was heading out."

"Oh," He holds on to his chest, folding into himself a bit. "No. Don't twist the knife babe."

"I'm sorry... It's been a long night. But I would really like to get your number. Maybe we can meet some other time? When I clear my schedule?"

"That's not a problem."

Escape

We exchange our contact information and as I move to leave, his next words stop me. "I'm coming with you."

"You don't have to."

He downs his drink, the glass cup hitting the wooden table with a light thud. "Babe, I got you," he says, removing cash from his wallet, placing it under the glass cup.

Nice... he drops tips for servers. Okay. This could lead to something promising.

We navigate through the moonlit path, the same path I walked with that annoying human being yesterday. Although there are no fireflies to celebrate my wins, tonight still feels magical. I won a lot on the tables—having less losses compared to yesterday—and I met Nonso.

"I was here yesterday. Didn't see you."

"Yeah." A slow smile begins on his lips, the moon highlighting his chiseled facial features. "I had some... tasks in town."

"I thought as much. You must be a busy man."

"For you, I'm not. I was wrapping up with a business partner when I saw you. I didn't want to miss the opportunity."

"Oh. That's good. Before the airport meetup, I knew nothing about you. But now I know you're a venture capitalist looking for what to do with your funds. And... you mentioning you were conducting business means it's okay to talk business."

His brow rises, his lips turning into an O, in mock surprise.

"Serious, I'm not kidding."

"That's refreshing."

"Yeah. So... now that I know you and what you do. Want to hear my business plan?"

"Sure."

"And you promise to fund it?"

He throws his head back, laughing. "Babe, I can't promise that. But I promise I'll figure out a way to make things work out."

"Alright." I explain to him my business idea, to be the number one stop Brand Management community for SMEs. A major conference every year, an app for vendors and resources to train small business owners. I also pitch in the fact that I know a badass graphic and web designer who is ready to begin work once all project plan is set. "And I know... it seems like a lot at once, but I want to start small in a big way."

"Hmm... That's broad and narrow at the same time."

I nod in agreement. "And I don't need to explain the return on investment five years after launch."

"You've got documentation?"

I tap his arm lightly, and he feigns pain, to which I smile. "I do. All I need is your email address."

"I'll send you an email you can forward it to. But jokes aside babe, I want to know how your stay has been. Tell me..."

"Eventful." I smile. The Hollywood guy at breakfast, the tour, last night... it has really been eventful.

"I'm sorry I wasn't here on time to entertain you."

"No. But thanks for being a lifesaver at the airport. I was..." Shaking my head to ward off thoughts of Robbie. "I was not in the right state of mind."

"I can imagine. Everyone needs a vacation from their normal."

"Preach it. How long have you been here?"

"Nine days. I've got three more days before I leave though. And when I saw you at the airport, I knew you were an answer to my prayers."

Me too! Well, when I read more about you online.

"Oh," I tuck an unruly strand of hair behind my ear, then look up at him. "Why do you say that?"

"Lola."

He remembers my name! And pronounces it perfectly. Oh mama.

"I don't want you running off the other direction when I tell you which of my prayers you answered."

"Bring it on."

His stops in his tracks and I follow suit, standing opposite him, my villa just few feet away. Closing the distance between us, he reaches for my hands, which I let him hold on to.

The corners of his mouth curves into a smile, his eyes twinkling. "I prayed for a wife."

I try tugging my hands out of his, but he tightens his hold.

"Babe... Please wait."

The confusion on my face tells him all he needs to know. His eyes plead with me as he relaxes his grip. "Please let me explain."

Finally having full control of my arms, I wrap them around my waist as the cool night air causes goosebumps to rise on my skin. Not now. Not when I think I am free of drama on this vacation and have found an investor for my business.

"Go ahead." This is a bad idea. Holding my breath, I listen to him.

"The first time I saw you, I knew you were the one. I don't know how I knew." He takes a step closer. "But I know you are the one."

Letting out a deep breath, I pinch the bridge of my nose. This is a joke. An unbelievably bad joke. Swallowing, I look him right in the eyes. "You're kidding right?"

He scoffs, shaking his head, then gives a small laugh. "No Lola. I'm not kidding."

"You just met me."

"Do you like me?"

"I think I do. But that's not a prerequisite to getting married."

"That's fine. We can start with that." He pushes his hands into his pocket. "Get married in a month?"

Joker.

"Not what I imagined for courtship or marriage."

"We can work around it."

Escape

I scoff, throwing my hands in the air. I'm not having this discussion. What's wrong with the men on this resort? Taking three steps towards my villa, I retreat, returning to him. "I'm sorry Nonso. Please forget everything we ever discussed. I'm not interested in your proposal—my business proposal."

He reaches for me, but I avoid his touch. "Babe... we don't have to—Okay. That's fine."

I turn to move into my villa, but his voice stops me.

"Lola, please wait."

Pausing, not because he asked me to but because I notice a familiar figure by my door. Nonso is too in his feelings to notice it, so I just swallow, like a deer caught in the headlights. What would he think about me now? That I lure men to my villa every night so I can post them online? Exposing their weakness?

"You know what?" Nonso catches up with me and I turn to face him, his hands holding on to mine again, "Let's start all over again. Like I said, I've got three days and if by three days you're not interested, then it's fine."

"Alright." I nod.

"Thank you." He squeezes my hand reassuringly, before releasing them.

I stare at his form as he jogs away leaving me to handle this annoying human without once noticing him.

Eighteen

Onahi

"BRAVO." CLAPPING, I REMOVE MY back from the door frame I've been leaning on. She turns at the sound of my voice and begins marching towards me.

"What do you want? I thought we agreed not to go near each other."

Her tone indifferent, her shoulders stiff. Her calculated steps have me transfixed to the spot. She's wearing another romper, not the same she had worn earlier, this one is more western, with flowers and stuff on it.

Escape

Pointing to the retreating form of her to-be-lover, I smirk. "That was a wonderful performance. Aren't you going to run after him?"

She hisses, stopping before me. "Excuse me. I need to go to bed."

I smile, trying to take her hands in mine, but she avoids mine. "I'm sorry Lola. I'm pissed I waited this long for you to return, only to be entertained by you and your... friend?"

"Okay," she says, her voice flat.

"*Okay*... your friend? Who is he?" I shake my head, my brows furrowing. It's remarkable how many men have their attention on her, in such brief period, it's impressive.

She squints an eye at me, which is weird. I just want to know who the guy is. That's all.

"Hmm." She folds her arms, her lips curving into a smile.

Lips I've envisioned more times than necessary, doing something more than talking.

"And why would you want to know who he is?"

"Well." I shrug. "He walked you home. I just want to know—"

"Jealous?" She leans on the opposite doorframe.

"What? Jesus, No—"

"You're jealous."

Never. I don't embody such negative energy. Never have. Never will. I'm just curious to know who was seeing her off. I did last night, and it was fun. The thought of anyone other than me taking such liberties has me balling my hands in a fist. "Believe what you must." I take a step closer, the light above us illuminating the dramatic roll of her eyes. "I didn't wait so long for that. I came here to apologize." I release my balled fist, flexing them to allow blood flow.

"For what?" She tilts her head to the side, observing my every move.

"For earlier. Lunch. Last night."

She drops her arms, shaking her head. "I wasn't holding a grudge. You were just unavoidably annoying. Wrong place, wrong time. No offense."

"Honestly, I'm sorry."

"Apologies accepted." Standing straight, she asks, "Now, can I go to bed?"

"Just a moment, I have another request."

She lets out a long sigh, muttering something under her breath about men and stressing out women unnecessarily.

"If it makes you feel any better, I've been out here since eleven... waiting for you."

"I never told you to wait for me."

"Well, I met this young lady last night who was quite fascinating. Then I messed up my chance with her at lunch today. Now... Now I want to make it up to her. Oh, where do I find her? Her villa. What time does an average guest return to their villa?" I check my watch. "Urm, around 10:30-ish. So, I set out to be a nice guy by waiting for her and wait I did. Fighting with insects, out to suck life from me."

She begins smiling,

"And oh! There she comes, but she's with another guy. Who is he? She doesn't say. Well, she said she's single, single, single and down for fun, so that doesn't matter—"

"Stop it." She giggles.

"—and I remember making a promise to be her personal guide, which I'm sticking to, if she would let me."

"Let's not do that." Her giggling stops, her shoulders return back to being stiff and her voice tightens. "Your friend."

"You don't even know her."

She places a hand on her face. "Seriously? A female friend? The friend is a *her*?"

"What? Now I'm not allowed to have female friends?"

"I really need to sleep," she complains, moving to open the door but I shove myself in her way. "I have an early start tomorrow. Please..."

"Can we please have a decent chat?"

"I'll scream." She threatens, her eyes darting between me and the haven behind me.

That's it. I'm done. Fuck everything. I let out a frustrated sigh. We'll start afresh tomorrow morning. But why? Why the fuck does she want to make this hard. I'm actually doing this for her sake. Since Robert has vouched for her, it doesn't hurt to entice her from her current firm to mine. It doesn't hurt to have a little fun while doing that.

"Please..." What the fuck has gotten into me? Begging for attention? Onahi... "I really want to show you around, but I need to clear the air around this friend you keep bringing up."

"Go ahead."

"Please," I motion to the swing on her front porch.

She eyes her door, me, then the swing.

I notice the slight hesitation, and I immediately say, "Thank you," before she changes her mind. I wait for her to lead the way, then follow her reluctant frame to the swing.

"So...?" She says when we're both seated.

I release a deep breath I wasn't aware I was holding until her prompt. "This is awkward."

"I know. More awkward when I tell you I can't remember your name."

My head swivels in her direction, my eyes widening. "You're joking right?"

She giggles, then hides it behind a cough, then giggles again. "I'm not."

Minx. I shake my head and I laugh with her. This lady is just fucking unique and different. Her laughter turns into a hiccup, and I instinctively pull her into my arms and begin patting her back. When she calms down, I feel her heartbeat thudding in sync with mine. This feels good.

"Onahi." I murmur in her ear, "My name is Onahi. Don't forget."

"I won't forget."

"Good."

She tries withdrawing, but I tighten my embrace. "I like it like this."

"Urm... we can't converse like this."

Escape

The vibration of my phone causes me to withdraw from her with a discontented sigh.

Her eyes sparkle in the dark and I want to know what makes them tick.

"I didn't take you to be the sappy type."

Scoffing, I pull out my phone to silence it. "Not sappy, it's just been a while since I felt a woman's touch. And you smell good."

"Sappy."

"Ask around. I'm not."

"I'm tempted to, but you're sappy."

"Yes." No need dragging the matter. She'll find out soon enough. "About my friend."

Lola adjusts on the swing and begins rocking it in slow motion.

"Her name's Janelle, Jay for short. She's special."

"Hmm..." A simple word that's laced with questions. She thinks Jay's an ex. The irony.

I smile. "Like a special child kind of special."

Her eyes widen and I note the sincerity in them. "I'm sorry, I didn't mean—"

"It's alright. She's not handicapped or anything."

Lola let's out her breath, her chest rising and falling in steady motion, to the sway of the swing.

"She's smarter than both of us combined."

"You wish."

"She was proposed to and couldn't respond, just froze." That's what the media says, and I don't want to send out a wrong message since I'm speaking to the brand queen here. "And decided to come vacation here, to regroup... think, something like that."

"So... you're the chaperone? The sacrificial lamb?" Her eyes are misty as they look at me in another light. I don't mind being stared at like this for a living.

I shrug.

"That's so sweet of you."

"Thank you. But... Last night, I noticed a gentleman friend developed interest in her—"

"Now you're the fairy godfather." She claps.

Always has something to say. I have forgotten she said she is the Queen of happily ever *afters*. "None of that. Apparently, it looks promising. He should be a good fuck—oh, sorry I said that."

Her eyes widen in surprise, and she chortles, shaking her head.

"She deserves her own share of happiness. Lord knows who Ahmed is shagging right now."

"So, you're encouraging her to sleep around while engaged?"

"She's not officially engaged."

"But they're dating."

"They're not."

"Pfft. Whatever. You and your friends are so confusing. It's like we live on different planets."

"I don't support cuckolding." Thoughts of Flora, then Heather assails me. "Fuck. It irritates me. You don't want me going into details of how much it does." I take a calming breath, letting go. "But when it comes to Jay and Ahmed's situation, it's different."

"Hmm... I just realized I answered this question earlier today, but you didn't."

"Which is?"

"Do you believe in love?"

"Hell yeah." I answer in a heartbeat. "But I don't believe it happens to everyone."

"Interesting. Have you ever been in love?"

"No. Not at all."

"Hmm... Are you scared of falling in love?"

"Oh, now we're moving to phobias?"

She shrugs. "Answer the question. Philo phobic?"

I scratch the back of my neck. Am I? I'm not afraid of falling in love. I love my parents, siblings, friends and even businesses but romance, I don't think so. "No. Because I don't have time for that. But—"

She hops off the swing to stand before me. "No buts."

Raising my hands in surrender, I agree with her. No need polishing it. It is what it is. "What are you afraid of?"

"Nothing...I love trying out new things. Everything."

"There must be something. I gave you a better answer."

"Hmm." She places a finger on her lips, her eyes scrutinizing me. "Ah!" Her eyes lighting up as the answer comes to her. "Travelling on water."

"You mentioned that the other night." I smile.

"I did?"

"Yeah. Said you wouldn't have made it here if you knew it involved boating to the island."

"Hmm..." She crosses her arms. "I must have said a lot."

Smiling, I stare at her as she brushes something off her skin. I'm glad she made it here and not Robert. Fuck. Where did that come from?

"Hmm," she yawns, covering her mouth. "Onahi." My name sounds beautiful from her lips. "I really need to sleep."

Getting off the swing, I follow her lead to the door. "Do you really have plans for tomorrow?"

She turns to me, her expression crestfallen, one of a child caught lying. "I really don't." She shrugs.

"Really?"

"Really." Awesome!

"Just say the word, and I'll resume my duty to be your guide. Like I said, Jay already has someone and I'm..." I shrug. "All alone?"

She scrunches her nose. "The word."

"Uhn?"

"You said, say the word," she smirks, feeling smart.

Escape

Oh. I laugh. "Perfect. I'll see you tomorrow morning then." I lean in for kiss, but she turns in time for my lips to land on her cheeks. Awkward. "I'm sorry, that was uncalled for."

"It's alright." She looks pointedly at me, still smirking. She knows what she's doing to me and I'm going to have her pay me in full. "Goodnight Onahi."

"You can call me Nahi. Good friends do."

"O...kay Hmm..." she says warily, opening her door. "Good night Nahi."

"Night. See you tomorrow morning."

Nineteen

Lola

WHAT? WHAT'S THAT SOUND?

Flipping over in bed, I spot Biftu. She pauses in action—hunched, a piece of clothing in hand, and the sandal I wore last night.

"I can see you. Just move." I yawn. "I'm sorry you have to go through that," I add, motioning at my discarded clothing from yesterday's adventure and the scattered closet.

She relaxes, letting out a sigh. "It wasn't my intention to wake you up."

Escape

Waving a dismissive arm, I begin searching for my phone between the sheets. "I know. It's me." Got ya! I scroll through my notifications and chats. "I'm a light sleeper. How was your night?" Watching her smile from my side eyes as she resumes putting away my clothing.

"It was good, nothing new. But I'm sure yours was more interesting."

Taking my eyes off my phone, I narrow them at her. "How do you know?"

She places everything in their deserving space, then walks cautiously towards me, a smile splaying on her lips. "The head butler told me I must come prepare you today, even when I told her you specifically informed me you wanted no morning service."

Head butler? Prepare me?

My confusion propels her to speak more, "I don't know much about it." She smiles coquettishly. "But you've got an event scheduled for today."

"Is this a resort thing?" I adjust and something begins vibrating beneath me. "What is that?" I kneel, holding the sheet to my chest, while searching between the rest of the sheet. Biftu watches, not knowing whether to join in my search or maintain her position.

Seconds later, I find trusty Zeus, buzzing angrily. I let out a breath, turning him off. Biftu still looks confused. I bet she doesn't know the pleasure and thrills I get from my trusty Zeus.

It's such a shame I'm on a resort with multiple men for the picking, even with blessings from my mother and I'm still stuck to a rechargeable vibrating wand. I had completely forgotten about it, but Onahi's visit last night left me wet and horny.

Placing Zeus in the blanket chest, I lay back in bed once more. "So... is this event a resort thing?"

Biftu puckers her forehead as she thinks it through. "No. No, it's not. I-I am not aware of any resort event."

"I didn't plan any." Dismissing her talk about scheduled events, I focus on other important things, like breakfast, food, still scrolling on my phone. "What's for breakfast? Is it the same offering as yesterday or a different menu?"

"A slightly different menu. But the *Sweet Morning Restaurant* is closed."

"Really?" True. The time on my screen confirms it's almost eleven.

"I'm sorry. I should have—"

A knock on the door has us staring at each other.

"You have a guest." She smiles brightly, hopping away to the door.

How does the visitor solve the breakfast crisis? First, I hear greetings, then murmuring, then nothing. Nothing at all. Just loud silence.

Sitting up in bed, I pull the sheet up my chest. What's happening? I was beginning to enjoy my morning chat with Biftu, and it is strange she welcomed the guests and did not return to the room. Who is in my villa? Now I must go and confirm what the fuss was all about.

Escape

Sunlight peeking from the curtain seams give me enough light to work with. *I'm sorry Biftu.* I ruffle through clothes she artfully arranged to find a loose white V-neck crop-top and colorful loose shorts. I've never taken to having pajamas or nighties. I love sleeping nude.

Feeling comfortable enough, I cautiously step into the living space and before me, on the floor, is a mini buffet, covered with transparent dome covers.

"Good morning..."

I jump at the sound of the voice, turning my head, to find Onahi sitting by the corner, watching me, one knee raised, the other stretched out in front of him. He's deliciously wrapped in dark khaki shorts, and loose-fitting beach shirt that's unbuttoned at the collar, showing off a smooth hairless chest.

What's he doing here? What's with the breakfast in here and most of all, where is Biftu? In my confusion, I smile, taking in the croissant, richly laid fruits, jam, steaming cup of brown drink—which I assume to be chocolate—and a green bottle in the mix. "Isn't it too early for wine?"

My voice breaks his attention, and he smiles smugly, a corner of his mouth quirking up. Is it from having lewd thoughts or remembering our first meeting? *Whatever, that was whiskey, not wine. And it was late at night. Getting me drunk, even before the day starts, is not the best way to get into my pants man, I already want to hump you! Those lips, oh lawd!*

"It's non-alcoholic. And it was added for... effect." He gives a slow smile, his eyes focusing on my face. "But if you like it strong early in the morning, I could arrange that," he ends with a smirk.

He's definitely not talking about the wine. Or is he? Nope. He is not. Clearing my throat, I swallow. "This is fine." Then walk further into the room, taking a seat on the floor. "Thank you."

"You're welcome. Love the wardrobe choice."

He winks and I look down to note the white V-neck is a see through. My nipples harden in excitement, leaving nothing to the imagination.

Looking back in his face, I shrug, and I catch him biting his bottom lip as though in pain. He nods, a smug grin in place and moves from his position, till he is seated by me. He begins opening, and arranging the buffet spread before us, acting unaffected. Hah! But I see his jaw ticking.

"How did you know?" I ask, gesturing to the food while struggling not to drool. I don't know if the saliva pooling in my mouth is because of the whiff of his evasive body wash, the sexiness oozing off him or the aroma of the food.

He shrugs, swallowing, doing everything in his power not to look at the amount of exposed flesh for his viewing pleasure, but fails. I can tell from the way his eyes darts from my face, chest, then to the food. It doesn't bother me—when he had the chance to know me better, he let it slide—I'm more concerned about the food.

"Instinct."

"Hmm... I like that. And Biftu?"

"Told her I'll handle everything from here. She wasn't happy about that, but she'll be fine."

He must be desperate to make true his promises. The buttery aroma of fresh croissant, intermingled with that of hot chocolate, assaults my nostrils and I can't ignore them anymore. "Shall we?"

He nods and I go for it.

"This was thoughtful," I say, biting into a croissant lathered with passion fruit jam. "Hmm...very thoughtful. And this, this jam..." I bite then swallow. "Is the bomb." Kissing my fingers.

He smiles, sipping a mug of hot chocolate. I never took him to be a sweet tooth, but what do I really know about him besides his vacationing plans and his special friend.

"If I had known you were a sucker for croissant, I would have asked for more." His gaze follows my movement as he nibbles on fresh blueberries.

"I'm actually not. I'm more of a bread girl." I try to place another jam-lathered croissant in my mouth, but a defiant jam falls splat on my top, right above my left nipple.

Oops.

I use a finger to wipe it off, then lick it. Yum... I shimmy, resuming to place the croissant into my mouth but pause when I notice Onahi's dilated pupils zooming in on my top.

Following his gaze, I spot the pink smear that my cleaning up had caused to spread across my nipple. Nipples that are hardening painfully in response to his scrutiny. I clear my throat.

He looks up, our gaze lock. He doesn't hide the need in his eyes.

Someone wants me now...

"Like what you see?"

He gives a lopsided grin that has the butterflies in my tummy doing cartwheels. Who gave him such smile? His eyes twinkling with a promise. I can't remember much about that night, but I know it felt good. Something I'll like to try again now that I've got a clear head on my neck.

"I can help with that you know?" Dropping his mug, he scoots closer to me.

I play along. "Help with what?" Intentionally picking my mug of hot chocolate, while his eyes feasts on my tiny movements.

"You know I want you. From day one." He carefully moves to sit behind me—his solid chest pressing my back—causing me to shiver.

I hold firmly to my mug as he continues, our legs touching, but not entirely doing the type of touching I want.

"And you are sending off mixed signals."

Blowing on the steaming drink, I take cautious sips, a curve of a smile on my lips. My mind noting how my legs are turning to noodles, with every steamy breath. If he touches my breast, this drink will fall from my hand, and I won't be sorry. Hmm... Every forced-steamy-breath causes my pussy to moisten.

Act cool. Make him beg.

He curses under his breath, before settling his hands on his sides. The action causing his warm chest to leave my back.

I stifle a giggle. Such a gentleman. Would not touch me if I don't ask him to but can barge into my villa when he wants to.

Escape

"Think of the men... The crazy things you can do. No one would likely know you." Carolanne's voice says in my head. I like this one. A better choice than Nonso who is asking for marriage, asking for commitment.

Lowering my eyelids, a plan forms in my head, and I smile.

"Lola... Do you want this?" He leans close, wrapping his arms around my naked midriff.

Just below where I want him touching. I shiver at his touch, swallowing more drink than I should.

He whispers in my ears. "This was not what I planned when I came here, but I'm fucking game if you are."

Taking a final sip, I place my mug on the arrangement, careful not to spill them as my hands are shaking with excitement. There's no use ignoring the chemistry that's between us. I'm sure he can smell my wetness even through the lingering smell of croissant and hot chocolate.

"Touch them." I command.

His hands close over my breasts and I lean into him, taking deep breaths as he first fondles them, massaging the sides. *Remove the top, it's not so hard! Touch my skin!*

"See what you do to me?" his husky voice fueled by desire murmurs in my ear as he presses his warm erection on my back.

Oh lawd. Fresh warm juice slips from my clit and I press my back to his chest. Anything to get this deep gnawing need of him off me. My breathing grows faster as he begins kissing my nape to my ear.

"You like this?" he murmurs, his hands weighing my breasts.

I can't believe I have no words to say but to lean into him, moaning in response. He begins tracing the buds of my nipples and they tighten, the pleasure of it all, causing my eyes to droop.

"Ah... Fuck yeah. You do."

My clit twitches as his words hits every core of my being. *Speak dirty to me. I love it! Freaking love it.* But shit! I need to—I clasp my legs together as his hand moves down to brush my crotch still covered in loose shorts. *Oh gawd*, my breath hitches, *I'm not wearing any underwear.*

He groans when he returns his hands to my crotch, settling there. The heat from my pussy becomes one with the heat from his palm. *Good lord... it's been so long.* Zeus has been a good boy on days I needed to release extra tension, but it could never tease me or murmur nasty words in my ear.

"Do you pleasure yourself?" He trails wet kisses around my neck and ear, blowing here, kissing there, nibbling my earlobe. One hand casually stroking my nipple, the other hand applying pressure on my pussy. So casual.

"Y-yes..." my voice breathless as I respond with a smile.

He pinches my nipples and I follow his fingers, loving the pain-pleasure feeling. "Love me a woman who knows what she wants."

"Sure, you do..." I turn in his arms, taking us down in the motion. We end up with me laying above him, straddling his lap. His eyes are heavy with desire, completely different from the annoying man I have painted him to be in my mind. All a ruse to hide my attraction to him.

He smirks when his eyes meet mine. *Yes. I want you. And yes, I'm going to have you.*

All my plans of leading him on until he begs goes out the window. Leaning in, I kiss him roughly on the lips. I've been dying to have those lips of his again on mine. My pride didn't let me accept it last night. Today is a new day.

He wraps his arms around me, as we go at it. My sighs mingle with his groan of pleasure. He slips his tongue over my hungry mouth, and I tug at his lips, then bite it.

He pulls away, scoffing. "You like it rough, uhn?"

Shut up and stop talking. Closing my eyes, I move to take his lips in mine again, but he maneuvers me, until I lay beneath him. *What the heck?* Opening my eyes, I find his mouth curved in a smug smile, I'm tempted to slap it off.

"I'll love to continue this." He presses his erection against me—erection I'm yet to touch because my whole senses have been overthrown by his lips, his voice, and his fingers. "But I scheduled a fun activity for you to face your fears."

Uhn? Fears? "What fears?"

"Water."

I make to push him off me, but he resists. "Get off me Onahi. That was a low blow."

"Hold on. I told you I'll be your personal guide and I promise you; you'll love this."

"Get off me." I push.

"Alright." He does and we sit facing each other. "Let me make it better. Want to go parasailing?" He asks, raising a brow. The eagerness on his face and how he quickly shifted from our earlier activity to this is so unnatural.

I begin straightening myself out. So, it is not just breakfast and fuck. He has a full day planned. *Isn't that sweet?* "You sent Biftu?"

"Had to. I was scared you'll sleep the whole day."

"I'm here on vacation. It's expected."

"No offense, but just this one thing... I have it all planned, and I've envisioned your reaction. I believe you're going to love it."

"I'm not sure about me loving it. Why don't we do something else? Like ride a bicycle?"

"I promise, if you don't like it, I'll learn to ride a bicycle."

Not bad. It would be great to see him flat on the floor after switching up on me. The mental image is too good to ignore. I grin, looking him in the eyes as I stand up, then begin walking backwards into the bedroom. "Hold that thought, I'll go get dressed."

Twenty

Onahi

IT WAS FUCKING SELF-DISCIPLINE AND control that had me dragging Lola out of her villa in time for our scheduled activity. Fuck! When she stepped into the living space, all I first saw were legs. Legs that went on forever. No matter how many times I see her, I don't think I'll ever get used to seeing those legs. I can't wait to fuck her out of my system, offer her my proposal, then move on with my life.

Goddamnit. But those nipples. Nipples begging to be sucked. Had I not known better, I'd have concluded she let the jam spill on that thin fabric she called clothing, intentionally. I tried my damnedest not to stare at them, even before the jam thingy happened, but fuck it. I'm human. A living human with red blood flowing through my veins.

I fought the urge to reach over and touch them, to put my tongue on them. To flick the sensitive bud till she cried mercy. And we were on the road to me doing that until the remembrance of why I was there, and self-discipline came to the rescue.

Lola and I watch the captain call out to his crew members on shore as we await other adventurers to join us aboard the boat. She looks adorable in a colorful hooded Ankara top and plain black bum shorts that matches mine in color. The lady has planned to have me knocked off my feet with her fashion sense and her flair for colorful clothing. When I ask if she specially shopped for clothing before arriving the island, she laughs, saying she rarely wore colors back home due to work. It must suck being an employee.

"I can't believe I'm on water again." Her attention on the crew mates helping others board, as she settles a pair of neon green sunglass on her face, stray hair strands dance to the beat of the wind, "And we're not heading to the airport."

Placing my arm on the small of her back, I smile, my nose catching her vanilla scent. "That's because I'm learning from you."

"Nope... this is you being humble. You can talk a tortoise out of its shell. Just so you know, you're riding a bicycle whether I like it or not."

"You'll love it. A deal's a deal."

She sticks her tongue out at me.

Escape

Chuckling, I throw a glance at the gangway to find Jay and her friend from the other night walking towards us. I had sent eyes and ears on his trail to find out more about him—something I should do with Lola, but I'm enjoying the mystery. It's making this vacation... exciting. Turns out Jay's friend is Tyrell, son of Chief Duabi Alagoa, from Port Harcourt, Nigeria. Runs his family's furniture business, *Raw Inc.*, with his sister who is getting married on the resort this weekend.

I like that he is responsible, diligent, and even a philanthropist, but with all his brain and accomplishment, he must be daft or something when it comes to women. I would have done something drastic to scare him off Jay, but she's a grown adult. She deserves a chance to be happy. Ahmed once revealed to me he might never get married. And I don't know if everyone's buying it, but his recent proposal coming not long after his announcement to run for office doesn't convince me one bit.

When Jay spots me, her eyes light up and she makes a beeline to us.

"That's Jay and her *friend*." I murmur to Lola, and she catches on fast, smiling as Jay closes the distance between us.

"She is beautiful." She is—an excellent result from the combination of a Nigerian man and an Egyptian lady.

I remove my arm in time from Lola's back to hug Jay's flying body.

"Onahi!" She grins, caught in my bear hug.

"Jay..." I smile as she slides down my frame. "What are you doing out here?"

She releases her hold on me, tossing her head from side to side, her eyes mischievous. "Who told you I don't know the fun things to do around here? And you," she pokes my chest playfully, still grinning, "you've been one busy bee since I got here."

I raise my hands in the air. "Never said that. It's just—" Lola's hip bumps mine subtly, and I grin. "Jay, please meet my companion, Lola. She's the one taking up my time."

Jay turns her smiling face to Lola; a look of feminine appreciation clouds her face. Lola on the other hand smiles knowingly, her eyes darting from Tyrell to Jay. There's a mocking question in those eyes when they land on me. *You think you're still her chaperone?* It's a different feeling when I have knowledge of people beforehand. In this case, Lola knows what I know and the smiles we share are deeper, knowing...

"Hello Jay," Lola's says, trying hard not to spill the question on her lips. Something like, have you fucked your *friend* already?

"Hi Lola." She smiles cautiously.

"I'm sorry I stole him from you. He—"

"No, you did not." Jay laughs. "I've been keeping busy with my new friend, Tyrell." She winks to the guy behind her who looks far from being friendly.

"Ah." Lola spares me a knowing glance and I ball my fist as my dick jerks to life. Down boy. I let out a whoosh playful breath, laughing with the ladies. This feels so weird—I still want to fuck her even though she's acting like a busybody sister, a friend—I've never experienced this combination of emotions with a woman I want to fuck. What is happening to the dynamics of our relationship?

"Have you toured the island?" Lola continues, giggling conspiratorially with Jay as they continue their banter like old friends just reuniting.

Focusing my gaze on Tyrell, he walks up to me, his expression not giving much, a handshake in tow. His grip is firm. Tight. Not a bad chap.

"Hey, I'm Tyrell." We're of similar height with a slight difference in build and muscle.

I nod, my expression bland. "Onahi."

"Oh." He arches his brow in recognition.

Our eyes had met at the bar the other night and I guess he understands better.

"What's up? Great resort by the way," he adds as we walk to the edge of the boat.

Leaning on the railings, I check to make sure the ladies know we're behind them. "Thank you." When Lola smiles at me, I turn my attention back to Tyrell. "I hope you're enjoying your stay?"

His gaze slithers towards Jay and sits there before he answers, a smirk on his lips. "I guess."

Idiot. What is he trying to prove? I'll smack that smirk off your lips in a heartbeat if you're out to disrespect her. Jay seems happy so no need to rock that boat—just yet.

Straightening up, I look down at him, the best way I can. "You know she's engaged, don't you?"

He straightens, and we return to being of the same height. "And you're reminding me of this because?"

I give a small laugh. He's got balls. I like that. I hope he can handle not just what makes Jay special, but Ahmed's wrath. He should be able to—he's a tough entrepreneur that made *Raw Inc.* what it is today.

"Have you met Lola?" Tyrell looks confused and I walk the short distance to the women who were laughing at something, but hush once they sense my presence.

Tyrell joins our party, taking Jay's hand and she instinctively leans into him. That's a good sign. Ahmed has a lot on his plate and I'm not involving myself in his feast.

"Lola, meet Tyrell. Tyrell is Jay's companion." I wink and we all laugh, save Tyrell who's not having the joke.

"I'm loving this Island," Lola begins when our laughing fit ends. "It's a wonderful place to meet wonderful people." Is she trying to make Tyrell comfortable?

Her eyes rake over him and I'm the only one chuckling. You better not be thinking of taking on Tyrell's attention. We're not done sorting this thing between us. "Be careful Lola, you don't want Janelle biting your ears off."

Lola and Jay laugh, while Tyrell remains stoic. What are his intentions? He had better not be planning something serious with her. I sigh... It's none of my business for now.

The boat roars to life, and both ladies, seated on my left and right keep chatting about the sights and the blue ocean. They pull out their phones, taking pictures, striking poses, making videos—all traces of fear erased from Lola's physique. That's a good sign. Their girly giggles and occasional gasps stop when Lola's phone beeps. I pretend to look at the water from Lola's view, but my eyes roam her screen and I spot the name, *Nonso*, and words like, *fun, spend time*. I ground my jaw.

Who the fuck is Nonso? The guy from last night or another guy? She's having fun with me and doesn't need another dick hanging around her. Speaking of dicks. I need to give Duncan a piece of my mind. I'd have scheduled a meeting, but there's no need for that when I'll be seeing the motherfucker tomorrow.

"That's true." Jay's shoulder bumps into mine, jarring me from my conflicting thoughts. "You never told me you are a descendant of the resort owners."

I shrug, taking my curious eyes off Lola's direction. She's so into responding to her message, she doesn't look up when I speak. "It's nothing important. Old family tales." What the fuck is she smiling about? What's the idiot telling her? This boat better make it to the middle of the ocean fast, so she loses network signal and focuses on the day I have planned out for her.

Jay rolls her eyes. "Whatever."

Lola turns her attention to us, a grin etched on her face, the wind blowing her messy packed hair all over the place, "You said?" She places her palm on my thigh and I instinctively reach out to hold them.

I give Jay a don't-you-dare-repeat-that eye and she smiles. "We're going scuba diving," Jay begins, "are you guys?"

"Not we're not." I answer, "We're doing something more daring for the lady." Addressing Lola, I continue. "She doesn't like water but loves flights."

Lola's cheeks brighten as I reveal her weakness to our audience.

"So, it's parasailing for us." I kiss the back of her hand, and she looks at me, wonder in her eyes.

God damnit. You're spending time with me and you're going to have fun. Not with some idiot somewhere named Nonso. Once we get back to shore, I'm putting my eyes and ears on him.

Jay gasps. "Oh. That's beautiful." She turns dreamy eyes to Lola. "You'll love it dear. I'm sure Onahi is the best person to try something like that with."

Lola's grip tightens in mine, and I trace my finger over hers. You heard it. The best person to try something like that, is me.

"Thanks for the reassurance." Lola smiles, pushing a strand of hair behind her ear.

"It's no biggie." Jay smiles in return. "I should also try that soon," she tells Tyrell.

"We will." Tyrell says with a tight smile my way.

Dude has got long-term plans. I'm here for this.

Twenty-One

Lola

"PERFECT WEATHER," THE CAPTAIN, WHO introduces himself as Asad in his heavily accented English, goes on and on about safety, precautions, and hand signals if the worst happens.

The worst? I toss Onahi a glare. Instead of cringing, he takes my hand in his—smiling, dutifully nodding his head when necessary, confirming we had signed waivers—giving the impression we're having a good time.

Great. If I die on this trip, he can say I gave them permission to kill me. Simply great. And I might never find out what Jay meant with her last question.

He had confessed to doing this before when we left the other boat for this speed boat. It irks me that he's so cool about this when my palms are so sweaty and cold.

The boat encounters a bump and I squeal in fright, rocking on my feet. Leaning in, Onahi says, for my ears alone, "It's alright, I'm right here."

Hah. Like you're Jesus. I should have called mommy or Carolanne before stepping out of the villa, but my mind was preoccupied with this roguish human being who curses at the drop of a needle but somehow manages to act like a gentleman. Now I'm about to try something stupid. Very stupid. An extreme sport I never had on my bucket list. I don't even have a bucket list.

Standing straight like a mannequin, I allow a crew member to fit me in a life vest. "For precaution. Nothing serious," he says, and I swallow an enormous lump down my throat. This is not my time to die.

I shoot daggers with my eyes at Onahi who is getting friendly with the captain, speaking a language I don't understand and don't want to because this is my life! What is happening? Why am I letting another stranger, sweet talk me into doing something I might regret?

Onahi turns bright eyes to me. "He just agreed to dipping for extra bucks." He hollers over the wind.

What is that supposed to mean when there's sweat pouring down my back and sides. My wardrobe choice is ill-suited for this activity and *perfect weather*–which consists of the sun burning at over thirty degrees Celsius.

He walks up to me, already suited with a vest, his eyes scanning my attire.

"Don't even say anything." I mutter, and he grins like a boy given keys to his first real car. He looks so yummy in the vest.

"I hope there are no sharks in this water."

That was the first question I should have asked when he suggested this crazy idea.

"Like Jay said, I'm the best person to try something like this with."

Hissing at his remark, I begin tugging at the life vest. "Know what? Tell them to get this thing off me. I'm not comfortable."

He blinks in confusion. "You need to—"

"Onahi no. I call the dibs here. I want it off."

"But—"

"Don't worry, I'm still going to do it, but I want this off first." I point to the life vest.

He eyes me, his boyish excitement dimming, then turns to signal a crew member.

I sigh in relief when the vest comes off, then I pull of my hooded Ankara top, leaving me clad in a bra top and bum short.

"You need to—" Onahi shakes his head then swallows as he takes in the sight of me. Good for him.

"Help please," I call out to the crew member and as he reaches to help me back in my life suit, Onahi nudges him away.

"I've got this."

I grin as he recovers from his shock, helping me into my suit.

"What game are you playing at minx?"

I shrug, feeling light, better than before. "I wasn't comfortable, but this feels so much better."

"And looks so much better," he adds, his lips taking on that lopsided smile. "I'm looking forward to our after party." His gaze lingers on my lips, and my nipples, although stuck behind a padded bra, perks up at his hooded eyes.

"Ready?!" Asad calls, breaking the moment.

Onahi leans in, giving me a quick kiss on my lips. "For luck." Then turns to Asad. "We are!"

The crew tells us to seat down, securing us with individual harnesses. I talk about everything and nothing—the weather, throwing up breakfast if this turns out bad, the wind, how safe this is, who will record my last moments—to keep my mind from what we're about to do.

Onahi chuckles. "I knew it."

I pause, glaring at him. *You caused all this. I could be on my bed, or at a yoga training, but here I am getting ready to be launched into the air tied with only a rope to a moving boat.* "Know what?"

"Don't worry about that, that's why we have one extra crew member. He's in charge of documenting our experience."

"Oh." My eyes light up and I reach out a hand to him. When he touches it, I pout a, *thank you.*

"And here." He shows me a camera attached to a gimbal. "I'll be covering the aerial view."

I flutter my lashes at him, and he gives a small laugh. The crew members prepare the chute and when they complete the task, they call us up and clip us in. We sit, and Onahi tries his best to educate me on sea life, but I've closed my mind. Too late.

They begin releasing the ropes and next thing I know; cold sea water touches my legs and I squeal, a mixture of delight and fear.

Onahi, the annoying human is chuckling. "Brace yourself darling."

Darling?

He is looking around us—at the body of water surrounding us—as the distance between the boat and us increases. He has no idea he just called me darling. I look down and that is a big mistake. What if the rope breaks? Are there sharks in this water? Does he know how to swim?

"Are you okay?" Onahi shouts at me through the rushing wind.

"I'm alright."

It's quiet now. Have I drowned? Where is Onahi?

"Open your eyes."

Uhn? What? I wasn't aware I had them closed. I squeeze them shut tighter. I let out a deep breath, holding the harness tighter. *I'm still alive!*

"Don't worry. Trust me, just open your eyes."

I do. And when I do, I notice two things; we're far away from the boat—the boat is like a dot on the water—and everywhere around us is blue. Nothing in the horizon, just blue ocean water.

OMG! We're flying! We're 800 ft above sea level.

"This is amazing!"

Onahi chuckles, and only then do I realize we're doing this together.

"Should I say I told you so?"

"Don't you dare." I sigh blissfully. "At this moment, it doesn't matter whether or not you say it. This view is breathtaking." *So, this is what being a kite feels like.*

"This is one part of it. Imagine you're actually above a busy city. That's also serene. Having a bird's eye view. We could go paragliding on our next adventure."

"Well, I'll need to survive this first before thinking of that."

He scrutinizes me, and I let my hands out, closing my eyes. "You're doing an excellent job."

Everything around us is tiny. This is what birds experience when they soar in the sky. From up here mother earth looks so peaceful and natural. The air is clearer and the colors are vivid. This could have been Robert and I, but he decided to go with miss goody two-shoes.

"Fuck You Thelma!"

Onahi shakes his head at me. His eyes asking, *who is Thelma?*

Escape

"She is an annoying colleague of mine. I wish I never had to work with her, but I did and here I am." I grin, taking in the scene. I don't feel pained about the situation anymore, because, here I am, enjoying myself, on top of the world.

"She's engaged to a guy I had my eyes on. And the guy," I click my tongue. "I don't like it when people know you have feelings for them and lead you on. Only for you to find out they've known who they want to date or be with all along. It's kind of like them feeling they have control over others. It's sickening. Generally speaking, if you know something, save me the stress, tell me. If you've got a question, ask away. It's better we fight now than when the stakes are high."

He snorts. And we move on to discussing nature and other light topics.

There's a strange sound coming from below. I think we're being reeled in. No. No. No. I like it here. I want to be a bird, not just any bird, an eagle, flying high up in the sky with no human worries.

Raising questioning eyes to Onahi, he confirms my fear.

"I wish we could actually do this longer."

"I've got other things planned for today." Like the after party? "Next time you visit."

I ignore the words he used. We're having fun. No strings attached. And it doesn't matter if I would never use my personal money to come here in the first place.

We're almost five meters from the boat, when my greatest fear happens. We lose momentum, crash landing in the water. Onahi keeps his cool while I scream in shock and fear. Sharks.

Sharks. I've seen sharks circle people in waters like this on Instagram.

"What do we do?! It's not my time to die yet." I thrash my arms in the water. The idiot, he keeps laughing, until Asad launches a jet ski to get us out of the water. Was this what he paid extra bucks for? Ah!

"So... Lunch while we dry out?" he asks when we return to the boat.

****

HIS LAUGHTER IS EVERYTHING—IT comes from deep within and makes me smile, even when I don't want to. And his smile... it's different—his lips tilts towards the corners of his mouth and it makes me think of our tongues clicking together.

"I'm sorry for not telling you I had this all planned out yesterday," he says as we make our way from the sandy beach to *Gobota Specials*—the place we had our lunch argument.

"It's fine. I would have gone anyway. It's a must-do life experience."

He raises a brow at that, and I shrug.

"And thanks for the video."

"You're welcome."

As we settle into a cane chair, he summons a server with the flick of his wrist. "What do you think about a day in town? Get to try other stuff," he asks, studying the menu.

"Sounds promising." Instead of looking for something that has bread in it, I go with roasted plantain, smoked fish, and spicy sauce.

I replay the videos from earlier, while he responds to messages on his phone. In record time, the server brings our meal and my tummy grumbles in appreciation.

"This is so good," I say, biting into the savory fish I had dipped in the spicy sauce.

"Yeah." His carefree expression has been replaced with a brooding one. "You never told me who the guy last night was."

We're back to this? Someone's jealous... *He's my fiancé.* I stifle a giggle. "That was Chinonso Kalu. Venture capitalist and serial entrepreneur."

"Hmm..."

"I'm actually thinking of starting a business, but I need funding and sponsors. So, he's helping me out."

"Makes sense." But there's an edge to his voice that says it doesn't. He pauses between a bite, his fork in midair. "Are you open to new opportunities? Like employment opportunities? Where you can wear colorful clothing to work."

Colorful clothing to work? Is that the best you can come up with? "I'm not sure. But I won't say never. My priority is my business plan for SMEs. Come to think of it, you never told me the nature of your job."

He gives a slow smile. "I have multiple businesses around the world. Hospitality, construction, and technology. Though I mostly do investments and sit on boards."

"Impressive, you look so young though."

"Don't be fooled."

We hurry through lunch, and he books a private shuttle, which I drive into town. It's been ages since I got behind a wheel because I mostly used shared rides back in DC. But once he showed me how to ride the shuttle, I took over and it was fun!

When we get into town, a feeling of nostalgia hits me, like I've travelled through time where people are in no hurry, laughing and greeting each other as they pass. There are no traffic lights, yet everything seems to follow a set order.

"Do you mind taking me to the market? I'll like to add to my collection," Onahi says.

"Collection of what?"

He grins. "You'll find out soon enough." Then gives me direction.

"Right here." I park in the spot he says is safe to and we walk the rest of the way into the marketplace.

He buys wrist accessories to add to his growing collection, chatting easily with the market women in their local language.

When we walk off from their stall, he asks if I want anything, and I shake my head.

"You can't just... come here and not get anything."

"I'll get a Gobota souvenir."

"That's so touristy. How about a scarf?" His eyes light up. "Yes, you'll love them. They're colorful but not as bright as you."

Escape

Pulling me behind him as we weave our way through the market, we stop by a stall selling scarves and sarongs of assorted colors, prints, and length. Carolanne would love something like this.

"Is *pareo*." The market woman corrects me when I ask for the price. "Name is *pareo*."

"He told me scarf." I point at Onahi who snickers. The butterflies in my tummy dance to the tune of his boyish charm and I smile.

Onahi banters with the woman, while I zip my light backpack containing my new *pareo*. After parasailing, to be a complete island girl, I chose not to wear my hooded Ankara top but stuck with my colorful bra top. Now the cooling evening breeze is getting to me.

"Done?" he asks.

"Yeah." I chest out, ready for the next challenge he's about to toss my way. My bad. He zones out for a while, focusing on my bra top and midriff. "Hello?" I wave a hand in his face, and he shakes his head, smiling smugly.

"You do that to me." He pulls me to his side, his fingers making wriggly lines on my bare midriff, and I chuckle. "Ticklish, hmm..."

I laugh nervously, a disguise to hide my growing desire. I want his hands somewhere else. "Let's go home."

"One final thing before we leave."

"What's that?"

"The fire water at my favorite local bar."

"That's a marula stuff, right?"

"Yeah." The setting sun has his profile looking soft as he goes on about the fire water, a local beer made from the marula, hot enough to knock me out.

"It doesn't take much to knock you out," he tweaks my nose, recalling my first night.

Duh, I was high on drugs. I thought we agreed to leave that night buried in the past.

"Are we going to do that now?"

He smiles ruefully, before brushing a stray strand of hair from my face. "I'm sorry it came out that way." His eyes meet mine and I believe him. "So... I know I've not told you much about myself but when I was younger, Gobota was like a second home. The fire water was something I smuggled back home when my family visited the resort. I want to share it with you. But now I'm thinking it's a bad idea."

So, he and his family have some sort of Twin Bliss membership card. Born in wealth, living in splendor. Not every billionaire wears a suit.

"No. No." I place a hand on his chest. "I also have something planned for tonight. Let's get it." Picking invisible lint off his shirt, I add, "I don't want Zeus tonight."

Onahi tosses his face heaven ward, letting out a frustrated sigh. "There's a Zeus too?"

Without batting an eyelid, I tell him, "He is, my vibrator."

"Holy smokes." His eyes widen at my revelation, then it turns into a knowing smile. He grabs my hand rushing me down the path. "Let's get this over and done with."

I'm about to get laid!

Twenty-Two

Onahi

LOLA APPEARS TO BE AN ardent student, imbibing the local language and also processing it pretty fast when we join in the karaoke at the local bar. When I ask her to sing back to me, her accent is so natural, it has me questioning her origins.

She takes a sip of the fire water, confessing it is too strong with the shake of her head.

"I can't," she laughs, her hand making a throat slitting sign as tears gather on the corner of her eyes. I lean down, dropping a kiss on her lips and we stare at each other with a knowing smile.

"Want to come see my villa?" I ask.

"The greatest trick of all time." She eyes me from top down, her eyes twinkling with delight.

She agrees to visiting my villa after dinner at a local restaurant. "A change of scenery." I promise her.

The sight of my private pool has her gushing. Surrounding trees gives each Cairo villa enough privacy from prying eyes. Multiple lanterns hung on trees illuminate the greenery and sleeping petals on the other side of the villa.

"This is the complete package! We're swimming in that." She points at the pool.

"I thought you didn't like water—"

"Travelling on water."

"And swimming?"

"Duh, I can swim in a pool, not in a moving, living body of water that can toss me aside or bury me."

"Good to know. Want to come inside? I've got something better than a pool and I'm sure those legs are killing you from standing all day."

She giggles, fluttering her lashes, then leans into me. "Is that an excuse to get me inside or to get inside me?"

I shake my head, before leading her into the villa.

"Wow!" she exclaims, taking in the greys and whites of the interior décor. "Your villa is like version 4.0 of mine. Oh..." she purrs, "you have a bigger mini-bar."

Mine is a custom-designed villa, a perk of being the resort's favorite. When customers visit regularly for about five years, they are offered the opportunity of having a custom-designed villa. It's a major source of income for the resort.

Dropping everything we brought in on the couch, I ask her to sit, so I can massage her feet.

"Scrap that. Lay down instead." I instruct her and she shimmies in anticipation.

Taking her long legs and placing them on my lap, I scrutinize them, my dick throbbing to life in anticipation. I've been watching her prance about all day on them, in this bum short that keeps teasing my senses. I never considered myself a legs man, but fuck it, Lola's a game changer.

"Hmm..." she murmurs, closing her eyes, as I slide my hands up and down the shin of one leg. A jolt of sexual energy travels through my core, settling in my tummy, waiting for release. Down boy...down. I breathe, grasping for any semblance of control. It would be so embarrassing cumming in my pants like a guy excited to have sex for the first time.

"Know how long I've wanted to do this?" I ask.

A sigh of contentment escapes her lips. "How long?"

"The night you injured your ankle."

"Oh. What stopped you?"

"You were drunk and—"

"Drugged. Drugged not drunk." I hear the smile in her voice. "Not the best way to make a first impression, yeah?"

"I wasn't trying."

"Uhn, you were so eager to—" I press my thumb to the underside of her foot, and she squirms, sitting up, laughing.

"That's ticklish!"

I give a small laugh. "I didn't want you telling the story like that."

"Yeah right." She lays back on the couch and I resume massaging and manipulating her foot. She sighs; looking flush, achy, sometimes thrusting her hips forward. My dick threatens to make an announcement, but I practice breath control. The yoga classes come to my aid.

"You like it?"

"Love it," she murmurs, her voice fading.

Don't you fucking sleep on me. That's not the plan. I lift her feet off my lap, and she gives a disappointing *oh*.

"This was not part of the plan." I smile, standing up, adjusting my shorts, not caring my hard-on is visible.

"What is the plan?"

"We shower... And who knows? I get to fuck this itch I have for you away?"

"The feeling is mutual."

"I'm glad we're on the same page."

She gives me a knowing smile. "So... Shower it is."

Getting up in a flash, she shimmies out of her bum short, while my eyes follow her movement. "Last to get in the shower is a squid."

I am expecting to see her in nothing but her birthday suit, but she giggles off in search of the bathroom wearing her bra top and panties that gives me a perfect view of her bouncy ass cheeks.

Uhn? Why the fuck does she still have clothes on? And that ass. Damn!

"Are you coming?" She yells. "Or am I taking this shower alone? Wow! You've got a jacuzzi!" Then I hear the water come on.

What have I gotten myself into? I pull off my shirt and short, leaving my boxers in place. This was not what I envisioned when I asked her over. We are supposed to make out, skin on skin, then head over to the shower, then sex. Jeez. Lola's a living, breathing, energy ball.

"Are you going to take off the underwear?" I ask, stepping into the jacuzzi.

She eyes me like a delicious beef kebab, and it has my dick fighting to come out of the boxers holding it in place. "And derive you the pleasure of taking them off?"

"Oh."

Her fingers trail the water. "You had this well thought out, didn't you?"

The fuck I did. And I am yet to get a kiss all day. Yeah, we made out in the morning, but that was ages ago. "Come here."

Lola stares at me from beneath her lashes, ignoring me.

Fuck it. I pull her legs and she giggles until she's close enough for a kiss. Her silky bra top, now completely wet, molds her hardened nipples.

"Nice choice of clothing." I pull her closer, enjoying the way the hardened pebbles poke my chest.

"Why?"

"Cos I can do this." I move the narrow strip of excuse for clothing and my hand meets her warm, perky breasts. She moans, thrusting them into my hand.

Fuck! I'm in heaven.

She breathes my name and my dick twitches. I need to kiss those lips. The giggly smiling lips.

Pressing my mouth against hers, we duel for control. Not so fast, but not slow as well. When she makes a shaking moan, I groan, pressing closer. Needing her. Wanting to enter her. But I need to slow it down. We've got all night.

"Nahi..." she moans.

"I like it when you call my name." I grin.

She pulls her lips from mine, laughing, pushing me back, causing water to splash on the sides. The housekeeper will take care of it.

"You're so full of shit," she laughs, while I spread my arms on the ledge of the jacuzzi.

"Not my fault. I have the most sought-after woman in my tub."

"My bra!" she gasps, cupping her breast, smiling.

"It's a skill."

"Oh..." Her mouth forms a cute, O, as she leans back studying me. "Okay..."

She goes on all fours, coming for me, while I spread my legs out. Water dripping off her body has her looking like a siren coming out of the sea. Her wet hair—deliciously plastered on her head—has her looking like a wet barbie. My wet barbie.

My wet barbie? Where the fuck did that come from? I shake the possessive thought off my head. No need spoiling the fun we're having by being an obnoxious prick.

"What do you like?"

I grin lasciviously. "Everything."

She smiles, cocking her head to the side. "It's obvious."

Her hands brush my dick which lengthens from the contact. *Down boy. Down...* I groan.

Leaning closer, her brows and I follow her line of attention. "You've got a tattoo..." She rubs her hand on the spot above my right breast. It was a statement but sounded more like a question. "I never took you for one to have a tattoo."

"It's the only one. I got it when I was sixteen. Worried I was going to mess up in college." I laugh.

"*I can... do all things through Christ who strengthens me?* Wow. A bible verse?" She looks at me, wonder in her eyes. "A tattoo and a biblical one at that. Mr. Onahi, you amaze me."

"My mom agreed I needed something to remind me of my strength and faith. I'm not an atheist or something. We all need to believe in something to make it through life."

Why the fuck are we talking about church and my mom when I have a hard-on and a willing woman ready to relieve me of my obsession? "Can we get to business?"

She giggles, dropping wet kisses on the tattoo, causing me to shiver.

"Better." I sigh.

"I like it," she murmurs on the tattoo.

I like that too.

Lola continues trailing kisses on the tattoo, then surprises me by closing her lips over my nipples. I moan in pure ecstasy. Okay. That's a new one. I've never had a woman do that with me. Just me doing all the work. I've never complained because, well, sex was good. But this was euphoric, and we've not gotten to the best part.

"Now say my name," Lola says between licks, flicks, and bites. Squeezing my eyes shut and clenching both fists to keep from dragging her out of the tub and into the bedroom, I concentrate on the tingling sensation from her warm tongue. Release builds up in my body. Then it stops.

I blink my eyes open. "What?" My voice gravelly.

"Say my name Nahi."

"Okay... okay." I smile.

She resumes her ministration and I and thrust my hips up, in search of hers. Murmuring something about taking our time, she begins palming my dick that's still enclosed in my briefs.

"Fuck... Lola..." I moan, between harsh breaths of control. She didn't have to tell me to say her name—she's in control, and I'm at her mercy. I need her touching my dick itself, flesh to flesh.

"Good job..." she mutters, tracing kisses up my collar bone, then stops at my ears.

I jerk and she says, "Shhh... Just repaying the favor." And she pays attention to those things I thought were strictly for listening. Fuck.

I groan in pleasure when she mutters something about her being excited to be pounded by me from behind, the image so clear and visible in my head. Forcing myself to break from her hold, I pull her off me. Her expression is not at all friendly.

"Give me your lips." Her frown slips, turning into a smile. I thrust my tongue in her mouth and she whimpers, rocking against me, her warm pussy rubbing my throbbing dick.

"I don't want us finishing before we start," I murmur in her mouth, "Let's get dry and fuck-ready."

Stepping out of the jacuzzi, I assist her in drying off, preparing for the main meal. With every dab, she giggles, causing me to smile. Since she still has her panties on, I use the moment to pull it down her waist. She giggles again, forcing the contraption off her body with those sultry legs of hers.

My giggling girl. Only Lola would giggle when it's time to have sex.

"So..." She fluffs her now curly hair, walking backwards towards the bed, while I stalk her. The back of her knees hit the bed and she sits on it sultrily, hands on both sides, legs spread wide. "What do you have in mind?"

"A lot. But first I want to kiss those lips of yours again." I stand between her legs.

"Hmm..." she observes me, then frowns. "You're not wearing that wet thing here..." tapping the bed.

"I need to—"

"Nope." She twirls a finger in her hair. "Take it off."

"You sure?" If I take it off, we would be done in a second and I want to take my time.

She snorts. "I'm not a shy virgin. Let's see what you've got."

I deduced that the first night we met. Her kisses were not that of a novice.

"You asked for it."

"Since you want to take your time, I'll concentrate on me." She slides a hand between her legs and begins touching herself. Her wet pussy makes smacking noises as she strokes it.

Gawking at her in awe, I watch as she moans, tilting her head to the ceiling, eyes rolling with every whimper, every moan. Fuck! When she falls back on the bed, a switch clicks in my head.

Shedding off the briefs and damning the consequences, I join her in bed, replacing her hands with mine.

She gives a small smile. "I thought you'd never make—"

Kissing the words off her mouth, I stroke my fingers on her warm pussy, the way I had seen her do it. "I need to taste you." I murmur in her mouth.

"What?" she pants. Delirious. She is far too gone to register my words as I get off her, dropping to my knees before her pussy.

Twenty-Three

Lola

ONAHI MUTTERS SOMETHING ABOUT MY legs being his favorite part of my body but now, my pussy is inspiring him. Then he pushes my thighs apart, burying his face between my legs.

Oh... My eyes roll in their sockets. I move my hand across my chest, flicking my nipples. Onahi stretches his arm, holding on to one of my breasts and I buck my hips into him. It's different when his hands touch them.

Oh... I smile deliriously to the ceiling... I'm fucking his face. I'm fucking his face!

"Nahi..." I breathe.

My moaning encourages him to increase his intensity. He takes his hand off my breasts to place it on the lips of my pussy. I miss those hands on my breasts, but they feel better down there, supporting every licking and sucking of his tongue. My hips jerks as he thrust a finger inside me.

Oh... God. Oh... God. My... God.

He pulls the finger out, then in, then his tongue flicks my clit. "Ooh..." A tremor passes through me, and my leg shakes.

"You're not laughing anymore?"

"Shut up." He chuckles into my core, the vibration causing me to press my hips against his mouth. Oh...

"Hmm..." He hums, the vibration sending tingling sensations all over my body. My legs wrap around his back. "You like that?"

"You're doing too much talking." I pull his head back to the task at hand and he chuckles. This is why I've stuck to Zeus for the past two years. Zeus doesn't talk or gloat, he— "Oh... Nahi... Nah... Nahi..."

He's humming something into my pussy and the vibration makes me thrash around but hold on to him.

Oh God! I'm coming... I'm coming... I swallow, looking up, closing my eyes. There's a weird sensation pressing on my bladder. It's too much. I can't take this.

"Oh shit. I'm going to pee!"

"Do it."

"Oh shit." I try to fight him off my pussy, but he keeps sucking, his fingers stroking. A myriad of emotions and tremors pass through my body. One hand holding his head, the other holding on to the bedspread I scream, tightening my legs around him.

Letting go, liquid gushes out of my pussy. It goes on forever, sending tremors all over my body—a thousand soul-shattering orgasm. Onahi keeps lapping at my pussy, wringing out all the shivers he can. When I remove my weak legs from his back, I feel the bed dip beside me.

I fling a hand over my face to cover my embarrassment, watching him from beneath.

"Did you know?" His voice filled with wonder as he reaches for my breast, stroking it.

"No. It's my first time."

"Wow." He leans in to place a kiss on my forehead, as though sensing my embarrassment. "You're full of surprises. All my years... You are the first squirter I've met."

Removing my hand from my face, I stare at him in wonder. "You liked it?"

He gives a warm smile, climbing above me. "You're a fucking goddess. What's there not to like?"

I smile back at him. "It's going to be hard returning to normal. But I'm glad I'm having this experience." Great way to return to the sex scene.

"And that it's with me?" he gloats.

I shrug. There's no lie to that. We have this chemistry we can't deny. I'm so glad we cut to the chase tonight. Have sex and move on. After all, I came here to have fun. "I promise to reciprocate later. Right now, this Guru needs you to take her on a joy ride."

He laughs, pressing his burgeoning penis on my abdomen. "A joy ride uhn? For the Guru."

He's talking too much. And smirking.

I pull his head down for a deep kiss and he pushes into me, a full thrust. Nothing slow or delicate. I gasp into his mouth as he fills me up. Tears threaten to cloud my eyes as his girth overwhelms me. It feels familiar. Like home. A memory from the beach night flashes through my head, but I shake it off.

"You good?" His tone strained as he struggles to keep control.

Good. I'm not the only one feeling this sea of emotions.

I nod, claiming his mouth again, then wrap my arms around him. I want more, need more. Zeus is nothing compared to this. This throbbing pain and pleasure.

Onahi groans, burying his lips in the kiss just as he buried himself in me and begins pumping me with fast strokes. I move my hips in tune his, matching his pace, even though my legs feel weak.

Oh no... Another orgasm. Oh Lord... I struggle for control, clamping my lips together.

He keeps thrusting. My hand frantically runs through his back, in search of what I have no idea of. There's something building in me. "I'm going to come again."

"You asked for this." *For what?*

He gets off me and, to my surprise, grabs me by my hips, turning me to my side. He settles behind me, raising one of my legs high into the air, then nudges his penis inside me, and resumes thrusting.

"Oh..." I say with a smile as he pounds me from behind.

So full... I feel so full... I can die like this. The angle of his thrust, his size, his balls slapping my ass... Everything. Perfect.

"Like it?" he asks, thrusting fast and steady.

Love it! But my response is a satisfied grunt. I bite my lips when he increases his tempo, groaning like someone in pain.

"Let it out."

That's all the command I need.

He pounds me, one leg raised, balls slapping ass, while I cling to the bedspread. Every hit is a banger, pushing me closer to another release. My legs are past their stretch limit, but I pay the pain no mind as I squeeze my eyes shut, seeking my release.

"Fuck it. I'm coming," he grunts, pumping harder, like a maniac.

No. No. No. Not yet. I'm feeling something.

He pulls out, then kneels on the bed groaning, holding on to his penis, as he finds release, his eyes shut.

So much for another release. I rub my legs together as I watch my pussy reduce him to nothing but a man groaning in pleasure.

"Want to see me off to my villa?" I ask when he opens his eyes.

Confusion mars his gorgeous face at first, but when my statement clicks, he smiles. "You want to leave? We can go another round."

I shrug.

He squeezes my leg with the hand that has no sperm on it, then climbs off the bed. "I'll be right back."

He returns moments later with a towel to clean me up, and a new bed spread to replace the one I had messed up. He teases me about squirting as we arrange the bed and I tease him about his ejaculatory expression.

Next thing I know, he is chasing me around the bed for tickles. He finally captures me, and we fall on the bed, engulfed in giggles.

When our giggling fit subsides, he spoons me, whispering in my ears, "Stay the night."

Twenty—Four

Onahi

LOLA'S WARM BODY IS CURLED in mine when I receive a message from the resort's security team, telling me to be careful as a shooter is on the loose.

Taking all necessary precautions not to jolt her awake, I leave the beautiful vanilla scented siren on my bed, spent from a night of lust, laughter, and pleasure. Not so vanilla when it came to the sex. Sometime in the night, we had gone at it again, slower than the first time.

My dick twitches in response when I peek her slender legs between the sheets. The memory of her sweet nectar when I sucked between them—Fuck. Not now. I need to head to the admin office to get more information on the shooting and God knows, what else.

An unidentified shooter shot at a guest named Asher alongside his companion on their way to the historical ruin. They had hired a private shuttle and wanted to tour the area themselves. From the reports drawn, Asher is a big name in the transportation industry. Well, over half of the fucking resort's residence is a big name.

The head of security swears he is going to bring in Theodore Coker-Briggs, Gobota's celebrity private detective if he had to, and I tell him to do everything to keep the guests safe. My phone beeps with a reminder Salewa had scheduled on my calendar.

Tennis with the boys.

Shit. Time has flown by so fast. I need to get out of here.

"You need to figure this out." I press my finger to the table for emphasis. "Filter all the resort's residents. Profile them. Contact the locals. We don't know if this was just a random shooter."

"I'll check if we have new hires too."

"Good. Keep me posted." I should have gotten extra minutes with Lola this morning, but the mother-fucking shooter messed everything up.

Making a quick stop at my personal office in the admin building, I toss a towel on my neck, then fill up a bottle with water. Perks of having a living space in my office. Lola and I could perform magic here; with her leaning against the glass walls fully dressed, enjoying the view, while I fuck her from behind.

The bottle doesn't screw properly so I have to start again. Ah! Mother-fucking shooter. A day spent on the court screaming at the boys should do wonders to my foul mood of not getting extra time between the sheets.

Strolling over to the tennis court from the admin building, I book a spa appointment for two on the app and have it delivered to an Addis Ababa guest. That should compensate for my disappearance.

It's over three days since I promised to return my sister's call—Lola's pussy has me acting all repentant and thoughtful. Better to sort my sister out now before she gets on a chopper with her newborn. She picks on the second ring.

"To what do I owe the pleasure of this call?"

A new lay that has me thinking about my priorities? Instead, I say, "What's up sis?"

"You know why I've been calling you, right?"

Here we go again. I thought time and space would have given her the opportunity to focus on her love for me, not this old story. "Is this something new? If not, I'll prefer we not have this conversation."

"Why don't you just pick her calls? She's worried about you, you know?"

I smirk. "I know. And I don't care. She has to live with the consequences of everything she has done. I can't absolve her of her sins."

"But it's not like you were going to do anything soon. Time wasn't on her side. And you know what people think about you."

"Newsflash, I'm learning a new skill."

"You can't change, bro. It's in our genes to be transactional."

"And my own bloody sister is taking sides with the enemy. I wonder where all the sibling loyalties lie right now."

"You know I love you, all day, every day, till death do us part. But one thing you should know is, when you're wrong, I'll never take your side."

"How does my... You know what? I've found a new girl."

"Tshewww. Nahi, be serious."

"I kid you not."

"You're on vacation. People meet people. It's bound to happen. Doesn't mean it will last forever."

"Don't tempt me on this, Dachi."

"Lord. I'm sorry to say this, but I feel sorry for the girl already."

I chuckle. "I really need to work hard on myself then."

"You're too old to change, you just need someone who can match your crazy." Perfect. She doesn't know I've flipped the discussion on her.

"Now you're talking like a well-meaning sister." I spot Rasheed, the dark-skinned guy I met the day Lucas landed, as we converge at a Y-junction. He's coming from the direction of villas and heading to the fitness and sports arena too.

I signal to him I'm on a call, and he smiles as we fall into step. "Anyways, I'm working on it. That's why I need the space. Stop encouraging either of us to speak to each other. We are grown adults, we'll clean up our mess ourselves. Eni is doing a great job not interfering. You should learn from her."

"Okay bra-da."

"Thank you. Last I checked, you have a husband and a newborn. I don't know how you find time to blow up my phone."

She laughs. "It is in between those sleepless nights of caring for them I find the time. And you're the only man I can call at midnight these days." She sighs.

"Focus on your husband." She chortles and I can't help but smile, resuming our usual sibling banter.

I wish I could hop on a plane to visit my sisters, but this vacation is what I need right now. Besides, there's Lola in the picture, and the ongoing corporate scandal.

"My sister," I say to Rasheed, as I end the call.

He responds with a tight smile. "Nice. Family."

"All we've got." I shrug, then scoff. "The one thing that keeps us on our toes. I have two and the annoying thing is, they're twins. You have any sisters?"

A fleeting dark look settles on his expression, then disappears. "Used to have two but lost one. My twin."

"Oh. I'm sorry. Childbirth can be scary. My sister just had—"

"Wasn't childbirth."

"Oh man. I'm sorry. Just assumed—"

"It's fine man." His lips twitch as he stares up the path, his dark skin reflecting the morning sun. "It's something I—"

"It's alright man. No need to go into details. Coming for the games?" He's dressed in loose gym shorts and a neon vest that suggests he could be. The day we had brunch with Lucas and Femi, much into our discussion, we had agreed to a match, although he didn't signal interest.

"No man. Heading to the gym, got an appointment I can't miss."

"Sounds like a woman's involved, but I won't say much." I do a zipping my lips motion and it's strange. Fuck! Lola is rubbing off on me.

For the first time, I hear Rasheed chuckle, and it causes me to smile.

"Be safe *outchea*." I tap his shoulder as we come to an intersection where we have to part. "The ladies are out to cause havoc."

"Thanks man," he says, and we shake over it.

"Alright then. Need to go school some grown men on the court. Since you're not coming, I'll have to find someone to pair with. Take care man."

Upon walking less than a mile to the court, I glimpse Duncan laughing at whatever Femi is saying—they look like buddies already—while Lucas is shaking hands with none other than the guy from last night's shooting, Asher.

Interesting.

Escape

"Manchi, this is your double, Asher," Lucas calls out, walking into the court to take his position, while I drop my water bottle and towel on a bench.

"I'll be a minute," I holler back. I need to set this white fox straight.

"If it isn't Onahi Akachi himself." Duncan says as greeting. "Fancy meeting you here." He has opted out of the game, deciding to sit it out.

"What the fuck did you give Lola the other night?" I ground out between my teeth.

Duncan raises a brow and I swear underneath my breath, giving him a withering stare. I'll fucking punch his lashes off his face if he dares deny it.

"She's an adult, she makes her own choices."

Motherfucker.

"Good. You're an adult, you make your choices. I never want to see you close to her. Make your choice." Giving him a once over, I jog into the court, taking my position beside Asher.

Asher and I shake—his grip firm—and we strategize. He confesses to be rusty in the sport, but I assure him it takes teamwork. For someone who was shot at last night, he doesn't show any sign of agitation, looking more like a tennis pro.

Minutes later, Asher and I are three points in with Lucas' team on one point. What's wrong with Nollywood's finest this morning?

"C'mon, Lucas! Pass the ball!" Duncan calls from the side.

"Serve. Damn it!" Asher hollers, bouncing on his heels.

"Okay. Okay..." Lucas calls on his end.

He adjusts his stance, tosses the ball in the air, then hits it with all he's got, but it doesn't go past the net.

I chuckle as Femi goes off, reprimanding him. He slams his racquet to the ground, rubbing his clean shaved head in frustration as he looks to Asher and me who are having a field day.

Lucas mutters something, then goes to sit on the bench, while Asher explains to Femi his special tricks. I move to pick my bottle of water, chugging down its contents, my eyes scanning the area, then Lucas.

He's got his eyes on a group of giggling ladies—dressed in form fitting gym attire—walking past and I almost hiss at his continuous display of stupidity when I notice his wife is part of the ensemble.

I knew it! This motherfucker is in love with his wife but doesn't know it. I smile at this revelation. Picking my towel, I dab my neck and arms, then walk to where he and Duncan are seated. Duncan pays Lucas no mind, engrossed in his phone.

"Okay, Dude." Femi calls from the court as he and Asher make their way to the bench too. "You've been acting up lately. What is going on?"

"I think I miss Nigeria, the cameras, locations and—"

"Sleek feminine bodies." Duncan laughs, taking his eyes off his phone.

"Maybe not," I say, leaning a foot on the bench while balancing my arm on my raised knee. Using my water bottle to annotate, I add, "You are deeply in love with your wife."

"What shit are you talking about? She is my wife, why would I be in love with her?"

What shit is he spewing? The urge to hit my water bottle on his head is tempting, but I hold the thought at bay.

"Okay, that came out wrong. But for fuck's sake, I shouldn't be feeling like a piece of shit because of my wife."

"That's the point Lucas. You have never loved any woman; it has been a rush thing for you. Wam-bam! And you're done. Off you go on another adventure." I end with my arm in Usain Bolt's signature pose.

"Goodness," he mutters, pulling his bag to fetch his bottle of water. "I have been married twice and have treated those women with respect."

"Have you? Really?" Duncan smirks.

"Shut up, old man." I glance briefly at Duncan, warning him it's not time to play.

Not wanting Lucas and Duncan to begin a squabble, I rein the conversation back to the matter at hand. "Think about it, Lucas. This could be your chance to actually build something beautiful. All it takes is your commitment to this one woman."

Lucas turns his eyes from me, distracting himself by gulping down water.

"I saw you were staring at her earlier. Guy, you were drooling."

"Shit." Lucas's gaze darts around our audience to confirm they had not seen him ogling his thick wife.

"Forget it bro." He shouldn't be bothered by that.

"What happened? What do you both know that I don't?" Duncan asks, curious to know.

Ignoring Duncan, I speak directly to Lucas. "I've met you and Barbie before and you never looked at her that way, even on your wedding day. You look at Muyiwa... differently. Like... you want her by your side, never out of sight. Even though you do the darndest to make it look like you're irritated."

Lucas's cheeks darken. "She is my wife, dude. I should know her whereabouts. That's what husbands do."

"You never cared the first day both of you arrived," Femi adds, "you didn't even want to pick her calls."

I shrug. "For a woman you are planning to ditch, you are showing a lot of concern." That should have him putting two and two together.

"And why shouldn't I? I brought her to this resort. I'm responsible for her until... you know."

"Is he going to wave this one farewell too?" Asher asks.

Oh. So, Lucas is popular, not just for his movie, but for his marital shenanigans as well. Way to go.

"He insinuated such over some bottles of beer the day they arrived. But I guess our man," I rub his shoulder, "is having second thoughts."

"Stop spitting shit, Onahi." Lucas drops his bottle on the bench. "You have no moral right to preach to me. All of you." His eyes darts from me to everyone, fingers pointing. "You guys don't even have your shit together."

Escape

"Calm down, Lucas. It's not that serious, I'm just trying to help."

"Sort out your own feelings first before preaching to me! You all should face your messy lives and leave me the fuck alone!"

He grabs his bag to leave, but I call him back, stretching his bottle to him. He stares at me with tight lips before snatching the bottle and does not bother inserting it into his bag.

Excellent job Onahi.

Sort your life before trying to help others.

Twenty-Five

Lola

OPENING MY EYES, I DART them left, then right—coast is clear. Last night was—gosh! I curl my toes in excitement before drawing the duvet to my chest. Sitting up to confirm he's not in the room—of which he's not—I grin like a fool.

Magic! That's the summary of last night and everything we got into.

I shiver, biting my lower lips, as my mind reels from how the night ended. *Was I moaning and screaming like that?* Sliding back into the bedding, I close my eyes, rolling around. *What if he comes out of the bathroom? Girl... act normal.* With that thought taking dominance in my mind, I stop rolling around. Ouch. My neck, abdomen, and knees feel sore. Like I went to the gym the yesterday.

It was worth it. Last night wasn't normal. It was episodic. Cataclysmic. Earth-shaking.

My phone beeps and I reach for it on the bedside table. It's a prompt from the resort app.

You are scheduled for an event. Please accept your invite.

Hmm... Another surprise activity? Looking up from my phone to the bathroom entrance, hoping to catch movement—nothing.

Wrapping the duvet around me, phone in hand, I walk to the bathroom to confirm my host is in there but, nothing.

Okay... I lean on the door frame before clicking on the notification. It reads.

Hey Guru,

You might wake up sore this morning. I booked a spa session for you with Jay from yesterday to help with that. Wishing I am in bed with you.

PS: I attached her contact to the appointment note.

A spa session! Settling on the love seat by the floor to ceiling tinted glass wall overlooking the ocean, I feel my ears burning.

Onahi...

He didn't have to do this. But who am I to say no? Hugging my phone to my chest, I look up, grinning, "He's so sweeeeet..."

There are two things on my morning to-do: one is to send a message to Jay, while the other is to figure out breakfast. After easing my bladder and brushing my teeth with only toothpaste, I return to the bed.

His villa is way bigger than mine, with a workstation in his bedroom. How much does it cost to have this type of villa? He must be a big shot. In such short time, this place is beginning to feel like home. I miss my villa already, or is it the early morning movement of Biftu I miss?

A note on the bedside table catches my attention. How come I didn't see that before? Picking it up, it is a note signed by him.

Hey Guru,

Need to sort some issues, would be back in a minute. And I know you love walking, but don't stress yourself today. Please place an order for breakfast using the app.

PS: You look edible in bed.

Wow!

I must have done a number on him. Two messages in one morning, after a night of passion. He's so worth all my flight hours. That's true, I need to get on with my day, before I blink, and it's time to get on a flight. Back to my reality.

Escape

In a hurry, I send an invitation to Jay, then decide against walking all the way to the restaurant for breakfast, using the mobile app to order instead. I'll miss the sound of the rushing waves and, of course, the ocean's view, but since Onahi suggested not to stress, I might as well indulge myself.

What is he doing right now? I look at the note again. *Would be back in a minute.* How long ago did he leave? Is he thinking of me right now? Missing me?

No. No. No. Stop it. I shake my head.

I won't let cupid mess this thing up for me. For us. We agreed to scratch this itch and move on, no need to make anything off it. *Stay the night* does not mean stay in my life. I should have directed them to send the meal to my villa. Now I have to eat here.

Wrapping myself in an enormous white cotton blanket that smells of him, I ransack his mini kitchen to make a creamy cup of coffee before moving back to the loveseat to watch the ocean in the distance. Placing my cup on a nearby stool, I put a call through to Carolanne.

"Hey babes what's up? I'm checking out at the grocery store. I'll call you right back."

Not when I tell you why I called. "We did it."

"You said?"

"You heard me right. Twice."

"Whaaaaaat. Hold on, give me a minute."

Was she speaking to me or the cashier? I hear her mutter stuff on the other end, then the beeping of a POS terminal.

"Babes wait let me get in the car. It's hot like crazy out here."

Who would believe that I, Lola, would sleep with a random guy? One I've known for less than a week. I bend to take the extra blanket spilling on the floor, before sipping from my cup.

A click and beep later, followed by the slamming of a door, her voice comes through. "Please come again."

I sigh. "I said, we did it..." Gritting my teeth together.

"What?!!! Baby girl! You are *dequeen*!"

"Shh... Stop screaming." This is not something we should be celebrating.

"What do you want me to do? I'm happy for you *gurlllll*. Oh my! Start spilling the beans. Which one of them?"

I begin massaging a toe—well best to start before heading over to the spa. "The annoying and brooding one. Well, it was kind of romantic."

"Hmm..."

"He came to my villa in the morning, we went out on a boat, yacht, whatever. Then we went parasailing. Ooh. Carolanne, you should try that stuff, it's amazing! It's like—"

"Hol'up Lola. I'll ask for more info on that later, for now, continue the real gist."

Who's telling the story? Pulling my phone from my ear, I stick my tongue out.

"I see you."

"Whatever." I smile, she knows me so well. "Well, after that, the whole parasailing thing, we walked the beach, ate lunch. Took a ride outside the resort and spent time with the locals. I got something for you."

"*Awwn*... Thank you. Continue."

"We visited a local bar, they had this karaoke thing going, so we spent the evening there, drank some local brew... Just chatting..."

"Yeah... Just chatting. You've been *dickmatized*. You can't even remember what you did yesterday. He must be so... good."

"He is good... Where did I stop? Oh... Okay, so we chatted. Then... we went to get food again because you know... hunger."

"Okay..."

"And one thing led to another. He invited me to his place. I said, why not? And you know. Gosh... he's so cute."

"You slept with him because he's so cute? Lola?"

"I think that's one of the reasons. Besides the fact that I'm getting to know him, there's this chemistry we have." I close my eyes, smiling like a fool. "Because it felt right."

"Chemistry. I see..."

"My internal muscles were exercised last night. And now he's booked me a spa session to ease my," I shiver, grinning, "external muscles."

"See why I told you to jump on the opportunity? Imagine you were here. Stuck. Looking at the blind fool who has gone and got himself engaged to—"

264

"I was there."

"I'm sorry I had to let it out like that."

"That's fine. I just experienced a life changing event and Robbie is the last thing on my mind."

"That's the spirit—who the heck is this? The light is green move! Sorry babe."

I smile. "I'm so glad I'm far away from that struggle." The thought of heading back to reality almost turns my mood sour, but the slight ache between my legs brings me back to my magical reality. "Anyways, I'm happy for them."

"You would never have gotten this guy if he hadn't pulled that stunt he did."

"I know yeah."

"Wait. Did you guys use condom?"

"Urm..." I'm too embarrassed to admit it but thinking back. "We didn't."

"Fuck!" I hear honking from Carolanne's. "I'm sorry." She hisses, then return to speaking to me, "Lola are you crazy?!"

"He pulled out and—"

"Is he clean?"

"He said—"

She switches to video call, and I can see she has arrived at our apartment building but is still seated in the car.

"Is he clean?" Her face set in a straight line, all playfulness gone.

Escape

My brows crease and I answer the best way I can. "I don't know!"

"Oh Lola," she sighs.

"I-I-he He said he was clean." I lie, then repeat the truth. "He pulled out before he came. We were too into the whole thing to remember using condom."

"And you did it twice. Can you hear yourself? Oh God." She stares up, then looks back into the camera, worry clouding her eyes. "I told you to have fun. Apologies that I didn't add *safe* fun. But seriously—"

"He's young and rich." I shrug. "I don't think he would have anything life-threatening."

"Look at you... When I say you're smart but not street smart, you'll start throwing tantrums. Don't you know it's rich people that have more illnesses but manage it well?"

"I believe he's clean. Keep your negativity to yourself." I won't even share with her my squirting experience.

"Okay... And pregnancy?"

"He. Pulled. Out."

She cackles and I paste a mock smile, *haha, very funny.* "You're so bloody innocent. Well, at least you'll have a rich baby daddy. Just that when you return, we'll have to make sure you're not carrying any form of disease. Because if you are, we are not sharing the same toilet oh."

"Whatever..." There's a knock on the door. "He's back," I whisper to my screen. Getting up, I adjust the blanket into a more presentable look. I should have dressed up, but the subconscious thought of having his pulsing penis inside me propels me to the door. "Talk to you later."

"Okay love. Please, no sex until you guys get a condom."

"I hear you."

Unlocking the door with a bright smile, it's only a delivery from the restaurant. The bright smile of the delivery girl dims, I'm not whom she was expecting to meet at the door.

"This is Mr. Onahi's villa." Her brow creases with a frown.

Giving her a tight smile, since she is going to be bitchy about it, I say, "Oh... Nahi is not in now. Can I have my breakfast please?"

Her expression changes to a fake smile, and I snatch the basket, shutting the door in her face. I don't have time for drama this morning. I've got a spa date.

****

INSTEAD OF LINGERING ON THE fears Carolanne planted in my head or the rude staff's statement, I rush my breakfast, order a shuttle to my villa, and get ready for the spa.

It's a war zone in my head as I pair up loose floral short, with plain matching sleeveless top. I decide against walking and order another shuttle that drops me off some walking distance from the spa's building.

You're pregnant. You've got infection. Nope. It's pregnancy. You're pregnant.

Escape

Stop! I need to focus on something else. Of the two, the scariest is being pregnant—motherhood is not for the fainthearted.

Jay is yet to send a response to my message; probably got herself hooked on the fresh meat she was all over yesterday. I don't blame her. It's like hot endowed men are part of the islands' package.

One just adjusted his sunglasses, entertaining me with a lecherous grin. If I wasn't so worked up about the fear of being pregnant, I'll have returned his grin, just to give him a taste of his medicine.

Heavens, help me. I'm not the kind of girl who has sex with strange men but since I got on this island, men have given me more attention than I've gotten my entire adult years.

Oh snap! My period. It was supposed to start yesterday and I'm yet to get even a stain. *Where are you cramp?* I would have gotten some warning cramp, but nothing. I can't believe I'm praying for a cramp as a sign that all is well with my reproductive system. I hope it's not what I'm thinking.

Calm down...it was just one night. Last night.

I can't get pregnant from just having sex last night. And even if I am, it doesn't happen overnight. Whew. Carolanneeee.

The contrasting cool air of the reception area hit me as I walk into the spa building. I've travelled into another space and time. There's an Asian lady arranging vials on a white shelf that goes on for days beside a front desk. Echoes of dripping water, entangled with soothing mediation music reverberate around the room. A light minty fragrance permeates the air.

"Hello, miss," the Asian lady coos with a slight accent and I smile back. "Do you have an appointment?" She picks up a tablet and walks friendly towards me.

"Yes, I do." I show her my QR code and inform her of my expected company. She assures me she will get her to me.

"Please wait here." She gestures to a plush seat and sits elegantly with me. Staring at her screen, her brow creases. "A deep tissue massage, full body and...sauna...." Then she smiles, looking up at me. "From Mr. Onahi." There's a twinkle in her eyes.

I offer her my most confident smile. "Yes, Onahi."

What's with the staff, staring at me like I've developed a third head for hanging out with a guest of the resort? What does she know that I don't?

"I'm sorry ma'am. It's not that. You selected to be tended by a male masseuse, but there are none available, only females." She smiles and I forgive her earlier, *from Mr. Onahi*, statement.

I wanted to live on the edge. "It's alright. I'll go with a female masseuse."

"You'll be pampered properly." She smiles, nod, then gets up and heads back to her corner.

Waiting to be called, I scour the internet with the keywords: side effect, one night stand. So many articles pop, and I open multiple tabs. When I begin reading a ladies' story of getting STD from the best night she ever had, I give up on my quest and close all the tabs. No need giving myself headache. I'll visit the pharmacy or speak to a doctor instead. *It's nothing to worry about.*

A lady beckons me to follow her, and I walk through a hallway that hosts multiple African artworks, blooming flowers, and creepers in pots. The sound of echoing water droplets soothes my wandering mind.

We arrive a private massage room decorated in shades of browns and green, with external bright warm lights. The massage bed looks inviting, with contrasting white and brown fabric, calling my name.

"Please change in the bathroom." She points to a door I didn't notice when I entered. "There are towels and robes in there. Then lay on your tummy on the bed. Your masseuse will be here shortly." She bows and I'm left alone.

It feels like hours, but I'm sure it was seconds after I lay on the table, a lady in Twin Bliss' official black and gold uniform comes into the room, introducing herself as Imade.

"Can you please take off your bra?" Her voice is light and feathery.

I scramble, sitting up. "I have to take off everything?"

She nods. "I can work with it, but it's a better experience for you if it's off."

I've seen videos and should know better than to leave my bra on. Truth be told, although I'm exposed and experienced, I've never taken myself out to be pampered. Food, yes. Gym, yes. But to relax my body, never.

Dragging my ass off the bed and walking into the bathroom, I do what's expected of me, but leave the towel tied above my breasts. When I step out, she smiles. She looks excited to touch my skin. Lord... what have I gotten myself into?

"The towel please." She smiles. "You can place the towel on your buttocks if you like."

I lay back on my tummy and adjust the towel till it covers only my butt.

Her voice comes from a distance, "You specified you wanted the marula oil used for your skin. Do you want me to go ahead?"

"Go ahead."

She dribbles warm oil in a wavy motion on my back and legs. The mild nutty scent of marula oil fills my nostrils and I make a deep sigh, adjusting until I get into a more comfortable position. Her hands gently knead my legs, and I stiffen.

"Your first time?" she asks.

"Yes... That was ticklish."

"Relax. You'll get used to it."

I've never gone naked in front of another lady, neither have I let another woman get this intimate with me, not even my sisters. She continues, applying different pressure and sometimes leans in so close. So close, that she's almost laying on me.

All is going well until she moves to my back and touches the sides of my breast. I flinch, my muscles tightening.

Oh, shoot me!

"I can see you're not comfortable."

Escape

Of course, I'm not. And it's not your fault. Just left-over sparks from my night with a stranger. I hold back a giggle.

"I will focus on your back." Her hand brushes my back and I hold my breath. "And when you're comfortable enough, I'll take the towel off, massage your butt. Then you'll turn to the front."

Oh snap! She's going to... oh no.

She must have sensed my shock. "Your appointment is for a full body massage." *I know!*

"Is it possible I do just the back massage?" I tilt my head up, waiting for her answer.

She smiles but it falters. "It's my first time here. I was trained by Di-Uno Massage, Nigeria. And I want to give you the full Di-Uno experience, ma'am."

"Hmmm..."

"Is it okay if I take off the towel completely?"

"Now?"

"Yes, please."

I don't want to be the reason she doesn't keep her new position. "Please do."

Cool air kiss my butt cheeks as they become exposed, and I talk myself into releasing my tightened legs. What a shame. I spent an entire night with a man, touching, screaming, and I can't lay comfortably with a female masseuse.

She dribbles more oil on my skin. Massage. Pressure. Lean in. Massage. I change positions as instructed, my mind going with the flow.

"Want to do something amazing?" Onahi says with a boyish grin, showing off his pearly white teeth.

"Ma'am?" Imade's voice calls out.

Blinking my eyes open, I realize I'm still on the spa bed and Onahi was only a dream.

"We're done ma'am."

I slept off!

I grin. "Thank you, Imade. That was amazing."

"Did you enjoy it?" She smiles, eager to please, handing me a new towel.

Accepting the towel, I clean off excess oil from my skin. My body feels light as a feather. Almost like the feeling Onahi triggered when he made me come last night. But this can't compare to it.

Walking into the bathroom, I check my phone to see if I missed anything. "Are you asking if I enjoyed it?" Nothing. I eye the robes folded on a shelf; if I wear that all the way to my villa, would that be odd? All I want to do is sleep. "I was nervous when I stepped in here and you did magic, girl! Where do I drop a review or something?"

For the first time since we met, she breaks into a shy laugh, "Thank you. You don't need to dress up yet, it's time to go to the sauna. A robe will do."

She places my clothes in a black and gold souvenir bag, while I tie the sash on the robe.

"Thank you very much, Imade." I say, collecting the bag.

"It was a pleasure."

"Can I keep this with you?" Offering her the bag.

"Oh, you can place it in a locker, close to the reception area. Please follow me."

Upon securing a locker, I am left on my own, with directions to the female sauna and that is when I sight her.

"Yay! You came," I grin at Jay. Finally, a familiar face!

"Yay! I did." She cheers, smiling.

Uhn? I blink. That was so fake.

It wasn't her response that had me blinking, but how she said it. Animated. Like I forced her to join me. Instead of focusing on that, since Onahi said she was a unique lady, I share more information on what we're doing here.

"We're having the full treatment." Even though she's late, and I've done the key thing, she can always return for her own massage. "Don't worry about this, bills on the house," I wink. "Courtesy of Onahi."

From outside, the sauna's glass is all steamed up. But once I slide the door open, the steam clears out, leaving a mist I can see through in its wake. The sauna already has occupants lounging, scattered on wooden benches, with robes and towels on. Jay follows me in, and I select a place to sit.

She settles beside me and begins making acquaintance with the lady, Muyiwa, Lucas Opeyemi's wife. I peer through the steam in search of another familiar face. *Yeah. Familiar face.* I've spent my time on this resort with only men, and I expect a familiar face to appear just like that.

First person I make out is the lady Duncan had chased after, on my first night at *Eclipse*. She spares me a malicious side glance, before carrying on her conversation with the lady beside her.

I sit up, squaring my shoulders. *Good. I know you not too.*

Relaxing my back on the wall, I try meditating, but my mind keeps going back to Onahi and last night. My pussy gets wet from imagining being here with him. *Get a grip girl.* I shouldn't be thinking of sex. It should scare me that I've been infected or worse, will I be a single career mom?

He hasn't called me yet. Is he on to the next lady? Hmm... Stop catching feelings!

I sigh, adjusting my sitting position.

"Are you okay?" A concerned gentle voice asks, and I turn to the source. It's a dark-skinned lady, with eyes so white, a brilliant contrast to her skin.

"Urm... I'm fine." I hope she can see my smile through the fog. "Just need to get used to the heat."

"Oh."

"Yeah. I just came in from the massage room." *She didn't ask you.*

It's not too late to make a female friend. I sit up for the umpteenth time as the mist clears. To take my mind off my new addiction, I focus on the present. "I'm Lola, and you?

"Melody. Dr. Melody."

Wow. A doctor. I am sitting amongst the big girls of this century. I can imagine she is some celeb doctor who does Botox or butt lift for young girls. Who knows?

Shut up. Shut your mind up and enjoy the moment. Turning my head to the side, there's a lady struggling to breathe through her mouth, but she hides it well. The struggle is real, we all have to deal with the heat.

Jerking as the sudden sound of forced air comes through the pipes, carrying steam, I hear Dr. Melody stifle a giggle.

"Pardon me. I couldn't help it."

I smile. "Enjoy my awkwardness. It only happens once," I say in a singsong voice. It feels like we're the only ones in the sauna. When I lean back on the warm wooden wall, I inhale deeply, now appreciating the warmth. "It's my first time in a sauna and I'm liking it. I don't spoil my body enough."

"Well, I'm glad you're doing so now. Most people never do so in their lifetime."

From her words and profession, she comes off as one who has experienced and seen all there is. The urge to know more about her tugs at me.

"So... What do you do? I always hear, *not all doctors are medical doctors*. You could be a Doctor of Psychology. Or some part of science I've never heard about."

She smiles, I am so sure she did, because there's positive energy emanating from her, making me feel happy.

"I'm an Endocrinologist."

"Oh..." Whatever endocrinologists do, I have no idea. "I've always wondered what it was like to be a doctor and I don't think I have any female doctor friends." I tilt my head to notice her nodding. "Maybe nurses, but not doctors, I don't."

"I'm glad that you can actually make an acquaintance of me. So, what about you? What do you do?"

Girly talk! Here we go... I tell her what I do, and she compliments me, asking if I'm available for consultation outside the resort. Of course!

"I know you said your medical focus is on endocrines. And I'm wondering... Asking for a friend. What do you think about pregnancy?" Snap. "That's not what I wanted to say. Sorry... I meant, d'you think pregnancy can happen from just one attempt?"

She takes a while to respond and when she does, there's humor in her tone. "Pregnancy. Obviously, a man and a woman have to come together for that to happen."

"Yes. But what if. Okay, what I'm trying to ask is... How soon can one know they've conceived?"

"Interesting question..." She turns to me, smiling fondly. Like an old aunt, but she looks so young. "Usually, it takes around five to eight days... Thereabouts."

It was only last night and—Oh snap! I sit up, doing everything in my power to control my breath. It's all coming to me! The night on the hammock. He penetrated me. No condoms. Oh no, no, no. That was about... Three nights ago.

"This only happens when the guy cums." I mumble more to myself than tell her. Nothing to worry myself about. But are there exceptions to the rule?

"You had it last night, didn't you?" The abrupt question comes from Muyiwa.

Shoot me. I've been having a group discussion. One I'm unaware of.

The steam has reduced that I can see faces of my audience and I am proud that I do not cower but own up to my words.

"What? Oh, no... I was only asking for a friend." Biting my lips, my brows raised, as she leans forward, squinting at me.

"He gave it to you real hard, *gurl*. Could smell it all over you." She leans forward and her huge breasts spill out of her towel.

I smile as she continues without a care.

"*Awwn...* You are blushing... You see... You like him." She chuckles, like a big sister, before straightening her face. "If you don't make up your damn mind to grab this man, then you need redemption."

Chuckling, I shake my head. "You are amazing, Muyiwa."

"I know, right? Everybody says that about me." She shrugs, then ties her towel, before leaning on the wall, forgetting I exist.

Relaxing into my space, next I hear from Muyiwa's corner is. "Okay, this is way better than sex. Who needs a man's problem when I can reach orgasm in this paradise?"

Muyiwa...

The ladies discuss men and their many infidelities. Muyiwa hosts the discussion, while Duncan's lady friend cheers her on. A random lady steers the conversation to the powers of marula being a solution to having loyal partners.

"Is that not a new style of *jazz*?" I blurt out. *Jeez Lola. Now you've won favorite sauna girl of all time.*

"I don't think it is new. Or that it is *jazz*." A collective 'hmm' floods the sauna. "I've been researching it and it has been in existence for ages. I honestly don't believe it's *jazz*...

Just normal trees and fruit and all that. Call it nature at its best."

Duncan's side piece adjusts her towel. "Sorry to burst your bubble, but I don't think this... this Marula thing works. If this thing actually works, I would have been married with child on the way by now.... All those things are just an old wife's tale and marketing mumbo jumbo. At least it brings people back to the resort."

These women need to calm down. It's not like men are so hard to get. *Says one who was eaten till she squirted.* I squeeze my thighs as my traitorous clit pulses in remembrance of last night.

Their conversations travel round my head in circles as my thoughts drift.

"Honestly sister, I believe it works..."

What if I was pregnant? What if being on this resort is all it takes? The tour guide had mentioned something about fertility. Or not.

"...tell me something new... Don't market it to me. I'll support your business from the sidelines though."

"...must be a *jazz-like kayanmata* total package..."

Turning to Dr. Melody, I ask, lowering my voice, since the ladies are much concerned about the potency of the marula. "What are the chances of someone getting pregnant without protection?"

"See, young lady, stop asking questions about pregnancy. Why do you want to get pregnant when you have access to things like this?" Muyiwa taps her crotch and I scrunch up my face. She didn't have to be rude and, I wasn't talking to her.

Escape

Jay dabs my thigh. "Did you come here with anyone?"

I don't know what that has to do with anything, but I answer, "No."

Her beautiful mouth curves into a knowing smile. "Oh, okay."

Muyiwa seizes the moment again. "See you. All you need to do is grab a man of your choice and enjoy your life."

Dr. Melody pitches in. "See... the thing with men is that they think the world begins and ends with them. But what they don't know is that we know how to get them." She taps her palm for emphasis and puts those same hands between her legs.

Urm... Is this some pussy power retreat? I didn't get the memo.

"Ladies, I'm not leaving you people," the lady breathing through her mouth earlier says, "but it's time for my massage." In a laborious breath she adds, "Ehen, you people should not forget that I work with a travel agency. In case any of you need to book places like this at a discount, I—" Her voice fades into a whisper and I watch her slowly crumble.

I watch everything happen in a bubble. Dr. Melody appears beside the lady before she hits the floor.

"We're taking her outside." Dr. Melody says in a firm but calm voice that betrays the tension in the air.

They move the lady out and I tail behind them. The contrast of the air seeps into the pores of my skin, which are open, thanks to the heat. Wrapping my hands around my numb self, I catch myself muttering prayers I haven't said in a while.

"Muyiwa, please fan her." Dr. Melody dishes out instructions as she kneels to perform CPR on the lady. "I think she's suffering from heatstroke. Lola, please call the medics."

Call? My phone is not on me! First time I would desperately need it and it's not close by.

"It's alright." Jay takes me into a hug, and I welcome her body heat. She releases me, then rubs my back.

"The medics," I mumble in a daze, watching Dr. Melody loosen the lady's clothing.

"Camilla called for backup already." Jay gestures to Duncan's lady.

A close call, Dr. Melody says as we watch the EMT guys roll the lady, called Sapphira, off on a bed.

Sapphira... She seemed genuinely nice and soft spoken. I hope nothing bad happens to her.

By the time I change to my shorts and top, there's still no message from Onahi. Was yesterday a hit and run for him? Is the spa appointment a, thank you, now get out of my life gift? Or is this a game?

I send him a text message.

Twenty-Six

Onahi

LOLA: WHAT'S NEXT?

The fuck? Lola sent a message hours ago and I'm just seeing it. Because I turned the damned device off. I was working on my laptop, going through documents, emails, endless spreadsheets, and PowerPoint presentations of proposals, when my phone rang for the millionth time. It's fucking unbelievable that the one moment, one moment, one moment I feel free from their drama, relaxed and in control, they decided to blast my phone.

But man! What kind of prick am I painting myself to be? Who spends all day with, and has mind blowing sex with a giggling enchantress without dropping a call in between the day, but pairs her up with his responsibility for a spa date to ease his conscience? This asshole.

I enjoy her company and she is interesting. Refreshingly so. Although I don't like how flighty she can be, there are ups and downs to it. She is quite adaptive. I have things planned out for her. That's if she is actually up for it. No need messing things up by bringing work up just yet. That'll be me becoming another Alberto.

Lucas was right. I need to sort my feelings for her. I don't want to attach anything to it seeing we're just going with the flow. Was it, three, no four days ago we met? Feels like I've known her forever.

Onahi: Busy day. Missed you.

On second thoughts, I can wrap things up fast and meet up with her.

Onahi: Heading your way in an hour. Please send location.

I resume working on reviewing the final presentation I have before me, while making mental notes on what to do tonight. Dinner at the *Vintage Archive* isn't a bad idea. Only problem is that it's a black-tie restaurant. I can always get Salewa to sort that out. I'm sure Lola will have something captivating to wear.

Left to me, I'll cut to the main meal by whisking her to a quiet place I can fuck that moist pussy of hers all night. I don't think I've gotten a full taste of the magic we can make together. I want to watch her play with her Zeus thingy. I know she'll giggle first, and when she gets down to business, her expression will change to that of pleasure.

Then I will have the honor of watching her cum, but I won't let her rest, I'll take over, slamming into her, till she moans my name in worship. So much so that even when she moves on to the next guy, she'll be moaning my name because I'll be a branded tattoo in her fucking-memory.

Leaning back, I review the presentation I have been working on. This looks good, my team can—

Shit. I toss my pen on the table, looking around the office space. How did I miss that? I stare at the numbers that do not correlate with what my team sent. There's no need pretending. I can't concentrate. I can't concentrate when all I want to do is ram into that pussy of hers and hear her make mewling noises. The moans and pleas. Nahi... Nah... Nahi...

I'm so not getting anything done. I might as well go in search of her, but before I do that, I need a quick update from the security team. While I wait for the call to connect, I envision what she has been up to without me.

During the spa session, had she thought about me? I should have fucking cancelled on the boys and returned to spend more time with her—fuck her out of my system. Scratch this consistent weird itch off. What was I thinking? One romp between the sheets would satisfy me?

"Hello?"

Fuck. What you're doing to me, Lola. "What's the update?"

"We've had the butlers subtly go through their guest rooms and are yet to turn up with anything close to what was used last night..."

I rub a hand on my forehead, wishing I had not bothered to call in the first place, as he shares his attempt and progress.

It is none of my fucking business how they run this place. All I should concern myself with is my ROI. But therein lies the problem—I'm not an ordinary investor. This is my heritage. A threat to Twin Bliss or its guests is a threat to me and my family.

"Fine. Send me updates via email from now on. And call me only if you get a major lead."

Immediately the line goes dead, another call comes in. Ahmed, Jay's fiancé.

"What's up man?" I exhale, long, leaning back in my chair.

"I'm on your turf!"

What?

"This place looks better than it is online. My investment must be doing wonders."

Fuck. Fuck. Fuck. Ahmed, not now. "Yeah... thanks man."

I begin my exit from the building so I can return to my villa, shower, change, and find Lola. We can do *Eclipse* or just stay indoors. I'll go with whatever works best for her.

Ahmed goes on and on about his trip to the resort.

"Jay says you've been a wonderful host." His double-worded statement doesn't perturb me. He knows my stance about his sudden proposal. They were not into any form of commitment, so his words didn't prick my conscience. News from the guys I placed on Tyrell's back say he makes her smile.

"Anytime," I say, getting into a shuttle.

"Want to host me tonight?"

"Sure." Just get off the phone, man.

"Okay. *Eclipse* sounds like a great place to start."

"Sure."

"You're not sounding like yourself tonight. Are you alright?"

"I'm good man."

"Alright. So, I'll see you soon?"

"Sure." Much later. After my thing with Lola. Whatever it is we're doing. I just need to get into a private space with her, hear her laugh and make funny expressions. I get lucky, we go for a quickie or even a full ride. After that, I should be back in full Onahi mode.

Sending a text to Salewa to research other hot spots in town in case Ahmed doesn't dig *Eclipse,* I raise my head and my gaze falls on her.

Who the fuck? I squint my brows as I watch a fake-smiling Lola receive a kiss on the cheek from a guy. It's the guy from the other night. The Nonso, VC guy she had mentioned on the boat. Or was he whispering in her ear? I don't give a fuck what they were doing.

She doesn't look comfortable, and that's all the sign I need. What the fuck does he want? He had better piss off because

Lola is mine till this whole thing between us is done. Hell. Till she says we're done. Her message was *what's next*.

"Stop right here." I tell the driver, then hop off the shuttle.

"Nahi..." Lola smiles brightly when she sees me.

Good, she's getting the hang of it. "Hello, darling." I lean in, intending to kiss her on her lips, let him know we are more than friends. But she turns in time and my lips land on her cheek. She flashes me a glare and impressively covers it with a warm smile.

"Hello," I nod at the guy. His expression is cloudy, but he masks it immediately. An evening of poker. I'm up for this.

"Good evening," the guy responds.

Ignoring him, I fall in step with Lola, putting an arm around her waist. It's rude. I'm intruding. But I don't fucking care. We had a good time last night, and she's not screaming me off her. If anything, I'm doing her a favor. She wasn't this cheery moments ago.

Lola does the introduction as we continue the leisure walk down the path to her villa, the sun setting behind us. From my side view, I notice Nonso balling his fists, but he can't do shit. The lady has made her choice.

"We just left the art gallery and the pieces they have on display are amazing," she gushes.

"Yeah, they've got lovely pieces. It's peak season so they make sure Africa's best are on display."

Lola and I banter about the pieces on display while Nonso struggles to put a few words in. I visited the gallery a week or so, before, so my memory of the pieces on display is still fresh.

Escape

When we arrive at her doorstep, he excuses himself for another appointment which he and I both know he doesn't have.

He leans in to give Lola a kiss on the cheek. "Tomorrow morning?"

"Sure." She smiles, and I am happy to watch him go.

"Good night Onahi." Her smile sliding off her face.

Now we're back to Onahi. She reaches to open her door, but I place my hand on hers, stopping her. She turns to face me, her brows raised, warning me not to push it.

Not now. I saved her from a boring long walk, which in turn saved her from fake smiles that could cause wrinkles. I deserve answers.

"What the fuck was that about?" My heart drums so loud in my ears, it's deafening.

"What?" she snorts.

"Lola, stop playing."

She tilts her head my way, all traces of the giggling happy-go-lucky lady gone from her face. "You, stop playing!" She pokes my chest, her tone low but menacing. "I sent you a text and never got a reply. If that's not ghosting, I don't know what is."

I exhale loudly, raising my head, pinching my nose. My bad. She should be the mad one, not me. "I got engrossed at work." Then I look her in the face. "And I sent you a message like an hour ago."

"At work?" she scoffs. "Look around. You're on vacation. You don't need to make lies up. I'm not some girlfriend or wife. Just courtesy."

Fuck. It's not time to explain things. I just need her to forgive me, we get make-up sex and move on. "I'm sorry about that. I just want to know why you agreed to go out with—"

She raises her brow at me, and I give up.

"Whatever. Got plans for tonight?" My tone, tight.

"Yes."

"I-I..." Why the fuck am I stuttering like an idiot? Is this because I had a taste of her pussy? I swallow. "I thought we could hang out with my friend tonight." I never thought of getting laid before going out to meet my friend. Haha. "And I wasn't expecting to see you with another guy so soon."

She sighs, a slow smile forming on those lips that promised to suck my balls. My traitorous dick twitches in remembrance.

"I'm here to have fun Nahi.... You and I? We are just... a thing. An itch. You said so yourself. I don't know anything about you, and you don't bother to share. No need having expectations."

"Yeah." I nod, not remembering anything but what her pussy does to my dick. "I love our open communication."

"Me too. The sex was good."

"Can I?" Come in? I smile.

She sizes me up. "Nope. Good night Onahi. I need my beauty sleep. Have fun with your friend. We had a swell time today."

She thinks I'm talking about Jay.

Escape

The sound of the door hitting the frame feels like she tossed a bucket of ice on me. Fuck! That didn't go as planned. I reach to knock on her door, but let it slide. Tomorrow it is.

Arriving at my villa, I get into the shower still thinking about Lola. My dick is hard as fuck, threatening to burst with my seed. She had not pushed me off when I placed my arm on her waist. That's a good sign. She's only doing this to punish me. Punish us. But she has Zeus to take care of her. Me? I've got memories of her.

Closing my eyes as water from the shower head rains down on me, I imagine her lying flat on her back, long legs spread wide with her knees up and the humming sound of her vibrator making her pant and moan. Conjuring up the feel of her body pressed closed to mine last night, I palm my dick, working it, one hand braced on the shower wall.

Groaning as I palm my feverishly throbbing dick, I picture Lola in a variety of positions. Up against the shower wall, her face pressed against the wall with a sensual smile and me thrusting from behind—we should have done that last night. Above me in bed, those long legs gripping me as she bounces, her breasts bobbing in motion—beautiful sensual mounds. Lola's mouth gagging on my dick—

"Ah..." I groan as my dick spurts cum on the wall. I wait for the cool water to wash over me, then begin preparing for my night out with Ahmed.

PART THREE

Twenty-Seven

Lola

AFTER SENDING A MESSAGE TO Onahi and not getting a response, it pissed me I thought for one second our one-night stand could become a fling. Coupled with my pregnancy-infection scare. Something I should investigate if I really love myself.

We had so much connection during our night together. I woke up to his gift and was feeling special instead of irritated that he had bundled Jay, his responsibility, on me. Then not one sound from him all through the day. Not one, 'thank you Lola.' I was anticipating his call, a response to my text, when I got a text from Duncan whom I only remembered because I met Camilla at the spa.

When Nonso called if I was available to hang out at the art gallery, I was excited to see where his fantasy of getting married to a random girl would lead. And it led to a boring night. Not that the artworks were not interesting, far from it, but Nonso was... Well... He was not Onahi.

He spoke briefly about why he was vacationing. It had been what? Three years since he last took time off work, and it was telling on his health. It was a painful decision to let his successful share riding business go, but he had to do it for his health's sake. It was like giving up a baby and hoping the foster parent would cherish it like he did.

Then meeting me at the airstrip. Just one look, and he knew I was the one. Our late-night walk from the bar confirmed it for him—I had a vision, I had plans. *Dude! You only just met me! On a resort, far from home.*

And so yes, I was excited to see Onahi when he came along. An appreciable change to Nonso's voice, which I once found sweet, but was becoming sour from talking about commitment and non-fun stuff.

My impulsive and curious nature caused me to agree to a second date with Nonso this morning while on our first date last night. Since Onahi had moved on—no call or text. Ghosted me. Of all things to use in covering up his tracks, he brought up work.

Who works during a vacation?

"Ma'am, you have a guest," Biftu says, and I hop off my couch to the door. Walking out of my villa, I find Nonso, arms folded, leaning on a shuttle.

He grins when he sees me, standing straight. "You look lovely this morning."

I'm wearing a monochrome romper that stops above my thighs with a sandal to match.

"Thank you. I thought we were going out." He is all decked out in sportswear.

"Yes, we are—"

I spot two bicycles with helmets hanging behind the shuttle. Yay! "What are those?"

"Our rides." He smiles. Then begins taking them off the shuttle.

"Urm... For?" What's the joke?

"We're trying out the Treasures of Bodo Cycle Tour. The weather is perfect, and I hope it remains so." Why do we have to do this early in the morning?

"Alright..." Eying the bicycles, I remember Onahi's promise to cycle if I didn't enjoy the parasailing experience. "You don't even know if I can ride."

"You've not said you can't"

"Are you kidding me?"

He smiles. "You've got athletic legs babe. And even if you don't want to, I brought the shuttle. You had a glint in your eyes when you saw the 'cycles. So, I'm guessing you know how to ride."

"Haha."

"Yeah. So...?" He claps his hands, wrapped in biking gear, mouth pursed, eyes squinting, anticipating my answer. His white vest is doing nothing to cover his hairy chest. "It's a three-hour trail, back and forth."

Is that supposed to sway my decision?

"Urm... why don't we get breakfast first then we would think this plan through." He didn't think to consult with me if I could ride or not. Good for him I can, but three hours on an empty tummy. Nope.

"Don't worry, I've got that covered." He brings two drawstring bags out of the shuttle.

"There's no breakfast on that bicycle, Nonso." I fold my arms, staring at the bicycles with contempt. "I'm glad you woke me early today in time for breakfast. Please, let's make use of the opportunity."

"Here." He tosses a bag at me.

"What's in it?"

"Open it."

What's this surprise now? Apples? Bread? Cake? Cookies? Peering into the bag, I bring out the content in awe akin to disgust. "Protection pads?"

"With chamois pads." He laughs.

I hiss, tossing him an irritated look. "I thought you had apples packaged for me or something."

"Don't worry Lola. Just go in and put those on."

I'll have to change my whole outfit. Turning to my villa to do just that, I turn back to him on second thought. "Treasures of Bodo? I don't think I've seen this activity in the brochure."

"I don't think the brochure covers everything that's offered here extensively."

Exhaling loudly, I march into my villa to change. With Biftu's help, I opt for a black legging, putting the pads in place, then a bra top with a transparent white tank top for effects

I join him, waving my digital camera. "We find a way to mount this, or nothing."

"Anything for you babe. These bicycles are top notch."

We mount the camera below, close to the front tires and my mobile phone in-between the handles and begin cycling. Not long into it, I relax into the motion, forgetting my empty tummy, enjoying the scenery.

He points to local women making *pareos,* farmlands and local eateries. This is a different route from the historic ruin tour the resort organizes. This is getting one and up close with nature and the people of the town. Almost similar to my outing with Onahi after our parasailing event. Why does he keep coming to my head? *You need to move on!*

"That's our destination." He points to a canvas tent between shrubs some distance away. I've been seeing similar tents on our path and when I asked what happens there, he had said it will ruin the surprise. "Common babe! You can do this."

I pedal with my strength at his praise.

Escape

At last! I smile in exhaustion at Nonso as we set our bicycles down, underneath a tree. We've been riding for what seems like days.

"I'm so not trying this again," I announce, attaching my helmet to the bicycle, before taking off my phone and camera. Following his lead, I walk towards the tent he had pointed out to be our destination in the middle of nowhere.

"What's here? Why didn't you allow me eat?" I say between ragged breathing. I'll be so pissed if we've come to stare at animals or some zoo shit.

"Oh!" My hands fly to my mouth as I stare at the colorful feast laid before us; some on a plush picnic mat, others in a transparent picnic cooler.

"Breakfast." He smiles at me, then walks back to pull me from my daze. "Come on."

Shaking myself from the wonder of this thoughtful gesture, even though he had been the one to rouse me from bed without telling me exactly what we'll be up to, I allow him to lead me. We sit on the picnic mat and the silence is deafening.

The tent has all the basic camping necessities, including a bed and pillow which I briefly eye before returning to the meal before me. The meal is worth every pedal, and I slightly regret I had the deep tissue massage yesterday. *I'll need another massage today.*

"First the art gallery, now this. Hmm..."

He shrugs, passing a hand sanitizing wipe my way. "You deserve this and more."

I give a nervous laugh. "Thank you."

Nonso begins arranging cutleries, asking me what I prefer on my plate.

"Can we wait for our bodies to cool down a bit?" I ask, just as my phone beeps.

Onahi: Good morning, Guru. How was your night?

"And do what?"

Ignoring the message, I focus on the present, filling a disposable cup with fresh, cold orange juice. "Talk?"

"Go ahead."

"I'm sorry about yesterday evening."

"It's alright. A lady of your kind will always have men at her feet. I was just not prepared for your status to change so quickly."

I almost choke on my juice, clearing my throat. "What do you mean?"

He pours hot water from a flask into his bowl of cereal. "I'm not stupid Lola. I know when a man has fucked a woman."

Okay. I swallow. Point of correction, we fucked—I fucked him and he fucked me.

He scoops cereal into his mouth, my eyes following his movement. "But it's alright. We're not a thing yet. So, I don't expect you to be loyal and all. We all have needs." He flashes a smile at me.

What the heck have I gotten myself into? This is turning into a scary movie. My phone beeps and I check.

Onahi: Talk to me Guru. I'm sorry I messed up yesterday.
Fat chance.

"That's an interesting... philosophy." I nod my head slowly. "And pretty creepy. Considering the fact that you knew all that and still chose to bring me out here."

A low laugh escapes him, and he looks into my eyes. What reflects there is grim determination.

"I keep my words, Lola. That's one thing you will come to love about me if we move past this..." He waves his spoon. "Stage. And like I said, we all have needs."

"Now I'm interested in your story." I bite into the toast that has been keeping warm in a picnic bag. "What needs do you have?"

He looks back into his cereal bowl. "You'll find out if we move past this."

Mystery. I see what you're doing, mister.

We talk about small businesses in Nigeria and the travails of owning one. As we wrap breakfast up, he starts telling me tales of businesses he had started and seen destroyed.

You're full of surprises. All my years... you are the first squirter I've met.

What's happening to me? Shaking my head, I nod at whatever Nonso is saying and adjust my position on the mat. He asks if I'm alright and I nod with a smile.

"Please continue."

"No. No. Now, let's talk about you."

He asks me about my career and how I started. I tell him of my family's migration, finding a place in America's corporate world as a first-generation black migrant and a woman.

"What?"

He shakes his head, then confesses, "You're beautiful."

You're a fucking goddess.

Onahi!!! Get out of my head.

"Oh." I smile, scratching my hair. "Thank you."

I'm ruined! Here I am, having an intellectual conversation, and all I'm thinking of is sex with the devil himself. Is being *dickmatized* a thing?

I sit up, then look out to find the sun high on the horizon, signifying it's either noon or past noon. Picking up my phone to confirm this, I let out a sigh of disappointment when I see no new message.

"Come on," he says, getting to his feet. "We need to head back."

I groan. "Seriously?" Getting atop that bicycle is not something I want to do straightaway. I stare at what's left of our breakfast. "Who's going to clean this up?"

"Don't worry yourself about that. They'll have it cleaned before the next guests."

"It's so strange that this place is far out here, and they manage it so well."

"I'll pin it down to great management. Come on." He stretches his hand towards me, and I grip it firmly, standing up. "Our time is up."

Escape

We say our goodbyes at my doorstep, and I drag myself in, my legs weak from a day of riding. Good thing I messaged Biftu before we left the tent to prepare a scented bath.

Dipping myself into the tub, which is smaller than Onahi's jacuzzi, I moan as pain and pleasure ripples through me. I just spent an entire morning with an amazing human being and I'm thinking of the rude prick.

Tshewww. I should have brought Zeus here.

My phone beeps, and I check. It's a message from Onahi.

What does this mean?

Twenty-Eight

Onahi

I'M TEMPTED TO PULL THE fucking chain innocently seated on my neck as I stare at her door from the shuttle. I shouldn't be going through with this. She didn't respond to my messages all day until I sent that one.

The hanging lanterns and the cutleries arranged on the table can perish in the ocean for all I care. I just want to spend time with her. Listen to her. Tease her. Hear her giggle. And yes, if possible, fuck her, in a thousand ways. But since this is the only way I can have tidbits of the things I want, I'll shamelessly take what's offered.

Escape

It's been a long day and having sent messages waiting for her response; I went around my normal day. But it wasn't so normal. I kept barking orders on phone, making demands, and pushing employees—who made it their business to remind me I'm on vacation—beyond their limit. I went crazy with worry when she did not respond to my messages and took a shuttle to hers only to find her butler arranging her villa.

"She went for the Treasure of Bodo Cycling Tour with a friend."

I didn't need to think hard to know who it was. I had warned Duncan off her and he had enough problems of his own to deal with.

Nonso had said, *Tomorrow morning?* So, I knew he was the one. She was out there, doing a three-hour plus cycle tour with a shooter on the loose, with that Nonso guy who is rumored to be in some BDSM club shit. I had him investigated earlier. I don't want to take chances.

The security team were narrowing down the suspects and this close to putting everything in the past. I told security to look out for her and her companion—as much as I don't want to interfere without her permission, her wellness is of utmost importance to me.

When I got info, *she is back in her villa*; I sent her a message asking for her presence for dinner, by the beach, where I'll tell it all.

A notification pops on my phone—Lucas' wife took up another villa under my tab? What the fuck is wrong with Lucas? Why does he have to mess things up thinking everyone was acting a role in a goddamn movie? I shouldn't be doing this when I plan to be on my best behavior tonight, but to get out all the nerves, I dial his number. He picks on the second ring.

"Manc—"

"Sonofabitch."

"Ona—"

"Why the fuck did Muyiwa move to a separate villa?"

"Oh that." He laughs.

"Yes, the fuck that."

"Calm down, man. The woman saw something and is overthinking it. I knew I should have—"

"Shut the fuck up, Lucas. You're a dick! Why do you have to mess things up? I can bet a hundred percent that you were the one who did shit to mess things up with your wife and now you're spreading that virus all over the resort."

"Where's all this coming from?"

"That's all you're going to say? Shit. I should have known you wouldn't have anything to say. No clever words spilling from your lips. No one to read your lines. Dude." I take a deep breath. "Make this shit with Muyiwa work or never stick your dick into another woman. I'll personally request for you to be castrated."

"Is that all?"

"Yeah." The fucking fool hung up on me.

Stepping out of the shuttle, I adjust my shirt then walk to her door, giving it a knock. In less than a minute, the door opens, and I swallow at the smiling image before me.

Escape

Gone are the colorful shorts and rompers she usually wore. In their place is a white one shoulder irregular sleeved gown, accentuating her curves. Although I have seen her naked and even worshipped her skin, the gown makes a great show of teasing me with one cleavage. It stops on her knees, and there's a v-slit in front that has my imagination running wild. Her legs, I swallow, remembering how they held on to me two nights ago, are wrapped in gladiator sandals that stop at her knees, beneath the gown.

Looking up, I smile into those hazel pupils of hers. She packed her hair up, but I'll have it down before the night is over, if everything goes well. I prefer it down and free. Like her. Free like her.

"You like it." Her voice! They're like music to my eardrums. Is this what it means to miss someone?

"I do." She had not asked a question, but I want her to know I love the dress on her. Anything she wore, she brought to life.

"I'm glad you approve. I tossed them in my luggage, knowing I would need them for some kind of beach event."

"I'm glad you chose my beach event."

"You don't look bad yourself." Her gaze trails down the white shirt I have beneath a sky-blue two-piece dinner suit.

The short shuttle ride to the beach is mostly silent and I hold on to her hand, threading wriggly lines on them. Her fingers are so slender and soft.

"Do you trust me?" I ask when we near our destination.

"Is this a test question?"

I'll not make headway with that question. Pulling out a sash from my pocket, I hold it to her face. "Indulge me."

"You want to—"

"Yes. Please."

She bites a bottom lip, her gaze darting from the sash to my face. "Promise not to dunk me in water or anything of such, because—"

"Shh... I need you to trust me."

Her chest rises and fall, then she adjusts till her back is to me. I place the sash on her eyes and confirm she can't see a thing.

"Hmm..." she hums as she turns to face forward, blindfolded.

And I hold her hand. "Trust me."

She resumes biting her lips and I'm tempted to lean in and kiss it.

"We're here," I say as the shuttle comes to a stop. I murmur my thanks to the driver, then guide her out of the shuttle.

"How did your day go?" I ask, placing my arm on her waist as I guide her movement. Not because I've been dying to wrap my arms around her, but because I'm a nice guy. Lies.

"It was good. I learnt more about the island... I went cycling."

My gut tightens at the thought of what might have ensued during her tour.

"Nice." It's not my business to pry, asking questions about Nonso and what the deal is between them. "I'm sure you enjoyed that." My business is to make it up to her.

"I did." Why does it hurt that she confirms enjoying time spent with another man? This fucking itch. But my dick is not twitching as it usual does when she's close by. "You?"

"Not as fun as yours." Best to come clean, since I confessed to telling it all. "I spent most of it thinking about you, making plans on how to get on your good side."

She snorts. I'm being truthful my dear.

"We are here my lady. Ready?" I ask as I move behind her to untie the sash.

She nods, then gasps when the sash comes off. Walking briskly, going round, she accesses the set up. The table is set for two and covered with a white cloth. There are solar powered lanterns scattered in the surrounding sand. The orange light from the lanterns gives a warm hue around our table. Before us, less than twelve feet, lays the ocean, with gentle wave sounds and occasional splashes. Behind us, night insects whisper to us from the distance. She turns to me, wonder in her eyes.

"Onahi..."

I shrug.

"You shouldn't have." But she rushes to hug me and her scent envelopes me. "And I deserve this and more." Such a feisty mouth. "Thank you..."

Just when I'm settling into her warm hug, she pulls away.

"Let's not have our meal getting cold."

Other ladies would have waited for me to pull up their chair and sit demurely, but no, not my Lola. Pulling out a seat, she settles in, giddy and excited, her gaze on the ocean. "Don't think you can bribe your way into my life."

I give a small laugh. "I'm not thinking about that."

She leans in conspiratorially. "If I'd written a bucket list of 1001 things to do before I die, this would actually be top of my list."

"I'm glad I'll never be forgotten in your life's history."

"Hmm... You like doing this?"

"Doing what?"

"Plan things? Plan people's lives?" She arranges her napkin on her lap. "Is that what your business is all about?"

"You've done your google search?" It's been a while since I did that on myself. Last time I checked; my online profile was clean. I don't care if she has found out who I truly am.

She rolls her eyes, picking up a glass of water. "I don't even know your last name."

"Akachi."

"What's that?"

She hasn't? I breathe a sigh of relief. "My last name."

"Oh. A-h-k-a-c-h-i?"

"Without the H."

She giggles, shaking her head, muttering something beneath her breath.

"What's that?" I arrange a napkin on my lap, wanting to know everything running through her head. Through her mind. Why is she giggling instead of bringing out her phone to google me up?

"Nothing." She drops her glass on the table and I reach out to hold her fingers. Lola studies our hands, then looks up at me.

"Please."

She removes her hand from mine, and I clear my throat, the moment lost.

"It's weird that I'm doing this..." Her hands flutter around, "dinner with a one-night stand."

"You're not regretting this I hope." She would google me when she gets home then. Would she be impressed by what she finds online? I hope she's not regretting this. Us.

"I'm not. I'm intrigued. My friend told me to try it and I'm loving it." Her eyes say another, but I don't push for answers. So. I'm the lab experiment. Is she worried something is happening? Like Dachi said, this is just a vacation fling. Nothing can come out of it. I wish I could meet that friend of hers, to thank her.

"What's yours?"

"My what?"

"Your last name."

"Arogundade. And my full name, Omolola Arogundade."

"A complete Yoruba princess."

"You're staring at one," she says, her eyes twinkling. "Now it's time for some genuine revelation like you promised."

Our standby chef introduces himself to us, promising us the most. Lola smiles brightly when he lists what's on the three-course meal menu, her eyes darting to mine from time to time. It's going to be a long night. A worthwhile one. She's asking for the wine menu while fluttering her lashes at me. Whoever that friend is, I'm willing to give her a million dollars in thanks.

Twenty-Nine

Lola

THE CHEF GOES ON ABOUT the Nigerian cuisine available. My jaws go slack in surprise when I notice Onahi leaning back on his chair, a hand on his chin with his lips splayed in that boyish lopsided smile of his. How did he know I have this weird thought of having Nigerian local dishes in a five-star restaurant? My best bet will be the first night we met.

When it's time to pick dessert, the chef encourages me to try something with marula in it. It is hard making a choice on the flavor to settle for. He tells me not to worry, I can have it all. I chuckle, commenting on the service and he nods, making a cryptic remark to expect nothing but the best. With a lingering smile still on my face, my gaze lands on Onahi who is looking rather smug.

"I'm not going to ask how you knew," I say, and he shrugs, sitting up.

What else did I tell him that night?

"You really studied in Nigeria?" I ask, nibbling on the last morsel of *Amala* I had dipped in *Efo-riro*.

"I did. Briefly. We were always travelling. It was fun."

"Hmm..."

"My mom—"

My eyes go round in mock surprise, taking my glass of wine in hand. "You have a mom?"

He gives a small laugh. "Common. I've mentioned her to you already."

"Honestly, I thought you dropped from the sky." I take a sip from the glass, hiding the heat flushing my skin, remembering vividly what we were doing when he mentioned his mom.

He bursts into laughter and the joy on his face causes a strange flutter in my chest. I blink rapidly, struggling to keep a smile, while placing my glass of wine on the table. What was that? Am I falling for him? *Keep your head in the game, Lola. You're having fun. You agreed to that. Stop catching feelings.*

"I didn't. I have a mom. She's alive and well. Two sisters too. Twins."

I'm tempted to ask if he took anything before now, but his message had said he was going to be open about everything. Is this the time I ask if he's clean? Or has had any infections in the past I should be aware of. Had he intentionally had sex with me without a condom? How does one approach conversations like this?

"That's impressive. No wonder your accent isn't easy to place. It's a mix of everything."

"Yeah. Constant travels. I've never really settled down."

I nod. "I get the memo."

He eyes me, taking a sip of his drink, clearly uncomfortable. "I didn't mean it that way."

A server comes to clear the table, replacing our empty plates with the last course, marula-banana ice-cream in a dainty cup.

"Why?" I ask.

"Why what?"

"I don't know. That's not what I meant to say."

We consume our ice-cream in silence, the ocean getting calmer as the evening wears on. It's been one long day and deciding to come out here was out of curiosity, just like every of my impulsive actions have been. Now watching his pink tongue flick on that dainty spoon is causing chaos in my vagina. I shouldn't be thinking of having sex with a man who didn't bother using condoms or discuss condoms. But my wardrobe isn't helping either as my thighs brush instinctively on each other.

He takes another scoop of his ice-cream, and a stray drop hangs on the corner of his mouth. He smiles at me, licking his lips. Wiping it off. Oh snap. Blood floods clit and I see stars, recalling the way he had eaten my pussy.

If we agree to use condoms, maybe we can try again. My clit is weeping and crying to have another round with him between the sheets. Anywhere. Of all the three sexual partners I've ever had, he is the first person I have ever gone bare with.

"What is going through that mind of yours?"

Nasty things... I smile, dropping my spoon after taking the last scoop. Ignoring my wandering thoughts and the mushy feelings trying to overwhelm me, I ask a question that's unrelated to the questions I should be asking. "How are you related to this resort?"

His brows knit as he thinks of the best potential lie to get out of that one.

"I'm not a dummy, you know. I have ears. I heard Jay that day on the boat, but it was none of my business then."

"And why is it now?" he asks, leaning forward on his seat.

I roll my eyes, "We had unprotected sex." There, I said it.

His eyes go round, shaking his head as he leans forward. "How does that—"

"I don't know. But I let you have unprotected sex with me. The girl who delivered my meal at yours stared at me weird. I deserve to know."

He gives a small laugh, covering a cough with his hand, looks to the ocean, then back at me, before relaxing into his seat. "That's not adding up."

"Whatever. I gave you access to my body."

Escape

"Is this some form of feminism stuff? Because I am a feminist."

"Onahi, stop joking around."

"I'm sorry about the condom stuff. Just so you know, I'm clean and my pull-out game was strong."

Yada, yada, yada. Show-off. "I was there."

"And I never go bare," he adds like I never spoke. "I'm sorry I—"

I snort when he doesn't continue his heartfelt speech, after trying to make light of the situation. We settle into a companionable silence, the ocean's waves crashing on the shore—our background music. "Now tell me. What's your relationship with this resort?"

"It's a long story."

"I'm all ears. We've got the night."

He looks at me through hooded eyelids, takes a sip of the wine, then gives up, sighing. "I own shares. A substantial percentage."

Impressive.

I nod slowly, assimilating the information, waiting for him to continue, but he takes another sip of his wine instead. So, he literally owns this place—I never thought of him that way and he never acted like it. No wonder he was averse to hanging out with me and my social media self.

"I'm waiting."

"For?"

"That's not all I want to hear. Impressive news. But I want more. The story. The *hows*. The blood connection."

He raises a puzzled brow. "Where are you getting your information from? I thought you didn't know my last name."

I snort. "I'm sure if I google you up, nothing tangible will surface."

"I'll tell you not to bother with that as well."

"I heard Jay, Nahi." So much for telling it all. "Okay, tell me about the marula. The branding and all."

He doesn't hesitate, diving back into the discussion. "It's something this island is known for. It's been growing here for ages and my family line started with a funny story connected to it. When I was younger, I saw the opportunity of mixing fiction with facts as a back story for the resort—shared it with my dad. And since then, we've been working with it, weaving the story around the resort."

"Now you're speaking my shit."

He smiles, getting comfortable in the moment. "A friend of mine recently told me she spoke with a ghost on the beach—"

"This beach?"

He shrugs, "So she claims."

"Oh wow..."

"I know right."

"Have you? Have you seen a ghost here?"

Giving a small laugh, he says, "I've visited this resort every year since my second birthday, and I've never set eyes on any."

"Too bad... It would be such an exceptional experience. Does the media post it?"

"Not that I've heard of. It's usually somewhat of a personal experience for them."

"Your family? Anyone seen a ghost?"

"Not that I know of. But my great, great, great—"

I giggle, "I get the drift. An ancestor of yours."

"You got that. My family has deep ties here. Long ago, it is said one of my great-aunts who loved taking long walks by the beach, lost her husband to some sort of sickness. She was still in mourning when she took her usual walk and never returned home." Creepy... "Years later, one of my great-nieces' heart was broken, and that great-aunt of ours appeared to her by the beach, telling her everything will be alright."

"And it did?"

"Not really. She found love again but died having her second child."

"Good that she found love."

"Hmm..."

"So, the legend is true?"

"Which of them?"

All of them! "The ghosts? The marula?"

"The ghosts are not in any way tied to the marula. And personally, I just think it's a family story."

"And the lady's story? The one in the brochure? Who had to be cooked with her child?"

He scoffs. "That's the ancestor my family line started with. The one that brought wealth to my lineage." He smiles fondly.

"And the marula magic? The one the tour guides sing about?"

"Those are just traditional jumbos mixed up for marketing. It's a mixture of truth and fiction."

"Anything to make rich people visit the island, yeah?"

A ripple of laughter erupts from him. "And beautiful ladies like you. Most especially beautiful Brand Gurus." I shrug, then smile, staring into his eyes as his words hit home. I've never fancied being called beautiful, and even when Robert called me Guru, it never made me feel the way I feel now.

After thanking the chef, we take a walk on the beach in silence, holding hands. I notice him stealing glances at me, but I ignore it. Occasionally, my hand will tighten when the wave rolls towards us, but he doesn't act fazed.

What was he thinking about? Was he thinking of us? What if a ghost appears to us right now? It would be so unreal. How would I react? What would I ask her? I think I'm falling for your nephew, although we agreed to be *just* fuck-buddies.

A substantial percentage, he'd said. Just how large is his percentage? I knew he was rich, but not this rich. Owning shares of this resort alone, ignoring the fact that it has other locations around the world, is wild. The cost of one night is someone's three-year wages in some parts of the world, and he just loosely said, a substantial percentage. Someone like him would have seen it all. Being in a relationship would not be a priority on his list when he can have sex with countless women. Women like me.

Escape

No. Stop it...

I am different. Oh snap. That's what all the ladies who have had sex or fallen in love with him might have thought. *Am I just one of them too? Lola... get your head in the game. We're here to have fun.* What if he wakes up tomorrow and finds out that I got here by deceit? Would he think what we've had is all a lie?

"Ready to head home?" Home... He flexes his hold on mine.

Jerked out of my reverie, I turn to smile at him. "Yeah sure. After such an interesting dinner, I think we should walk."

"And waste the food? Or the precious time you're sparing me?" He stops walking, bringing out his phone, one hand left in his pocket.

"It's not wasting." I smile fondly, brushing aside his phone. "Don't do that." I know he wants to book a ride, but what better way to end this romantic night than to walk home?

He drops the hand holding the phone, then suggests, "How about we walk half-way then continue with a shuttle? It's a win-win situation."

Pretending to think about it, I fold my arms. He dips his other hand with his phone in his pocket, looking into the ocean, his profile to me. The man is adorable. "Since you put it that way, I think it works for me. I can't wait to fall on my bed."

He turns quickly to me, his eyes on mine, a shadow of vulnerability I've never seen in them. "I assumed you were coming to mine."

"Why?"

"Mine's closer." He looks at his watch, then back at me, grinning, trying to play it light. "And it's late."

I shake my head. No way am I letting his sweet mouth talk me into going to his place again. I've had as much adventure as I should. Now that he's told me an estimation of his net worth, he might think I'm with him for that.

"Please..." He comes closer, wrapping his arms around my waist. "I've missed you like crazy Lola." He whispers to my forehead. "Please come over. I promise to make it up to you."

I shake my head.

"You're more than an itch. Please?" He places his fingers on my chin, raising them up and I meet his lust filled eyes. He traces my lips with his thumb and my treacherous lips quiver with the desire to taste his lips one more time.

He gives a small laugh like he knows what's happening inside of me. "Fuck. I've been barking at everyone all day. And been slapping myself for not seeing your message on time."

I swallow. What is he saying? What is he promising? Is he confessing something?

Placing his second hand on my chin, I am forced to listen to his promises while I battle with my why. "I want to make it up to you. Please let me. I want to taste you again. Hold your hips while I pound into you. Please you till you lose control and shatter into a million pieces."

Yeah. Make it up with sex. Good old sex. After all, we're supposed to be having fun and the Queen of happily ever *afters* should know better than to think it is more than sex with someone like him.

Escape

I press my lips against his to shut him up. For a fleeting moment, I consider withdrawing, but his hands travel through my back, settling home on my ass—grabbing, squeezing. I moan into his lips.

Instinctively, I part my lips under his, wrapping my arms around his neck. He groans and my vaginal wall clenches, releasing more than enough juice for us to complete the makeup session he was begging for.

God help me. I heft myself off my feet, wrapping my legs around him, and he supports my weight, still holding on to my ass., We exchange our breath between urgent lips, our tongues fighting for control. Lips biting. My mouth devours his; my tongue stroking beneath his, the roof of his mouth, his lips, then back inside his mouth again.

It's okay if our one-night stand becomes a fling. I'm not settling for less, just choosing to enjoy the moment.

I pull back, skimming along his lips, absorbing the moment.

I taste his smile as he says, "Still demanding." He bites my lips and I giggle, every breath forcing juice out of my clit. "And still giggles." The throaty vibration of his baritone causes my clit to clench and unclench, seeking his penis.

Leaning back, I admire the work of my lips as the moonlight illuminates his pink wet lips and causes shadows to form beneath his hooded eyes.

"Was that what you wanted?" I ask.

His response is to pull my lips back to his and plant a hard kiss on them. Like a full stop. The end. I giggle and he lets me slide down the length of him. His erection poking my abdomen.

Placing both hands on my smiling face, he brushes a thumb on my lower lip that's sensitive from the bites he gave me earlier, shaking his head, like he can't understand what's happening to him. Me too!

He smiles, then pulls away. I miss his warmth already. "See that light over there? Beyond the trees?" It's not so far. "First person to get there decides where we sleep tonight." I'll be a fool not to take advantage of him and our situation, to go back to my place.

"Bring it on."

"On the count of three..."

Thirty

Onahi

IT WASN'T EASY OPENING UP and being vulnerable with her, but I tried my best. I was on the verge of telling her about my issues; why I don't date, what my friends think of me, and so much more. But we are just fuck buddies. There's no need clogging our vacation by sharing irrelevant information.

The condom stuff—if she hadn't mentioned it, I'll never have thought about it. I never forget to use a condom. Never. Even the rare times I'd had drunk sex.

For the first time in my life, all I wanted to do was bury myself in a woman's essence—Lola's essence—and it was worth it. It hurt me to see our night of passion troubled her. And that she wields it over my head like a sword.

After the race—which I let her win—she complained her thighs were killing her from a day spent cycling. As I placed an order for a shuttle, I sent instructions to my butler to have a warm scented bath prepared. Scrolling through my notifications, I realized Lucas had called me some minutes ago. I ignored it, not wanting to hear from him. Not because I was angry at him, but because I didn't want my evening ruined by his dramatics.

"Just step in, I'll stay right here." I motion for her to sit in the jacuzzi, while I sit beside the jacuzzi, on the chair I carried in moments ago.

"Onahi..." I love it when she breathes my name in awe. It's something I'll never tire of hearing.

From the door, her eyes take in the candles and sparkling glasses of champagne sitting on the shoulder of the jacuzzi filled with rose petals, then returns to rest on me.

"Don't get irritated if after this experience, I stalk you— demanding your love and attention." She struts to the jacuzzi in a two-piece triangle bikini, that reveal more than they conceal. "You're spoiling me."

I had the honor of taking her dress off earlier, in between kisses and moans of pleasure. What had started as a foot massage had my dick hard in seconds, her legs wrapped around my waist. It was self-control that had me taking myself off her to confirm my butler had done as requested.

Fuck. Those legs.

"I don't mind." I swallow, watching her settle into the jacuzzi with a satisfied sigh. It's something I want to watch over and over again. I think I really wouldn't mind her stalking me. I would save her the stress by asking her to remain with me, but I'm not in the headspace for that right now.

She takes a glass of champagne by the stem and sips, her eyes scrutinizing me above the rim. "Champagne. Roses and music." Clicking her tongue. "You're a complete romantic."

Me? Romantic? I laugh. What the fuck! Anthony needs to hear this. Fuck! Everyone that knows me needs to hear this.

"What's funny?"

"I don't think you meant what you said."

"You being a romantic?"

I snicker. "That's out of the question."

She sits up, setting her drink down. Leaning forward, she rests one arm on the jacuzzi edge, the other cradles my chin. I watch as rivulets of warm water trails down my chest and settles on my boxers. "Look at me Onahi."

Taking a deep breath, I stare at her lovely innocent face. A face on a body that houses a beautiful soul.

"You don't think you're a romantic?"

Shaking my head, "Well... I-I..." What the fuck. Say it! I don't have a heart. I'm a fucking transactional human being. I want to fuck you till I can get this itch off—no matter how long it takes. Then offer you a mouth-watering position. The HR team will have no reason not to hire you. You're good at what you do, and it has nothing to do with us ever fucking.

She raises her brow at me.

"I don't."

"Hmm..." Letting go of my chin, she relaxes into the jacuzzi. "So, what do you call organizing the parasailing thingy to surprise me?"

"Tsk. I wanted you to try something more fun than visit bars and restaurants."

"And the spa?"

"Sort of a—let's not talk about us?"

"Okay. Setting up eyes on Tyrell for Jay?"

I scoff. "Jay. Jay is a good friend."

"But you fancy the idea of her finding something good with him."

"Nothing serious there. Just because I don't see myself as romantic doesn't mean I don't wish it for someone else." So much for wishing romance for someone else. Ahmed's arrival yesterday changed a lot of things. I stayed for a while with him at *Eclipse* but the torn expression on Jay's face had me running out and over to the gym. Okay, not just that, Lola's rejection too.

"Whatever. You've been nothing but romantic." She sips her drink. Her brows furrow and she adds, "That's after our disagreement at the restaurant."

"Nice. Thanks for the thorough analysis of my nonexistent romantic side."

"You're welcome."

"Relax and enjoy, I'll be reading *You Are a Badass* by Jen Sincero." I pick up the book the butler had placed on the side. I grew up reading books before bedtime, especially nights

Escape

where I find it hard to sleep. It calms my senses, giving me insight into other people's world—perfect way to declutter from screens. But since I met Lola, reading ceased to calm my senses. I've masturbated to sleep one too many times, thinking of her.

"Interesting choice."

"Read it?"

"Nope. Heard of it."

"I'm glad." Flipping the pages, the sound musical in my ears, I stop at the very beginning. "Okay, the introduction. *You can start out with nothing, and out of nothing, and out of no way, a way will be made.*" I begin.

Just as I complete the second paragraph, she giggles. I look at the book in my hand, then back at her.

"I'm sorry. It's not you. My mind wandered and when it came back, you said, *unimpressed.*"

"Are you?"

"Slightly..." Oh... I'm doing something wrong. "But instead of reading while I soak in here at this odd hour of the night, why don't we spend our time doing something more fun?"

I raise my brow. Here I am, trying to settle her in, make her feel comfortable, make it up to her, but she wants to rush things. It's taking every fucking will power of mine to maintain control over my body—Okay, my dick—And just like that.

"Nahi..." I glance up at her. "I'm sorry, I didn't mean it that way."

"It's fine." I get up, wearing nothing but my boxers and a withering erection, placing the book on one side.

"I really would love to hear you read to me, but that's not what you promised." Her eyes sparkle with mischief, raking my form. My dick, so shameless, rises at attention to her lewd stare.

"Come on... Get in." She waggles her eyebrows. "I know you want to." Her perky breast bobbing above the water.

Fuck chivalry.

Picking up a glass of champagne, I gulp everything at a go, then turn on the jets and she squeals, excited.

"You had that all along?" Her voice cloaked in giggles, wiping off water from her face.

She makes room for me, still wiping water from her face, and I get into the jacuzzi. "You're going to beg me to get off you soon."

"Have I ever?" Her eyes throwing a challenge, which I heartily jump on. Closing the space between us, my finger finds her bikini clad pussy and I flick it, to which she yelps in surprise before grinning at me.

"Kiss me," she commands, and I obey immediately, clamping my lips on hers. My mouth coaxes hers with slow, languid kisses. My hand continues strumming her pussy through the thin fabric. She moans, thrashing, a throaty sound coming from her throat that sends all the nerves and blood in my head to one location.

Fuck! I've missed her. Her kisses are usually fierce but this time around, they follow the slow pace I lead.

"Does this impress you?"

"Sit right here." She taps on the high pads that look like steps, then lowers her head to my nether region. "A lot. That I want to suck your balls."

Don't say another word.

I take off my boxers and my dick bobs in attention. Her hand goes around it, leaving me groaning in response, closing my eyes.

I have to force my breathing to go back to normal when her head dips to take my hard, throbbing dick into her mouth above the bubbling water. Occasionally coming up for air, she licks the head of my dick over and over, then fully takes it in, sucking and slurping.

Fuck! Tightening my hold on the arm of the jacuzzi, I use another arm to hold her bobbing head. Fuck. Fuck. Fuck.

"I'm going to come if you continue." Thrusting into her lips.

She grabs my butt when I make to pull out, forcing me to remain under her control. The slurping sound of her wet tongue in contact with my dick. Watching her worship my dick. Her knowing smile. Everything. Fuck! I buck repeatedly, then groan as the head of my dick rests on the rooftop of her mouth.

"Lola... Fuck. Fuck." I can't believe I'm whimpering like a baby, all the veins in my neck forming a tight cord as my body shudders. "Yeah..." Releasing cum into her mouth. That fucking mouth with fucking kissable lips.

Cum drips on her face as she releases my dick from her lips and in between my crossed eyes, I notice her smile. She dabs water over her face as she swallows my seed. Fuck! A tremor passes through me, and I relax my back, sliding down the tub.

I give her a light kiss on her lips. "Stalk me. I'll never get irritated."

She giggles.

We get out of the jacuzzi, clean up and head over to bed in our birthday suits.

She sits on the center of the bed, watching my every move as I place the clothing we had discarded in a hurry earlier, on the love seat. Yawning, she covers her mouth, falling flat on her back. "I think it's good night from me."

"Not so fast my darling." I climb atop her, and she's doesn't giggle or struggle. My giggling girl has lost all the energy in her.

"Tired. The cycling."

"Let's help you get ready for sleep then." I scatter kisses on her forehead, cheek, neck, collar, making my way down.

"I don't have the strength for this Nahi."

"I can do this without your help."

She tries closing her legs when I get to my destination, but I gently nudge them apart. "Open them. I need you relaxed." Brushing my fingers on her pussy; they're not as wet as they usually are.

"I'll fall asleep and—" she ends with a moan as I begin licking her clit.

"It's just a tongue massage. Nothing to bother yourself with." If I'm lucky, I'll get her squirting. "This pink lady and I have unfinished business."

Escape

I instruct her to place a pillow beneath her waist and resume my task, with the intention of putting my fingers and tongue to use. Spreading her open with my fingers, she shudders when I run my hand through her thighs and leg, prepping her for the main meal.

Flicking her luscious bud that's now releasing sweet nectar, I taste the juice—rich and warm. I swallow in anticipation, then put my tongue to the task, sucking her bud slow—going up and down.

She stretches her legs, moaning, when I clamp my mouth on her, causing me to feel the beginnings of an erection.

Down boy...

Her legs wrap around my neck, her frantic hands stroking my head, demanding more.

Penetrating my greedy tongue into clit overflowing with sweet nectar—swollen and thick from arousal—I tongue-fuck her like a miner who just struck gold.

She doesn't say my name, but I feel it from the tightening of her legs, the feverish movement of her hands pushing my head, the bucking of her hips, her attempt at cussing.

I don't let go until she gives in, completely spent and boneless. Reduced to whimpering, but satisfied woman.

One final fond kiss to the pink lady and I move up to watch her. She has her eyes closed, trying to catch her breath.

"Impressed?"

She snorts, then smiles, opening her eyes. "Beyond a doubt."

Pulling her against my body, lying on our sides, her back to me, I nuzzle her neck. My erect dick pokes her ass, but I'm too tired to do anything about it.

"I like you. Sex with you is amazing." I like spending time with you. Exploring with you. Eating with you. Eating you out. Arguing with you. Everything. I can't put a finger on what this is, but that's what I have narrowed it down to be.

"I know you do."

That was not what I want you to say. Fuck. I wasn't expecting anything. But that's a good start.

Much late into the night, I wake up with a start. Where's she? She was—I breathe a sigh of relief when I notice her wrapped in a duvet an arm's length away. I roll over, putting my body beneath the duvet then hug her to me, my dick happy to be resting between her warm ass cheeks.

As I drift to sleep, she murmurs inaudibly in her sleep, then wriggles her ass. Her hands squeeze mine that lay beneath her breast.

"Nahi..." she murmurs, and I realize it was her voice that woke me up earlier. "Make love to me."

I move my hand to her pussy and confirm it's wet. I don't think twice about it. When it comes to Lola, I realize, she's becoming an exception to everything.

Thirty-One

Lola

NOT AGAIN. I BLINK AWAY tears as I heave out the last thing I believe is in my tummy. Taking quick shallow breaths then hitting flush, I sit on the floor, picking up my phone.

It's alright Lola. Don't panic. He is rich. Don't panic. You'll be an exceptional mother.

Squeezing my eyes shut, I let out a muffled cry. I blink my eyes open; I need to be strong.

Running my thumb across my phone's screen to turn it on, an email notification pops, reminding me my flight is scheduled to leave tomorrow morning. Time has flown by so fast—from that evening in my bedroom, till now—it feels like a lifetime. I bite my lips, then send a text to Carolanne.

Lola: I think I'm pregnant *woman shrugging*.

What if I truly am? I flip my phone continuously. If I tell him now, how would he react if we eventually find out I'm just overreacting.

Is it possible to get pregnant so soon? So fast? The doctor from the sauna had said it took about five days. Today is my... the bar, the bar, his place, the art—oh no. Today is my sixth and last day at the resort.

I clutch my arm to my tummy, folding my knee to my chest. I glance at my phone screen. Nothing. No response.

Common Carolanne.

What was I thinking last night when I asked him to... Oh God? His penis was so warm. And hard. Poking my butt. I had to feel it. I bite my lips to stifle a moan, sighing as I vividly recollect him biting into my shoulder as he thrust into me from behind. My traitorous and addicted clit is spasming, looking for his penis. I shake my head in mock disgust.

I like you. His deep baritone scared the shit out of me when he said it. I don't trust whatever he says—he has been hiding his identity from me. Thinking I don't notice. I didn't come here to catch feelings; I came here to have fun.

"Lola?" Onahi calls from the room where I had left him. We had briefly discussed the lack of condom use last night and he apologized for his shortcomings. We agreed not to make it an issue since his pull-out game is strong and we're both clean. He was so forthcoming on his STI status, he showed me a scanned copy of his test results from two weeks ago. If I didn't know better, I'd believe he wants to plant his seed inside me.

"Coming!" I get up hurriedly, looking around, ensuring the space is clean, then close the toilet seat and sit on it. "Toilet!"

It's not his fault what happened last night. I'm as much to blame. It's not like we're teenagers or that he's my first. I swallow, pushing down another bout of nausea.

Maybe it's food poisoning. The meals from yesterday.

My phone beeps.

Carolanne: OMG!!! How do you know?

Another message comes in.

Carolanne: *Big grin* Is it a boy or a girl?

Stupid girl. She thinks this is a joke. My life is hanging in the balance here, my career, my dreams, my plans, my body!

Lola: It's too soon to know that. And read again, I said '*think*'! *Rolling eyes*

She tries calling but I decline her call.

Lola: Can't talk. At his.

Carolanne: *Tears of joy* You went to get dick again? *Woman dancing*

Lola: Focus on the problem at hand. You might be a godmother sooner than you expect *smirking face*.

Carolanne: *Rolling eyes* It's soon to know you're pregnant.

Lola: That's the thing. *Grimacing face* We had sex the first night I got to the resort.

Carolanne: *Woman facepalming*. And you didn't tell me?

Lola: Suggestions please? Should I tell him?

Carolanne: Confirm first. Then tell him.

Lola: Thank you. There should be a clinic somewhere in this resort.

Carolanne: Did you use protection last night? *Smirking face*

I'm not answering that.

Getting up from the toilet seat, I flush one more time—for effects. Then on second thought, since I've not had the chance to, I send her another text message.

Lola: Google, Onahi Akachi

I never wished for this. It's not something I want. It all started as a joke. If my fears are confirmed, I'm going to be living with a joke for the rest of my life. When I have children, I don't want them having multiple homes. Even though he had said he enjoyed travelling the globe with his parents, that's not what I envision for my kids.

I'm throwing up. I've had unprotected sex multiple times. If that's not a sign of pregnancy, tell me what it is. *Oh God, I promise I'll never do it again.* I murmur a silent prayer as I step out of the bathroom, belting the sash of his robe tightly.

Maybe I'm the exception. Maybe that's what's happening to me right now. I'm carrying a baby I'll never know I'm carrying until the final day, when it's time to deliver the baby.

Onahi has his phone to his ear when I walk into the bedroom. He smiles at me, then holds a hand to his nose,

signifying that I stink. I pick up my clothes and begin donning them. Biftu had brought them earlier after Onahi persuaded me to spend the rest of my day with him.

"I need to visit the clinic." I tell him immediately he gets off the phone while tying my gladiator sandal.

A line appears between his brows. "Are you okay?"

He stands up, reaching for me as I make to walk around the couch, pulling me into a hug from behind. "Is everything alright, Guru?" He plants a playful kiss on my cheek.

"I think I have food poisoning." Leaning into his warmth, I rest my head on his shoulder. "I've been throwing up."

"Oh. I... I could call in a doc—"

"It's fine. I already ordered a shuttle. It's just a visit to the clinic—pharmacy."

"Are you sure?" He walks round me, to look me in the eye. "I could have someone come here to—"

Things rich people say. I smile. "It's alright. I'm fine."

He scratches his neck, sizing me up.

"What?" I chuckle nervously.

"It's strange." He lets out a long breath, folding his arms, studying me with a wry smile. "I think it's the first time you're ordering a ride for yourself without being coerced."

I shake my head at him.

"I'm coming with you." He says, picking up a shirt from the closet.

"Whatever." My phone beeps and I swipe the screen.

Carolanne: Is that our baby daddy??!! Gurllll! *Smiling face with heart-shaped eyes*

By the time we arrive at the clinic, my tummy feels twisted—inside-out. I winced with every slight bump during the ride.

Onahi is still on the phone when I tell him not to bother coming in with me. After registering with the medical person on duty, I sneak into the pharmacy and discreetly purchase a pregnancy test kit.

It's the least I can do to confirm my fears. I don't need to scare the man with my random thoughts. We're not emotionally involved with each other. *I like you.* What's that? A declaration of love? Or the best he has to offer? I'm not some puppy he can like today and give out tomorrow when he's bored. I am my own woman, here for fun but making a mess of my life because of *amazing sex.*

The ride back to his villa isn't as stressful, but I have worked up an appetite and a craving for sugar.

"Can I get that same ice-cream from last night?"

"Your tummy's no longer hurting?"

"It's not as painful."

"I can help you with something that would make you feel much better."

"Everything's not about sex." I smile at him as we alight the shuttle.

A line appears between his brows. "Did I mention sex?"

I roll my eyes.

"Oh. Don't worry, I can do that if that's what you want." He brings out his phone to place the order. "Yeah... The ice-cream can come to bed too. We could try out a couple of things."

"I give up."

"No, you can't. We still have, how many days?"

I smile. "I leave tomorrow." He stops in his tracks, and I do the same. "What is it?"

"Wow." He shakes his head. "That was so fast. And I'm yet to show you half of what I want to."

"So sweet. You've done a lot. Enough for me to daydream of you being my happily ever after." I wink. "Now let's make sure we maximize my remaining time here. You've been a rather... Nice guide."

"Yeah." He holds my hands, his face registering an emotion I've never seen him wear before now. Something kicks in my chest. Would he ask me to stay? Would he ask for my home address? Would he confess to loving me?

How does one know they're in love? This is absolutely different from what I had for Robert. This is something more. Compared to this, the feeling I had for Robert was a crush. Oh... I think I am in love.

"Thank you." I put my arms around his neck, raising my face to his, and we kiss. Nothing serious. Something light. His lips taste yummy. He pokes his tongue at my lips, and I sigh, granting him access, leaning into him. Stroke for stroke—our tongues do a slow dance.

My legs tremble from the flood of emotions rushing through me and I sag against him, weak.

Onahi growls low in his throat, releasing himself from our lip lock. "Let's go inside. I want to bury myself in your warmth all day."

Leaning back, I pluck invisible lint from his shoulders. "All day? Hmm?"

He winks. "All day."

"Well, I have plans." Withdrawing myself from his hold, I smile impishly, skipping out of his reach, making my way to the door.

Catching up with me, he flashes his villa card in preparation to open the door. "What plans?"

I should as well enjoy my last day here and with him. "Well... Having warm fluffy bread and ice cream on bed isn't such a bad idea. Can you add that to the order?

He has a baffled expression mirroring mine as his door opens from just touching it. "I remember locking up before we left. Stand back." He mutters, stepping into his space.

I follow closely behind him, not heeding his command. It's probably the cleaners here to do their job.

There's a strange perfume lingering in the air, very feminine. The smell of trouble. I know when he spots the source, because he freezes, stopping in his stride, and I bump into him. He doesn't shake but stands rooted to the spot.

"What the fuck are you doing here?"

I move from behind him and my gaze lands on her.

She looks polished, sophisticated, and relaxed, sitting on the couch, a glass of whatever in her hand. The type of women the media rarely talk about. A high-power executive woman.

Is she the type of woman he dates? I turn to find his skin flush, his nostrils flaring.

I want to scream at him, at them. Who is she? Why does she have access to your villa? Why haven't you told me about her? Who are you? But I watch in silence instead.

"I see you moved on so fast." The woman's eyes move from me, to him, then to the glass of wine in her hand.

"You have no right to walk into my properties, Flora." Onahi's voice is cold—cold like ice.

She gives a bitter laugh, looking at her drink for answers. "Why did you treat Anthony so bad?" Then looks up to Onahi, "He came here to apologize—"

"The fuck he did."

Wrinkles frame her eyes when she squints at him. She drops her drink rising from her position. "Don't use that tone on me, Onahi."

His lips tighten. "You don't tell me what to do, Flora. You had the opportunity to, but you misused it." He smirks.

"And I don't regret it. One bit, I don't. Barely three weeks ago, you were engaged to me and now..." She turns to face me, a patronizing smile on her lips. "I feel sorry for her already."

Onahi raises a hand, tilting his head to the side. "You. Leave her out of this."

She scoffs. "So, she doesn't find out how you use people for your personal gain and when it doesn't work out, you toss them aside?"

What?

That's not the Onahi I have spent time with. The Onahi I know is a brooding man who hides the fun person he is within. Looks out for others. Adventurous too. And... And...

"What the fuck are you talking about?" His face tightens in anger, and he nods as though realization just dawned on him. "Anthony." He says calmly, his hands flexing.

He walks towards her, his shoulder drooping, completely forgetting I exist, then decides against it and moves to the seat on the couch. "I should have known." He flexes his fingers on his thighs, looking off into the distance.

"Hello Flora?" That's what he called her right?

She deems me worthy of a glance, her stance haughty and irritating. I only want to clear the air and not let her involve me in their drama.

"I am Lola. And I was not in any way doing anything fishy or sneaky with your man." I smile. I look from her to Onahi, who has moved on to pour himself a drink—I'm obviously not needed here. "With that being said, I'll just go... Allow you guys to finish this... Business." Even as I say it, I feel something break into a million shards in my chest. Hope? Love? My heart? Whatever it is, I am not ready to analyze it here. Watching him act like I don't exist. Of which, I actually don't. I was just a means of escape. From his reality. From his world.

A living breathing fiancée. Here I was thinking something magical was coming out of this when—Jeez, I'm just a rebound.

I turn to leave, but his voice stops me in my tracks. "Lola, please stay. She'll be leaving soon."

Escape

"Yeah, just like you." Flora pounces on the opportunity. "Just like you always leave. Don't give me that silent treatment, Nahi. Don't even try it. You were never there, always trying to control things from whatever part of the world you were in."

"That's because I know what's best for you. And look at you. Just look at you, settling for less."

"Less? You think you're God's gift to humankind? You who look down on people? Knowing who is worthy to do what or what not?"

"I don't fucking look down on people!"

"Oh, I see that. Because you're hanging out with her, you think you're doing her a favor? Does she even know who you are?" She pauses. "I thought so too. You think no one can handle you? Everyone is a fucking transaction to you."

"Flora, shut the fuck up."

That's enough. I am done listening to their bickering. I can't even make sense of their history and relationship. Slamming the door violently, I pause to take a deep breath—Vacation is over.

Thirty-Two

Onahi

"ARE YOU HAPPY NOW?"

"I've been calling you. Been dropping messages. But you don't want to answer."

"And when someone doesn't answer or return calls, it means you leave them alone and move the fuck on with your life."

"Yeah. I notice you've moved on already."

"How does this even make sense? What the fuck are you doing here?"

Escape

I don't wait for her response. Lola has left, of which it's the decent thing to do, but for some weird reason, I want her here. "You know what? Before I return, I need you out of this place."

Her face is contorted in malice. She was mean to Lola, unlike her quiet, easy-going self.

Opening the door with more force than necessary, I leave to chase after Lola. I need to clear Lola's head of any doubt our altercation might have caused in her head. I grab her arm just before she steps off my villa's walkway.

"Please. I promise you. She's about to leave." I say, when she turns to me.

Her response is a smile.

Why the fuck are you smiling? A random stranger—to you—just said a lot of shady things about me and you're smiling? I want you angry. Mad. Pissed. Anything, but smiling like nothing happened back there.

"She doesn't look like she is to me." She scrolls through her phone, her other hand clutching tightly to the bag she had collected from the clinic. "And it's fine, no worries." She smirks, glancing repeatedly at me as she swipes her fingers on her phone. "Funny how today, when I want to book a ride, the app is malfunctioning."

"Lola, please. Don't do this."

The hand holding her phone drops to her side. "Do what?"

Words fail me. I make to speak, but it's only a snort that makes it through.

Tilting her head to the side, she studies me. "Are you okay?"

I try again, leaning on one leg, trying my best not to make a mess of our *situationship*. "Don't make us sound trivial."

"Hmm... Trivial?" Shaking her head, she folds her arm. "Onahi, I don't know about you, but when we started this..." She gestures with one hand. "We were simply scratching an itch. I was. And I think you were as well because you mentioned it too."

"That was before—"

"Before what?"

I make to speak, but she cuts me off with her next words.

"Before I found out you were engaged barely three weeks ago? Seriously? You couldn't tell me that?"

For fuck sakes, it has nothing to do with you. That was my past. You and I are the present. We chose to have fun together. Nothing serious.

But why did you feel betrayed when she stepped out of the room?

"I didn't have to tell you. You shouldn't feel entitled to know."

She turns away from me.

"I'm sorry," Holding her arm as she makes to walk away. It's a miracle I can breathe, as tiny pinpricks of pain shoot through my chest—like a single splintered bullet has gone through it. "I promise you, what—" My voice cracks.

Snatching her arms from me vehemently, she turns to face me. Her chest heaving, her eyes glistening with unshed tears. "Can you please stop with the promises? You don't have to rub it in. I get it. We have nothing going on, but please... please. Please, Master Onahi. Give me the permission to act emotional."

"Emotional?"

"I'm sure you don't know what that word means."

"I told you I liked you! Just last night. I got so emotional I spewed shit out and all you could say was, I know you do. And you say I don't know what emotional means?"

"Yes! Yes! I said I know you don't because people take time to process their emotions. Their feelings. And in order to properly do that, they need to know who they are dealing with to some extent!"

"And you think you are the saint in this situation?"

She squints, her chest heaving. The emotions I've been looking for coming in full force. She spreads her arm. "I've got nothing to hide."

It comes from inside, deep down in my tummy, rumbling out through my chest—I laugh. Place a hand to stretch the skin on my forehead, then drop it. This is incredible! Absolutely perfect! Lola the saint. I scoff. The Brand Guru. "You believe so? You think you're innocent in all this?" At some point later today, I'm sure I am going to regret this, but I won't let her paint me to be the bad guy and she, some sort of martyr in this *situationship*.

"I wasn't the one hiding my connections to the resort—"

"How the fuck did you get on this resort?"

Gasping, she blinks, then, bites her lips, thinking of a comeback.

"Yeah. Saint Lola. Answer the frigging question."

"I got in here with a ticket. A gift."

"A stolen gift you mean."

She gasps, her eyes going round.

I give a bitter laugh, serving her a little dose of her own medicine. "Yeah. Robert—"

"How—how. How did you know?"

"Cut the bullshit, Lola. You think I would be interested in you on a normal day? You think I randomly met up with you at *Eclipse Bar*? Think again." I lie through my teeth. Her legs, those legs. They would stop me and forever haunt me. And then discovering her giggles, they linger so sweetly in the air.

"But you..." She shakes her head vigorously, her lips drawn in a thin line. "So, you've known all along, and you've been playing me? You've been acting like you knew nothing about me and kept stewing me for information?" I shrug. Two can play. "You had me investigated, didn't you?"

"That would have been a waste of resources now, wouldn't it? When you were happy to share everything about you."

"Fuck you! Fuck you, Onahi." She pokes my chest.

"You already did." I smirk.

"You're a piece of shit! A piece of shit wrapped in gold!"

"An expensive shit. That's good. Nice one."

"And I didn't steal from anyone! You can't prove it!"

"If you were smart as you claim to be, you would have actually found out who sent Robert the invite." I sneer.

Escape

Her eyes go round, and her jaw goes slack. I have overdone it. I've hit sensitive spots I shouldn't have. But with Flora appearing out of nowhere, being scared we were being attacked by resort staff that have gone off the hook—no thanks to Lucas—and her walking away instead of standing with me, I wanted to lash out. Now look what I have done.

"You." She mutters through tight lips, backing away from me

"I'm sorry I never meant to say that."

She smiles, nodding her head slowly. "Oh, you did." She turns to walk away, then returns to stand in front of me. In my face. Like that first night on the beach. Everything started from that night.

"You know what? You deserve that lady in there." Her nostrils flare in anger. I have hurt her pride, saying she is not smart. What had gotten into me? What the fuck was my problem! We had something good going on.

"And do you know why I went to the clinic? The real reason I wanted to go to the clinic? Not because I wanted to know if I had food poisoning. But to confirm if I was carrying your child." That's impossible! What hand is she trying to play here? Even Flora has never pulled this trick on me. But then again, she's the first lady I'll ever be going bare with.

"How is that possible? We spoke about this, this morning. I always pull out—"

She laughs bitterly. Obviously seeing the confusion on my face. "True. How is that even possible? Science, Onahi. Science can prove us otherwise."

"What—what are you talking about Lola?" How did this conversation go from embers to flames? When did we factor a child into this situation? A child. My child. How the fuck is this even possible?

"Don't concern yourself about it, because as it stands, I don't want to have anything to do with you. Look at everything she said in there and with all the signs I've been seeing, that is exactly who you are. A-a-a control freak." She stabs my chest with her finger. "Who wants to control everyone's life. Was I a mere transaction too? Did you collect enough in kind for my stay on the resort? No. Don't answer. Save it. I don't want to know. I will not have you control me or my tentative child."

Control freak. That's a new one. Something Flora has planted in her head.

She ignores me, pressing her phone, muttering things beneath her breath. If she had said transactional, I would have agreed to that, but me being controlling? And the baby? If she truly is...

"Lola." I exhale, trying for a much calmer tone. "Please, can you just wait so we can have a reasonable discussion that does not involve us shouting at each other? I know I've revealed some things and said some mean stuff—"

She scoffs. "Some mean stuff you say?"

Rubbing my hand on my neck, I sigh. "I'm sorry. Please just wait for me. Let me send Flora off. And-and we can actually discuss all this and whatever pregnancy or baby you think we're having together. It's fine. A baby is fine. Just wait."

She snorts, shaking her head. I can't believe that moments ago, we were planning to spend the day together. I had spent time on the phone speaking with Williams, Salewa and the Head of Security to clear my schedule for the day.

A shuttle arrives, and it's obvious it's hers. What she had been booking on her phone while I tried to make sense of everything she had spilled.

"Lola."

She doesn't look back. Doesn't respond to her name. I watch as she gets into the shuttle, her profile straight, biting her lips, her jaw grinding. The pain in my chest intensifies. Blocking the flow of air through my lungs.

What I would give to have her giggle. To have her turn and do her mouthing zipping stuff. To have her say we just played one of her many games, like the ones we played on the ride to town after parasailing.

Enough for me to daydream of you being my happily ever after.

Last night when she had said that, against my will, something in my chest had jumped and pranced around— Maybe she was the one. This could be it. But alas, there's something missing. Something so essential we don't have. Trust.

Stepping into my villa, all the fight gone out of me. "Why are you still here?"

"We need to talk." Flora turns from the floor to ceiling window, not hiding that she had watch our showdown. I hope we put on a good show.

"If you really want to talk, now's not a good time. Actually, I would prefer you never return."

"I scared her away? I'm sorry."

"Don't push it."

She shrugs. "I'll be back."

Thirty-Three

Lola

HOW COME TIME BECOMES SO slow when things are boring, but fast when it's fun? It's shocking that it's just past noon. Feels like I've been sitting here for a thousand years already.

I told Biftu to get my stuff from Onahi's and she sent a maid that returned with everything even before I was done giving the instruction.

Sitting cozy on my couch in nothing but a terry robe, and a bowl of ice-cream Biftu got from wherever, I blindly watch a comedy show, while Carolanne rants via my phone—way cheaper than paying a therapist.

Did I overreact? I was only trying to excuse myself from his private conversation with her. And to find out she was his fiancée just weeks ago. Jeez. So, I'm the rebound. I thought we had something good going.

I like you.

What's that supposed to mean? Is that some sort of trophy? Or was he the trophy? Just because he told me about his roots last night—bout the size of his wealth. Did he think I was interested? Or no—threatened by that?

Don't make us sound trivial.

For heaven's sake. We agreed to scratching off the itch we have for each other. But he doesn't place importance in relationships—He had encouraged his engaged friend to carry on a clandestine affair. So, we were obviously nothing. Just... Just... Just a *situationship*. An itch to be scratched. A chemistry we had to put to test, that has exploded right in our faces.

If you were smart as you claim to be, you would have actually found out who sent Robert the invite.

He got me on that one. Big time. I felt like slapping the smirk off his face. I should have dug deeper. Checked the email it was forwarded from. Paid more attention to the sender. I would have saved us all this drama and avoided him throughout my stay.

You think I randomly met up with you at Eclipse Bar?

Control freak. Planner. Orchestrator. Maybe he had sent Duncan my way, to drug the answers out of me. But Duncan hadn't forced the pills down my throat. I had actually pushed him into giving them to me. Evil Genius.

I'm so glad it's my last day here. So, so glad! Even though the flight would go on forever. It's way better than breathing the same air or walking the same path with that traitor.

"Lola?" I had zoned out when she kept ranting about men being childish, and secretive. She had found little about him on Google. And the little included annual reports from different companies with his name listed there as investor or board member. Whatever. I'm no longer interested in knowing more about him. He can rot in hell for all I care.

"Yes?"

"The test. Have you done it?"

"Is it necessary?"

"Don't make me fly down there babe."

"I'll be home in a couple of days."

"Don't you want to save yourself the stress of reaching out to him later?"

"This is for you."

Picking up the package I had gotten from the pharmacy, I make my way to the bathroom. Carolanne and I read the instructions. Taunting her, I ask how many times she has done this, but she ignores my question, telling me to confirm my fears.

"There's no pee Carolanne." All that ice cream couldn't make pee?

"What?"

"Pee isn't coming!"

"Then drink some water."

Ugh. The pressure is getting to me. I have always envisioned getting pregnant on my own terms. Not from a casual fling. My first casual fling! And to the resort's owner, no less. Like I'm paying my landlord in sex. What a wonderful how I met your dad story.

"I'll be right back." I excuse myself from Carolanne's presence, leaving my phone in the bathroom.

Two cups of water, that's it. Sheesh. I shut the fridge, then gulp down water. Placing the cup back on the mini-bar, I hear a knock.

Who could it be? I wasn't expecting Biftu or room service. This is so not a suitable time. Opening the door in my terry robe, my eyes land on Nonso, who's bearing roses. No waiting shuttles with bicycles, thank God.

"Hello, babe."

Not the name-calling, please. "Hi." I smile, not giving him room to enter, and he as well doesn't push. "Long time no see." I jest, giving a small laugh that sounds like my lungs is filled with phlegm.

"For you." He hands me the flowers and I stare at them for the longest time. Such a sweet person. He deserves someone who would reciprocate his love, and that someone isn't me.

"Thank you." I smile, memorizing the details of his face.

"I need to be off this island, and my flight leaves in an hour. Business." He dips his now empty hand into his pocket, and I nod my head. "Not to waste your time, I'm here to know if you're interested."

The smile slides from my face. "Your proposition?" I haven't mulled over it throughout my stay. I've been hanging out with the devil. There was no time to think about you. Marriage is not on my agenda.

But being a baby mama is?

"Yes." His chiseled face goes into poker face mode.

"I can't." What more can I say to ease my answer? Even if I wanted to, I can't walk into his life knowing I might be carrying another man's child. That would be heartless of me.

"Okay..." His poker face is still on, but his eyes graze over me in admiration. "I love your spark, your zeal."

I nod.

"Don't think I've forgotten the documentation for your business. Please send it to my email." He pulls out his phone and types—the email address? "There. Please, send it."

"I don't think—"

"This is not about us or what we could have been. It's about others and solving a problem."

It truly is. I need to take myself off the table.

"Whenever you're in NYC, please ring me. We could catch up over a cup of coffee."

"Sure."

"Goodbye Lola."

"Good luck Nonso."

That was easy. Shutting the door and leaning on it, I exhale and inhale loudly. The fruity-citrus scent of the freshly cut flowers doing wonders to my soul. I smile, taking a sniff of the bunch. He would find his bride and live happily ever after. He deserves it.

Urgh, I want to pee.

Immediately I lift my back off the door, another knock reverberates. Did Nonso forget something? He seemed so collected when I told him no. The flowers? He wants me to return them? That would be so petty. Flowers still in my arms, I open the door to find the last person I think would ever be on this island, Robbie. No. It's Robert. Robbie was my imagination.

My heart doesn't skip, leap, or jump. I don't feel any form of excitement like I used to whenever I stepped into office, knowing Robert was there.

What is he doing here? Did Onahi put him to this? How long has he been on the resort? Why did they keep such secret from me? Robert, I'll forgive this one, but Onahi, this is a low blow.

"Hi." That's the only thing my head can process and add a sound to.

"Lola."

"Hi." Oh, why did I have to say it twice?

He shuffles his feet, puts a hand in the pocket of his loose pant trousers. "It's been a while."

Yeah, whatever. What are you doing here? Have you realized your mistake? That I'm the one for you? Too late, I'm already falling for your nasty friend. Your nasty friend I've done nasty things with.

I really don't want him to, but I ask, "Do you want to come in?"

"I thought you'd never ask."

"One moment." I grin. "I need to..." I glance down my terry-robed self. "Clean up?"

"Sure."

I shut the door before he agrees to my suggestion, then lean on it, my eyes closed. What?! Robert? On this island? What are the chances? Breath, Lola. Breath... I drop the bunch of flowers on a stool, pick up the ice cream bowl, and shove myself into a romper after scattering my wardrobe. *I'm sorry Biftu*. Glancing around to confirm everything looks okay in the living space, I walk gently to the door. It's the first time he's visiting me, and it wouldn't do for him to find my place in disarray.

"Ah... pleasant space," he says with a smile, looking around. That smile. It used to cause me butterflies. Not anymore. Someone else causes the butterflies in my tummy to do cartwheels and live shows now.

"I was actually concerned about you. I mean—" He clears his throat. "We were concerned about you."

Yeah. I left his calls unanswered the first two days I missed work and after that, he stopped calling. So much for being my work husband. But thanks a lot for the parting gift.

"That's all? After you lead me on for months. You can do better."

He adjusts on his seat, clearly not comfortable. "I'm sorry it came off that way. I thought you were joking with me too."

Oh really. Men. Bunch of Jokers.

"You know you're way out of my league. I just never thought serious about us."

And the projects we worked on together? "The late-night calls after work? Asking what I ate or what I'm doing?"

"I'm sorry, Lola. I just—Thelma and I happened. I wanted to see if you liked her—if you approved. Which was why I asked her to be on the project..."

He continues and my mind travels through time. Snap. It all changed when he told me he was assigned to work on a project with Thelma six months ago. Oh snap. Snap. Snap. And I'm only just figuring this out. Best to let go. I've moved on and I've got other issues.

"It was a mistake." I blurt out, cutting him short. "I'm sorry I made use of your tickets."

He looks up, baffled. "Urm... It's fine. I certainly understand and get it now."

"I promise you." I smile, shaking my head. Remembering the lady who was in Paris, hating on him. "It was my first time doing something like that."

He shakes his head, his blue eyes warm. "I understand Lola. It was totally out of character. And this place looks good on you. You look different."

I shrug. "The weather." It's not. I think I've fallen in love. And with the *wrongest* person. I thought we chose those we love. It's so...

Escape

There's a knock and Biftu steps in with towels.

"My butler."

"Oh."

"Would you like anything?" I cross my legs.

"No, thank you." He stands up, smiling, adjusting his shirt. "I actually came here to confirm for myself you are in good shape."

"Thank you."

What should I say next? I want to ask about the project. The one I had abandoned because of some childish office crush. Something that wasn't real. And where is Thelma?

"And Lola, I've got good news—They approved the project." Great. Perfect. "And you're still an integral member for the execution."

"Oh." I wasn't expecting that. "And the budget?"

"We actually got more than Thelma thought. Their 50th anniversary needs to be a blast." He grins.

Take that Thelma. Haha!

"That's-that," I tuck a stray hair behind my hair. "Splendid. Thanks a lot. And I am sorry I just jumped ship without warning. It was a trying time for me. You know? I had to clear my head."

"I know." His tone, very understanding, the reason I thought he was mine. "Every creative deserves time off. And the resort? Enjoying your stay?"

"Yes, I am. It's been great. Best decision ever." I wink and he smiles. "I've made new friends and I've been documenting my stay. Don't be shocked when I make a movie."

Robert chuckles at my optimism and I smile. "I hope you don't change."

I hope I don't too. I love myself.

We walk to the door, and I reflect on how a lot has changed in the past weeks. Their engagement. Me leaving for Twin Bliss. Meeting Onahi. Then Nonso's proposal. A lot has happened.

"How's Thelma? The bride to be." My grin is wide and blinding. I thought asking was going to make me puke, but I don't feel a thing.

"She's actually around. We got in not too long ago and she advised I saw you first."

Hmm... What does that mean? I'm sure he has told her what I did. Why isn't she here telling me what I should and shouldn't do? A question is burning on my lips did they pay for their lodging?

"That's so thoughtful of her." At least she has figured we're not friends. Might never be. Oh, snap. My bladder.

"Yeah. I told her about us."

Balls.

"She's understanding of the situation and said if I make it out of yours with two legs, I must invite you to join us tonight at *Eclipse Club*."

Too sad it's not coming from you directly.

Escape

I shake my head. I just want to stay indoors and mourn my choice of men. Then make plans for my unborn child.

"Please Lola." His voice and eyes pleading. "For old times' sake? Hangout?"

I need to use the bathroom.

Pressured to pee, I find myself smiling, shaking my head but saying. "Yes. Yes. Please send me the details."

Bidding him farewell, I run over to the bathroom and almost relieved myself in the bowl when I remember the test. Picking up the cup I had set up for the experiment, I giggle at everything playing out.

"Carolanne?"

Stretching over to get my phone, I find the call ended twenty minutes ago and she tried calling back. Well, I guess I'll find out for myself and tell her the news of being a godmother later.

Would I ever visit this resort again? To show my child where he or she was conceived? An act of lust. No. No. He had said he liked me. That's something. I'll tell my child we loved each other. It was love at first sight on a tropical island where I escaped from an uncaring boyfriend. *Okay, Lola. That's over the top.*

Thirty-Four

Onahi

A BLUE AND WHITE STRIPED fish chase down a yellow smaller fish. Whatever fish communication they were having, the smaller fish was not interested. It hides between the man-made rocks, bidding time for the bigger fish to forget about him since they are fish brained. It doesn't take up to three seconds for the smaller fish to forget he's being chased and returns to open water.

I smile when the smaller fish join similar fishes moving in a school, happy to belong. While the bigger fish turns around,

quitting his play with the smaller fish, bored, looking for another fish to either play with or bully.

"I thought I'd find you here." Flora's voice drifts over. I was so engrossed watching the fishes and their antics, I didn't hear her footsteps. There isn't much crowd here as the aquarium has lost its appeal—there are other late-night activities to indulge in than watching fish.

"Can I join you?"

I shrug. "You're here already."

The light airy scent of her signature perfume tingles my nose as she settles comfortably beside me. Completely different from Lola's vanilla fragrance. We both sit in silence, watching the fishes and their antics. In our one year of dating and six months of engagement, this is the longest I'll be sitting beside her without having a meal or work document between us.

Watching fish is a calming and relaxing hobby, someone had told me in the past. Not as relaxing as spending time with Lola and talking about everything or nothing. Lola. I don't understand how we came from kissing by the door to lashing at each other. What would it take to have Lola here instead of Flora?

A lot has happened in the past six days, with so much information swarming in my head. From work to personal and with friends. It relieved me to receive a call from the Head of Security about Asher's shooter being found, then an update of Lucas' misadventure in town last night. I placed a call to him, and he explained what had happened. He is in a worse state than I am with his now almost ex-wife. A long, refreshing walk to clear my head was what I needed, then I found myself here.

"I've actually missed this view." Flora says. "It's wider and there are more species."

It's one of my new favorite spots in the resort—after the gym. A couple of times, Flora and I had visited the resort together—for work. I had spent most time here and even told her to check it out whenever she bugged me to leave work and enjoy. I wanted to bring Lola here this evening, after a day spent indoors—just the two of us. Before I get my team to make her an offer.

"You know, before our big fall out," Flora folds her knees close to her chest, her arms encircling them, "you asked why I got an aquarium."

I recall that vividly. She used to dislike the idea of having pets and suddenly, she's embracing having a whole aquarium in her living space.

"It was because when I started seeing my therapist about my confusing emotions, he told me to watch fish."

Against my will, I ask, "Watch fish?"

"Yeah... It's a hypnotizing method of relaxing the mind and easing muscle tension."

Hmm... It's hypnotizing, alright.

"You just watch them swim back and forth, releasing control and not trying to know which fish just left which spot, but just watch for their motion."

Escape

I've been following the blue and white striped fish, and when I lost focus, I was adamant to pick another fish, waiting for it to resurface. "So, it's better to watch several?"

"The more the merrier. The merrier the calmer."

Bullshit. "Nice." I try this time round, watching the fish move, without trying to follow anyone in particular. My eyes cross and I rub my face, giving out a small laugh.

"You good?"

"Yeah." I try again, trying to let go, trying to relax, letting the fishes move with my eyes and not my eyes moving with the fishes. "It's not working." I snort, turning my face to Flora. She has her lips curved in a smile.

"It takes time and practice. As time goes, you'll find that your heart rate has reduced, your blood pressure, lowered and you'll catch yourself smiling at their antics—antics that makes you happier."

How the fuck am I supposed to focus on a group of fish? I turn to the aquarium, practicing what she mentioned earlier. The blue and white striped fish is back to the forefront, floating by a sea shrub. I wish I could nudge it towards the other side of the aquarium where a similar fish is. But it's out of my control. So, I just watch.

"Watching that guy lonely over there isn't making me a happy philosopher."

"Which guy?" She leans forward, following the direction of my finger. "Oh that. How do you know it's lonely?"

"Because it was walking with similar fishes, got derailed, found new friends, then left alone because they are of different species."

"Hmm..."

We watch them in silence. Occasionally, I feel Flora's eyes on me.

"For what it's worth, I am sorry."

When I say nothing, she adds, "I'm sorry for everything. And I am not here to get you back or do that dramatic stuff they do in movies. I-I just wanted us to clear things out and you know how I am. I am always looking out for the best in people. And I have your best interest at heart."

"No, you didn't."

"Onahi."

The hurt in her voice causes me to face her. "You think this hurt you more than it did me?"

"You've moved on."

I snort, turning back to the fishes. "She's gone. It wasn't even something serious."

"Onahi, I'm sorry." Her voice plead with me to see reason. "You-you were always on lockdown. I found it hard to speak with you. Always busy. I needed a friend. I was going through a lot. And Anthony—he was available. He came to apologize." She sighs. "We didn't plan for it to happen. We didn't plan to fall in love. It's different with him. And we've never kissed or had sex. Never. I want this to be something you are okay with; he wants it too. He's a good friend."

To you.

And I'm the villain. The bad guy.

She was spending more time with Anthony. How they found time between our busy schedules is beyond me. She works on the frontline for her family's charity organization. Anthony and I were always on the move. But he always had time to help me follow her around—times when I was busy doing something more important. Time spent with her was nothing like time spent with Lola.

They haven't had sex or kissed, and he dared visit me after confessing he had proposed to her and she accepted. Which man does that without tasting the fruit? That's a pill I'm finding hard to swallow. Flora and I didn't connect on other levels, but we connected on sex. She loved having sex with me. When she couldn't get through to me, all she had to do was seduce me and I was game.

Anthony. He was a good friend. The fixer. The one I entrusted with my girl—that's if she was ever my girl. After doing all that he thinks we're going to remain friends. Although I'm actually over that—I'm over the betrayal—but remaining friends is impossible

The blue and white striped fish has moved from its spot but keeps missing its own school. All it needs to do is move to the left! Move to the left, man!

Her palm rests on my shoulder and I freeze, my breathing shallow.

"Did you hear everything I said?"

"I did."

"And?"

"I couldn't hate you." I turn to face her. "I forgave you long before it happened. I just wished you had spoken to me more. About how you felt."

"You wouldn't have listened." She shakes her head. "You knew what was best for everyone."

I chuckle and she joins me, smiling. I acknowledge I can be dog-headed sometimes, and we speak of times when we could have done things better. Communicated better. Resolved fears together.

"I'll always have a spot in my heart for you. And I hope he makes you happy."

"I learned a lot too." She stares at the aquarium whimsically. "I'll make him know when I'm not happy." Turning to face me. "I don't want a repeat of this."

Swallowing, I resume watching the fish. "That's good."

The blue and white striped fish finally finds another lonely fish. They spin around each other, elated to find themselves.

"You see... They found each other." The fuck they did. After all the telepathy messages I sent their way. "Because they know they are in the same world."

Hmm.

Both fish follow each other's tail. The previous school of smaller fish return and begins acting still, floating on a spot. The sight is ethereal.

"I know you didn't ask me, but I think she is beautiful and has got balls."

Turning to her, our eyes lock. "When you said you didn't plan to fall in love, what did you mean?"

She sighs, squeezing her eyes shut, looking heavenward, murmuring a prayer. When she looks back at me, her eyes are

Escape

sparkling with delight—I've never seen this side of Flora. Having Anthony as her fiancé might be a good deal, after all.

Thirty-Five

Lola

THIS IS PEER PRESSURE. THIS is guilt. This is unfair. This is life.

I left Biftu in my villa— she was packing my suitcase in preparation for my early morning flight—while I take a much-needed walk to the *Eclipse*. I have little extra stuff, except for the *pareo* and local jewelry I got the day I went into town with Onahi.

I've kept myself indoor for the remainder of the day, hiding. Meeting Thelma and Robert at the club is also another form of hiding. The room will be dark with colorful lights moving around, so I don't get to see her genuine expression. She has never liked me. And I don't give her reasons to. Any comment she makes sounds like an attack. I would have preferred this was done when I resume work, so I can prepare myself for any form of confrontation.

I spot them. Close to the location I first saw them—the night Onahi walked my drugged and drunk ass back to my villa.

We have a lot of that here.

Fireflies. They have a short lifespan, just like mosquitoes, just like my thing with Onahi.

We have a lot of that here. Sounds more like they have loads of flings here. A lot of short-term relationships. Like Jay and Tyrell, and a complete load of others. And I happen to have caught feelings.

He has not tried reaching me, and I have not bothered sending a text. I have a lot to process and plan. There's more to my life than a casual fling with a random stranger on an expensive resort. I'm returning to DC to begin afresh. There will be a lot I'll need to adjust to and now that I've learned more between the sheets, my standards have gone up a notch.

Any interesting men over there? Yes, mommy! I met one and had mind-blowing sex with him. He pretended he didn't know much about me and has been playing me all along. Now I'm finding out he's a rich dude who doesn't give two cents about other human beings and has only been playing me all along. Did I mention that before? Playing me all along? Yeah, he's played me like a string.

You shouldn't settle for less. I don't want to be his baby mama anymore. Never wanted to. So, it doesn't hurt to find out that he doesn't deserve me. He's been so sweet, but everything has been a lie. The smiles, the ringing deep laughter I looked forward to eliciting, and his brooding face. That brooding face caught my attention the first time we met. If only I had known he was thinking of how to get me to pay for being in his resort, on his ticket.

I don't regret the times we spent together. I enjoyed every moment. If I could, I'll make the memories be on replay, but I'll erase everything that happened this morning. Even the result from the pregnancy test.

When I had checked the results, it was a complete negative. Maybe that's why I'm so negative and bitter. Did I really want to carry his baby? Have a piece of him? Somewhere down in my heart, a little spark was there, hoping that indeed I was pregnant. A piece of my glorious moment here on this island. A trophy to be taken home and nursed with Carolanne.

Not happening. I wouldn't even have the time to care for a baby when my career is still on its high road to something big. All it was, was a pregnancy scare. I made a fool of myself in the sauna for nothing.

And all the cramp. nausea and pain I had been feeling all day was because of my period, which is currently a bloody mess. It's like a vein on its way to my heart—burst—is gushing out. It's my broken heart. No. It's not. I was only beginning to feel something for him, not like I love, love him.

My hormones are the reason I feel high one minute and low the next. This same hormones have not helped me think straight. The delay in seeing my period could be a result of the long ass-flight or change in environment. Sheesh, I wasn't even ovulating when I was being promiscuous. I have not been thinking straight since I landed here and I'm so glad I'm not pregnant. So glad I won't be saddled up with someone who tricked me into bed, whilst thinking the worst of me.

Have I judged him too fast? Maybe I should call him. Hear him out. Understand his point of view. But it doesn't matter anymore—we had a fling and I'm not pregnant. Besides, we're from different worlds.

Terrific work Lola. You've got it all figured out. The plan now is to club tonight, ignore alcohol and Thelma, then get out as soon as possible. I need a good night's rest for the long journey back to my world.

Not wanting to search for them within, I send a message to Robert.

Lola: I'm here. Outside.

Taking a deep, calculated breath as I study people going in and out of the building, I spot Robert and Thelma, searching for me. He's holding her hand and they look so good together—It makes me want to cry. Why does she deserve to have him when I don't? Something melts in my heart at the sight of Thelma's smile when she recognizes me in my African print romper.

"Hey, Lola." Thelma pulls me in a hug, and I inhale her scent. It reminds me of late nights spent in the office, brainstorming ideas and a whole lot of misunderstandings.

"I'm sorry." She whispers for my ears only, then squeezes tighter. "For everything."

"Careful." We giggle, withdrawing from the hug. "You don't have to force me into forgiveness." Through cautious eyes, I watch for her response—she grins. Okay... A new Thelma. There must be something in the air.

"How was your trip? Down here?" Awkward...

"Girl..." she begins, waving her arms by her side, her purse hitting her lap. "It was bat shit crazy!"

"I thought as much." I give Robert a courteous nod. As usual, with Thelma around, he's got all his attention on her. Oh, what I would give to have Onahi look at me that way. How come I never noticed it in the past? I always thought he was just thinking, his mind a mile per minute, but alas, every word that spills out of Thelma's lips enchanted him.

"To come here alone? Oh, girl, I thought it would never end. Probably find ourselves in heaven or something. But I had to remind myself it was worth it. What, with all the perks I had seen online, we had to complete the trip,"

Who is this sister? What changed?

"Once you settle in, you start to feel it. It becomes fun. Try para—" I begin but pause as the memory of that day comes back to me. I had cursed her loud and clear in the skies. So close to God. *Oh God forgive me.*

"What's that Lola?"

I blink, then give a fake bright smile. "Parasailing. They offer that here. You should try it."

"Okay. I'll keep that in mind."

"We plan to spend about a week here." Robert adds.

"Too bad. I leave early tomorrow morning. It's been six days of bliss and adventure." And sex. And heartbreak. I'm sure feeling the heartbreak part more, because watching

Thelma look occasionally at Robert when she says something, or the slight squeeze of their hands which they think is not visible, makes me wish.

No. No. No. No Lola. We're not going down that train of thought.

"Okay ladies." Robert says, clapping his hands.

"I completely forgot you were standing there for a minute." I say and Thelma smiles at him, a palm on his chest. "He's always like that." The perfect couple. No, I will not cry.

Robert shakes his head at me. "Let's go inside. The night isn't getting any younger."

"Yes daddy." I mock.

Arm in arm, we walk into *Eclipse*, and yeah, the party just got started.

I do one shot with Thelma—a toast to new friendships. Another that includes Robert—a toast to the success of the project. One more shot for... I think successfully arriving the resort in one piece.

So much for not touching any alcohol. But hey... the flight will be miserable either way, so why not start tonight?

Alcohol pumps in my veins as the music becomes heated. Swinging my body and worries side to side, I lose track of Thelma and Robbie on the dance floor.

"You've got great moves!" A voice shouts into my ear.

I turn to find a tall hunk with a low cropped beard and geeky glasses grinning at me. Unlike Onahi, he squints his eyes when grinning. Not a bad idea for my last night at the resort. Just to prove to myself and Onahi that everything I did with him, I can do with others. I'm not even going to ask for his name. Unnecessary complications.

"Thank you!" I shout back as he closes in and we begin a well-coordinated unchoreographed dance to the song playing from the speakers.

"Whoo hoo!" I clap as 'Werk' by DJ Cuppy and Skuki come from the speakers.

"Come on Mami!" He shouts in excitement.

I'm giving it to you, boy.

Mami work, work, work, Skuki goes on the track.

I hop a couple of times, turn my ass to his crotch in the most intimate way, then move my upper body to the side. He seems to get the hang of it and in no time, I am grinding on him—moving left and right—my laughing eyes holding his excited ones.

Okay. That's enough. Haha.

I turn my eyes from him as I get up and I lock gaze with Onahi's. His eyes are dark and clouded. Worse than the night he saw Nonso and me walking from the art gallery.

Oh shit.

Thirty-Six

Onahi

WHEN FLORA HAD DESCRIBED LOVE, it was not like this. No. She didn't describe the short, quick take of breath or the pain that comes with seeing your person having carefree fun when you're languishing in agony. How you will almost gasp for breath like an asthmatic patient from pure rage baked in jealousy. All these are emotions I am currently feeling, as I stare at my person, my giggling girl, laugh someone else.

There she is, staring at me from across the hall while that guy—whoever the fuck he is—keeps rocking her. Didn't he notice she is no longer interested in their dance? Fool.

If anyone had told me one week ago that I'll feel like beating up a man six ways from Sunday for coming close to a woman I like, or even perceive to love, I'd have laughed—in their face.

Onahi feels nothing romantic for anyone. He doesn't understand why people do what they do for love. When people love, it's a problem—time consuming with unreasonable expectations and demands. Romantic emotions are far-fetched. Onahi is transactional. He believes in family, loyalty, and agreements. He doesn't let his emotions run him.

BS. Not this Onahi. Manic rage is blinding this Onahi.

There's a high chance our passionate encounters have made an exceptional being who would enter this world in nine months. I won't let her take that joy from me. She would also have to come to the understanding that we were more than itches to be scratched.

Striding purposefully towards her as she balances herself with those legs for days in slow motion, as though surprised to see me here, wriggling bodies blocks her from my view. Is she feeling what I'm feeling? Does she care? She had confessed to being a romantic. If she did, she wouldn't be dancing with him. Whoever the fuck he was. If she cared, she would have waited when I begged her to and we would have trashed everything needed, then decide on how to go ahead with whatever we were feeling. How is it possible to fall in love with someone in less than a week?

Love? I shake my head, making my way through the crowd.

Escape

Almost there. Close enough to pull the motherfucker who dared to laugh with my giggling girl when we were not on smiling terms. The mother of my unborn child.

The mother of my unborn child?

I lose all the steam in me and decide to turn the other way. Weaving through bodies, I make it to the elevators to get out of this space, before I do something I'll most likely regret and then get unnecessary press coverage.

Lola is a grown woman. She makes her choices herself. Fuck. She already has. She doesn't need me to babysit or follow her around to save her from her impulsive acts. I don't need to put up a fight or a show as evidence that I care about what she thinks of me and how I see her.

Flora had said I need to work on myself—I need to let people close to me make decisions for themselves by themselves. She even brought up the shares game I was playing with Ahieni, my sister.

Stepping out of the building, my sandals hit the sandy ground one step at a time.

Defeated. Tired. Step, step.

Worn. Used. Step, step.

Fuck. I let out a long whooshing breath, scanning the horizon. I should be angry. I was used. She not only took a gift I meant for someone else but came into my life and made me realize what I had been missing all along. Now I know what this love thing feels like, and I won't be able to settle for less.

Did you come here looking for the one?

No! I didn't even know what that term had meant when I had answered that question. With every thought, and every feeling oozing through my head, my heart, I think she was the one, and I blew it by hiding myself, giving her bits of me, trying to figure her out instead of giving her the opportunity to figure me out. With the bits and pieces of me I gave, I don't think it's possible for her to think I'm worth the bother.

The sound of the waves from afar comes crashing into my eardrums as I find myself at *Gobota Specials*. Everything that has happened in the past six days seems like a blur. Unlike me, I don't wait to be served; I place an order for something strong and walk to an unoccupied seat.

The crowd here is calm, mostly the older population who do not have the energy to hop around in a dark room with flashing-colored lights on a Friday night. Who will not grind on a man's crotch after getting up from another man's barely twenty-four hours ago. This is me. I'm not an *Eclipse* guy, I'm a *Gobota Specials* guy.

I've left *Eclipse* for her. I can't be in the same room with her and pretend it doesn't hurt that she rejected me. God. I'll leave all my wealth at her feet just to have her giggle with me again. For her to be free with me again, so I can bare my heart and thoughts with her.

A second chance.

My phone beeps and my heart races a mile a second as I unlock the device. Has she reconsidered us? Does she want to meet up? I'll go anywhere. She just has to send me the loca—I hiss when I read the message.

Lucas: Leaving for Lagos tomorrow. Thanks for everything.

Escape

I quickly type an obligatory message.

Onahi: It was my pleasure. I'm sorry man. Have a safe trip.

"Hey!" a familiar voice calls out, but I shake it off. Just my imagination.

"Hey. I'm talking to you." One hand clamps my shoulder and I freeze.

It's real. She's real. She's talking to me. She's here, right behind me. I close my eyes, whispering a silent prayer and hoping this will not be a confrontation—I don't want that anymore. I'm terrible at being nice when fighting.

"Don't act like you can't hear me."

Opening my eyes, I turn and there she is. Looking hot and ravishing. The heat from the exercise she had been indulged in earlier oozing from her skin. Light sweat sheens on her caramel skin. Under the moonlit sky, her skin glows like a mirage.

She belches. "Sorry." Then giggles.

Typical Lola. She's tipsy or probably drunk. "How many shots this time?"

Raising her fingers, she signals three but says, 'one' with a cute smile.

It can't be. I smile, shaking my head, then looking up to the sky before looking back at her. She's real. Almost the same Lola I had met six nights ago.

She looks at me, then the beach, then back at me.

What is it? What's wrong? Was it the guy from the club? I'll make sure he doesn't know what hit him. All you have to do is tell me his name. I'll make sure he never goes near a lone woman in a club—ever.

"What's—"

"I'm not pregnant."

I rock on the balls of my feet as her statement rings home.

Calm down. It's alright. Does that mean I don't have any excuse to visit you when you return to your normal life?

I had assumed we would share the responsibility of being parents. Of seeing her become a splendid mother.

She bites her lips, then looks off into the ocean. Lips I want to kiss, even though I'm pained she left me standing in front of my villa, looking like a fool.

Folding her arms, she looks back at me. "And I'm sorry I used a ticket you meant for someone else. To be sincere, I've never done something like that in my whole life. There was just a lot going on, and I needed to escape my reality. It was a perfect getaway."

Robert had said as much during our phone call. "I know."

She eyes me suspiciously, tendrils of her hair swaying with the wind. "Since when?"

"I've always known." I look away from her piercing stare. "I was waiting for you to tell me yourself."

Her lips form a straight line. I can see the war on her face as she battles whether to run or stay. We have a lot to trash out and plan, and it will hurt what's left of my pride to see her walk away.

Escape

She swallows. "What else do you know about me that I don't know you know?" Her voice is tight.

Is there? A lot. But there's no need to pull that up. We just need to work from here. Start all over again. "Nothing."

"Haha. No." Panic flashes in her eyes. "You seem to know things about everybody and everything." She puts a finger to the bridge of her nose, taking deep breaths. Probably counting one to ten. "You said you tracked Tyrell, had eyes on him. Did you do that to me?"

"Not in the way—shit." I let out expletives as her expression changes. "I've messed everything up, haven't I?"

"Don't avoid the question. How many times? And when?"

"It's nothing, really. Nothing serious. I really wanted to get to know you myself."

Her nostrils flare.

"Okay. Twice. One time I called Robert and then I had security watching out for you during your cycling with that Nonso guy. And..." I scratch my nape, avoiding her eyes.

"And what?"

"I ran a background check on him?"

She raises her brow.

"That's all. I just wanted to be sure you were in safe hands."

Snorting, she continues her interrogation. "Why didn't you tell me about Robert? If you really wanted to know me, why didn't you ask the questions that matter to you?"

Moving closer, I pull her shaking hands into mine. Is she shaking from anger, fear, or cold? She has mastered blackjack so well; I can't tell which it is.

"Lola... Please. I don't like us fighting. I've enjoyed the past few days knowing you and I'm sorry for everything I did wrong."

She scoffs, pulling her hand from mine. "You can't escape that. Don't play that line on me. Tell me. Everything."

I hope she doesn't take it the wrong way. She's asking for it and although we had agreed to make everything light—nothing serious, I started slipping last night. Hell. I started losing control a long time ago. When I asked her to stay the night. She controls me—If only she looks closely.

"Tell me Onahi."

Sucking in the longest breath and letting it out, I close my eyes, hoping she doesn't run the other way. I'm actually not settling for anything because I'm not in the market. I just want to have fun. She didn't come here looking for the one either.

"I wasn't supposed to fall in love with you."

She gasps.

"I didn't want to find reasons to. But I-I came to life when I first kissed your giggling lips. You had me when I knelt between your legs. With you, I never think of who I am, or who my friends say I am. You put a new heartbeat inside of me. There's this connection we have—When I first met you, I had plans. I thought all I—all we needed was to scratch this itch away. Had calculated how it will go... But I guess it's pointless now." I smile cynically.

Escape

"Excuse me sir, your drink. I went to your table twice."

We stare at each other, ignoring the server who has a tray balanced on one hand and a towel on the other. Lola's chest heaves with every breath she takes. It takes a while for the server to get the hint and leave us alone.

Lola blinks, breaking away from my sincere gaze. She stares at our surroundings and I only just notice the clinking of glasses and occasional laughter. She turns to me and something in her eyes blows on the ember of hope left in my chest.

"This place seems a bit noisy. Want to go for a walk?"

When I hesitate, she adds, "I'm not going to hit you with a rock or something. For fresh air? And privacy?"

That's scary and I wasn't thinking of that. But I get the memo—we need to talk.

Thirty-Seven

Lola

HOLD ON GIRL!

He didn't say I love you. He said, and I quote; *I wasn't supposed to fall in love with you.* What did he mean? He doesn't like the idea of being in love with me?

Looking off into the distance as we silently walk towards the ocean, my gaze lands on the hammock from the first night, and I smile fondly. Walking to it, I sit on the edge, and he stands beside me as we observe the lapping waves.

Escape

"Why—" I clear my throat. "Why do you think you shouldn't have fallen in love with me?" I brush a stubborn loose hair strand behind my ear, bracing myself for the worse.

He snorts, kicking sand, then looks at me. Shrugging. "My friends and family believe I am a transactional human. I don't get emotionally involved because—"

"What transaction were you carrying out in this relation— No. During our time together?"

He closes his eyes as though in pain and lets out a string of curses.

"Tell me."

"This is doomed anyway." He swallows. "I've been trying to get my mind off my disastrous engagement. So, when I saw an interesting puzzle happening within the administrative resort, I wanted to discuss with one of the brightest minds I know." Licking his lips, he nods. "I sent Robert an invite—nothing direct about my plan. Just to get him here and have him access things. And then you came."

"I did."

"You changed the plan. Had me curious. I got close and you sucked me in. I was—still sexually attracted to you. Robert said you were good at what you do, and I had this urge to arrange something... I don't know what I was thinking— get between the sheets with you, thank you for coming with an offer—a remote executive role in the shaky Twin Bliss Global Communications team."

"I see... And you believed I would have taken this offer?"

"I don't know Lola." He rubs his nape, then stops. "From our discussions, it sounded like you needed something else. You weren't happy at your place of work."

"You want to tell me about Robert being on the resort?"

"That was a mistake. I wasn't thinking straight when I sent him the invite after a call. I..." his voice trails.

It had better.

"Okay... And you don't get emotionally involved because?"

"You really want to hear my sappy story?" He smiles and the side of his mouth goes up.

Oh. My heart goes a jig. *Calm down, will you!*

"I do. You can join me here." I tap the hammock.

He glances at it, sits on the edge, giving me enough space.

"Go ahead, please."

"There's no story Guru."

"I'm waiting."

"Seriously Guru. I get more than enough love from my family. My parents are crazy in love. Couldn't wait to leave their businesses in our hands so they could travel the world together. And I've never lacked for attention from all sexes."

"Hmm..."

He scoffs. "I read a lot of psychological books growing up—finding my footing in business. Learnt a lot about people. I guess being transactional became my go to. Although people say life is all about give and take, there are two universal relationships: symbiotic and parasitic. I never want to be caught in the latter."

You can't live your life like everyone is a business! This is a lot. It's a lot to take in. "And Flora?"

"She's really my ex-fiancée."

"And?"

"Flora was a good catch; she had the connections and all to make a good wife. I proposed, she was happy. She expected me to—since we're now in a relationship, be more attentive, but..." He shrugs. "I don't know. It's not easy breaking a habit when there's no overriding reason. I was twenty-nine, ready to start a family. I avoided deep talks, spending time with her and well... My friend was happy to keep her company."

"She cheated with your friend?" That's despicable.

"I never caught them. She said it never happened. I want to believe her, but she fucking accepted to wear his ring while wearing mine."

"Hmm."

"It's all cheating to me. It didn't have to be sexual for it to be tagged cheating, but if that makes them sleep well at night, then so be it."

"How did you find out?"

"Find out?" He snorts. "I didn't. They came to tell me and I lost it. Made my way down here."

"I'm sorry. That's... painful."

"Not as painful as watching you walk away from me."

"Onahi..."

"I need to say it. I didn't plan to fall for you. With you, it was different. You intrigued me. I never knew I could overcome what had happened so fast by just interacting with you. I wanted—I want to spend time with you. I want to know your thoughts. I want to hear you giggle, moan, be naughty, loose control with me. And if it meant me playing along with your stunt, I was game."

"Onahi..." My cheeks are hot from his confession. "You've got a pleasant way with words you know." I chortle.

He slashes a daring look at me. "Honestly Lola, I love you. And this was not how I envisioned telling you. Fuck. I never envisioned telling you this. It's too soon. It defies what I know. And I want to try it for real. Explore it. Why not take a chance on us? See where it leads?"

Stop it Onahi. His look is fierce. Honest. Uh-oh. *It doesn't look like you're joking. Are you under some kind of influence?* "How long have you been in the club?"

"Not long... I only just got in when you saw me."

"Look at me." I shift till our legs are kissing, then lean in to smell his breath. "So, you haven't been drinking, smoking or doing anything suspicious?"

His eyes take on a glossy look. Are you listening to me? "Onahi? Answer my question."

"Fuck." He shakes his head, coming back to me. "Yes. I heard you. And no. I haven't."

"What were you thinking?"

He shakes his head, smiling, "It's sappy."

"I like sappy. I told you before. You are the one who fights it."

Escape

Leaning closer as we sway on the hammock, he whispers, "I want to kiss you, but I need to know we're on the same page. You know I like you and I've told you I—"

"I love you too."

"Lola? You do?"

"I figured out a while ago, but I wanted to stick to our bargain."

"Which one?"

"The one at the restaurant that afternoon."

"You're kidding me." He leans away, giving a small laugh.

I smile, missing his laughter. I can't wait to hear the much deeper one, but that's a wish.

"I'm not some girl who takes things that don't belong to her. I do my stuff and watch things fall in place."

"I know Guru. If I had any doubt, it cleared when I asked you about Nonso and you came clean with it. What's happening with him?"

"He left."

"You broke his heart."

"Would you rather I—"

"Never." His eyes graze my lips and I lean closer until our lips meet. He cups my face with his warm hands and my traitorous body want to roll into him. Breath him. Savor his soft side. But he was my escape and I, his rebound.

"Stay..." he murmurs as I pull away, getting up from the hammock.

"Easy for you to say. I've got work and business plans waiting for me."

"I didn't mean it that way. I don't want you to give up your life."

"This is the point where you allow me think, and make a decision."

"I could stand over there." He points to a tree less than six feet away, "and—"

"Onahi, let's not rush things. I leave tomorrow. Thank God for technology, we can work around things if we decide to go along with this."

"We are going along with this."

I raise a brow.

"Sorry... I'm trying." He admits with his boyish charm.

"Good."

He shakes his head, smiling. "Why is your impulsive self not coming out to save me from this dilemma?"

"Hmm... Because it knows it's going back to the real world and has done enough here."

He nods slowly in agreement. "So... What's the plan?"

"I'll take a walk—alone—and we'll see... Later."

"Promise to see me before you leave?"

"I promise."

****

Escape

HE LOVES ME. HE LOVES me not. He loves me. He loves me not. He loves me!

Good job Lola. I smile.

Clapping my hands clean, I watch as waves from the ocean come for me. I had intentionally picked an uneven number of sea shells after a long mindless walk, committing this place to mind. I'll miss this resort. It was initially too good to be true. Just like Onahi's confession of love was too.

My conclusion is this: if we decide to test what we have, distance will be a barrier. He's a traveler and although I love flights, I love having a sense of home. Clicking my tongue, I shake my head—I foresee heartbreak in three months.

"Hey."

Doing a slow turn with my head, I find a petite lady in a cropped top and bum short.

"Can I join you?"

Taking in the glinting light coming from different spots on the beach, I purse my lips. Why here? Why with me? Can't you see me trying to get some alone time?

"Sure." I smile. Misery loves company, it doesn't get better than this.

"Thank you." She says breathlessly as she sets herself beside me. "Care for some?" She pushes a bottle at me. "Fire water."

Smiling, I push it back to her. I'm done acting the spoiled child. Besides, I had some with Onahi the other night in town. "Thank you."

"It's alright. I got in yesterday with my second husband and he's sleeping like a log. Was restless and decided to come out."

Second husband? She's wearing it like a badge.

She looks down the shoreline. "Seems like everyone has company tonight—no offence to you—so I chose to sit with you."

And some people like their time alone too.

She chuckles, like she heard my inner thoughts before taking a swig of her drink. "You're wondering if I'm divorced?"

Shaking my head, I smile, turning back to the ocean. "No. Not really."

"Well, my first husband died in a fire accident."

Oh, snap. I'm stuck with a talkative drunk.

"And I never got the chance to tell him how much I appreciate everything he does for me. For us. We even fought the morning he died. Funny, when my now-husband started courting me, all I saw was my first husband in him. And he'll never know."

Curious, I ask. "Never know what?" I turn to look at her and she has pain written all over her face—her mouth set in a grim line.

"That he is my restitution. All I see is my first husband when I look at him."

What am I supposed to say? "I'm sorry."

Shaking her head, downs more drink. She gives a shaky laugh, covering the awkward moment. "It's fine. Thank you. What about you?"

I snort. "Nothing." I won't spill my heart to a stranger. I was tipsy before, but now my head is clear. "Know what? I need to leave. I've got an early flight."

"Oh. Good night." She takes a swig of her bottle, still watching the waves.

Weird.

By the time I arrive at my villa, my phone's screen reads 2:06 AM. There's someone by my doorstep. Oh no. I look around suspiciously. What's happening? Ghosts? The figure stretches itself and stands straight.

I laugh. I will always know whose frame that is. "Onahi..." I skip forward, closing the distance between us.

"Hello, Guru." His warmth engulfs me as he wraps his arms around me. Sniffing him, a sense of calm washes over me—he feels like home.

"I told you we'll see later. This isn't later." I giggle as I unlock the door, his nose sniffing the curve of my neck, his arms wrapped around my waist from behind.

"I couldn't wait. I wanted to convince you before you make your final decision."

I chuckle, shaking my head. "What about the agreement we had of you leaving me to make this decision myself?"

He begins trailing noisy kisses on my neck. And I lean into him, smiling. "This is me trying."

"With sex? Seriously?"

"That and the chance to tell you 'I love you' a million times. I hope that influences your decision. I read it works on women a lot."

"Oh."

"Yes. Is it working?"

"You might have to try harder."

We don't make it past the living space. Falling on the couch, with me between his legs, he continues.

"I don't know when. I don't know how. But I know these past few days have taught me a lot about you. About love. About communication." He says each point with noisy kisses on my neck, chin, behind my ear and I giggle. He pauses in his play and his voice turns serious. "About relationships—Flora gave me a speech. And no matter the decision you make, just know that I'll always love you."

I'll always love you too. And the good memories we made on this resort.

Closing my eyes, I bask in his words. He resumes kissing my neck, making slow but urgent moves. His hands travel to my bare shoulders, and I gasp, my eyes shooting open.

"Your hands. They're cold."

"They're fine."

"No, they're not."

He sighs as I extricate myself from him, rushing over to the mini kitchen space. "I'll make tea for you. Just stay over there."

But he doesn't listen. He joins me, taking up my space, clouding my head. "This is why I love you."

"Onahi..." I giggle, shaking my head. "You want to taste the tea first. I'm not the most domestic person. Ever."

He smiles. "It's the thought that matters." He spins me and begins kissing every nook and cranny, making promises I lose track of.

Escape

Sunshine creeps gently on our naked, entwined bodies—the tea things are still on the sink, unmade—with only my padded panties between us. How far we've come and how much we've learned of each other in less than a week is something most people think happens only in movies.

I splay my hands on his tattoo—*I can do all things through Christ who strengthens me*— then flick his nipple.

"Why this?"

"When I was to get the tattoo, it had to be something that reminded me of everything."

"Everything like?"

"Family, faith, work... Love?"

We keep silent, watching the sky turn purplish with the early morning sun.

"I love you."

He heaves a euphoric sigh of relief, closing his eyes. "I thought I would never hear that soon."

Laughing, I tap his chest. "Why? I said that not too long ago."

"We've got limited time, Guru. Want to show me how much you love me?"

I giggle as he tosses the sheet above us. "I need to call my mom..."

Epilogue

San Francisco, USA

Onahi

TARA STARES AT ME AS she receives the cookie that had been thrust in her face by a chubby arm—a sort of peace or friendship offering. She knows I have eyes on her and would not let her out of my sight.

Good girl. Give it back. You don't collect things from boys. Especially random boys in the park.

She shakes her head, moving her chubby feet as she toddles after the boy who had escaped from his parents. The boy turns, surprised, and my big girl thrusts the cookie back in his face. She turns to me, an unsure smile on her face and I wink my approval.

That's a good girl!

She claps, giggling, just like her mother.

"Nahi. What is she doing?"

"I spoke to her via telepathy to give the cookie back."

"You wish."

"But she did."

"Tara, come back to mommy." Lola signals as she sets Gozie down on his stroller.

Lola decided it was good for us as a family to spend time in the neighborhood park and so far, it's not been great for her. First Gozie became cranky immediately we arrived at the park and had to be changed there and then. Tara, decided she wanted to spend time with the kids of the family beside us.

It's been four years of marriage and endless bliss. Carolanne—whom I had never met before then—helped in organizing a surprise intimate marriage proposal two weeks after Lola left the resort. According to her, she had seen how often Lola was smiling after her return from the island and I was a good influence.

In one of our chats before the proposal, Lola told me she had opened up to Carolanne on my transactional way of seeing love, in her curiosity to know what changed with her, and Carolanne had told her I was demiromantic. I had to google it and claim that was me.

Ten weeks later, Lola walked down the beach with me— family and friends in attendance. We said our vows at Twin

Bliss, then honeymooned there for a week before travelling to a safari close by.

"No, Tara..." Lola cries. "Don't do that. Don't put diaper cream in your mouth."

She struggles with Tara until she gets the diaper cream from her, while I chuckle at the scene.

"It's not funny, Onahi. You promised to take care of her while I concentrate on Gozie and filming." She looks at me, then back at Tara, who has found that plucking the grass and putting it in her mouth is more appealing than diaper cream.

"Alright Princess," I swoop in, picking her up, then toss her into the air. "Who wants to watch Bubble Guppies?" She giggles, wriggling. "Uhn? Who wants to watch Bubble Guppies on mommy's phone?"

"Me! Me!"

"That's my girl."

"No one is watching Bubble Guppies. And not on my phone." Lola pats her hair in place using the camera of her phone screen. "We're making a family video, remember? BTS for the Hawaii trip."

It's the first time I'm agreeing to be in one of her lifestyle videos and I never knew so much went into the creation of her shoots—I thought it was only the filming.

She successfully launched her sixth masterclass for small business branding three months ago and after the last batch of classes for the season ended, as promised, we travelled to Hawaii without the kids for one week, leaving them with my sister, Dachi.

Escape

Lola who had insisted on the trip because Gozie never consumed breastmilk, only formula, started whining that she was a terrible mother two days after settling in. She had missed them every day of the trip, but now that we're back, I think she wants to send them back to Dachi.

"Okay. We're set to go."

"And Gozie?"

"Don't worry, I take a cut of him sleeping. It will be cute."

I nod slowly, not understanding why she's so excited to do it, but happy to be a part of it.

"Tara love, please look at the camera... Say hey..."

"Hey..." Tara flashes her teeth, waving chubby fingers, knowing how to act in front of the camera—most of the time.

"Good girl." Her mother's daughter. "Now, on the count of three, everyone says hey guys and I'll kick it off from there. Ready?"

"Sure."

"Tara?" She looks up from her position on my lap, her cute lips pouting. "Did you get that?"

She nods.

"One. Two. Three."

"Hey—" Lola and I say, while Tara says something like, "Water" in her toddler language.

Lola bursts out giggling.

Tara's curious brows scrunch up and in no time, she joins Lola, giggling.

My queens. My happily ever *afters*. They have my heart and I'll do everything in my power to keep them giggling, making wonderful music in my ears

.

About Margaret Adetimehin

Margaret Adetimehin, also known as CAMAA, is a bestselling author and storyteller with a refreshingly unique style that borders between reality and fiction.

As a true ambivert, when she is not reading or writing, she likes to imagine she enjoys traveling, tasty food, and research. She is not married with kids and dogs, but if you follow her on social media @camaa_pearlwrites, you'll be one of the first to know.

She blogs on her website, margaretadetimehin.com

Books by Margaret Adetimehin

Standalone

Nine Hours Till Five

Butterfingered

Flawed Perfections Series

First Impressions

Crossroads

Velvet Tamarind

Romantic Illusions

Twin Bliss Resort Novel

Escape

Lagos Lovin' Series

*Gaga Crazy (Spring 2022)

Anthologies

Hell Hath No Fury, An African Christmas Romance
Anthology

Nights at Club Nova, An Erotic Romance Anthology

*Dates are susceptible to change

CAMAA's Recipe

Let's roast/bake plantain in the oven!

I enjoy this meal and it's so easy to prepare at home. Living in away from Nigeria has thought me not to take street food for granted. Roasting/baking plantain is healthier than frying them.

So, to create yummy roasted plantain that Onahi and his guys, including Lola, enjoyed in Escape, at home, here's all you'll need.

One ripe plantain (with 10% green on the peel so it doesn't end up being too soft—this is my preference.)

- Pre-heat your oven to 350F.

- Cut and peel off the plantain's skin.

- Place plantain on the oven's rack, or if you don't want it getting messy, place it in a tray (this might take longer time to roast.)

- Bake for 20 mins, then turn and bake for another 20 mins.

- Serve with any sauce or dipping of your choice. Best accompanied with fish!

ENJOYED THIS BOOK?

THANK YOU so much for reading *Escape*.

As a reader, your voice has power, and as an independent author, I deeply appreciate your help in spreading the word about my books.

If you've enjoyed *Escape*, please consider leaving a **review on social media and all bookish platforms of your choice.** The review could be as brief as you like. Please avoid spoilers in your review out of courtesy to other readers.

Getting addicted to my stories? Sign up for my newsletters to get previews and updates of ongoing projects bit.ly/margaretadetimehin.com. Stalk me online using linktr.ee/camaa_pearlwrites.

If you have any comments (or find some pesky typos!) please don't hesitate to contact me via info@margaretadetimehin.com.

Find your favorite characters on Instagram: @twinblissnovels

Much Love!

XoxO

Love The Twin Bliss Resort Series?

Be the first to find out about promotions, news, and exclusive content! Follow @blackfemaleauthors on Instagram and Facebook.

Sign up for the Black Female Authors e-newsletter and connect with our book club where you'll find your next favorite African Romance Author on msha.ke/blackfemaleauthors/

Now it's time to read:

Haven by Timi Waters

She's autistic; he's gay. A marriage of convenience seemed like the perfect plan. Until it wasn't.

Tyrell Alagoa, a die-hard romantic, only believes in one thing—loving the right woman. When he found his missing piece in Janelle Lafayette, he wasted no time beginning plans to seduce her. Then he discovered she was not only engaged to be married to Ahmed Gusau, a northern billionaire and influential politician, but Ahmed also had a burning grudge and an unsettled score to even out with him.

Delight by Glory Abah

Destiny has failed in many things, but she is not a quitter. When an opportunity to research a new business idea during an all-expense paid High School reunion to Gobota Island comes her way, she grabs it with both hands. Unfortunately, Rotimi Daramola, her high school nemesis turned popular singer is going to be there.

Rotimi has always loved Destiny, even though she views him as her worst enemy during their high school days. The trip to Gobota Island is an opportunity to win her heart. Will he be able to turn her hate into love?

Euphoria by Jessica Tagbajumi

Duncan Dugo, a charismatic, driven multi businessman with his fingers in many pies across the world. A trauma from his past has him dependent and addicted to things best left alone.

Carmilla Grey, the beautiful, confident, and demanding girlfriend of Duncan desires commitment and stability but her flippant attitude may just have become a thorn to her own needs.

Together, the couple go on an adventure at the luxurious Twin Bliss resort situated in Gobota Islands, but will the tides of the past and Duncan's randy habits pull them apart?

Paradise by Rosemary Okafor

A vacation to twin Bliss Resort is all Muyiwa needs to strip herself of the lies she calls marriage- her celebrity husband is not worth the five years she has already given.

Lucas is not a one-woman man. Getting married to Muyiwa is a mistake he plans to correct soon.

It takes the flirtatious eyes of other men on his wife and the jealousy that almost tears Lucas to pieces, for him to realize that he still loves her so much and has to reclaim her heart at all cost.

Rapture by Mobolaji Olanrewaju

Asher Fabian will trade anything for peace of mind. An unknown force existing long before he was born wants something from him. The solution might lie with a mysterious young woman, who he met through his company's General Manager, Lishan Wilson.

Sappirah Wilson's wants to leave a legacy for her twin brother, Lishan. Asher seemed the perfect candidate for her plan. Can she achieve her plan with the help of the legendary marula?

Sparks fly and there is sizzling passion. But time, fate and an unknown foe from the past become obstacles set to keep them apart forever.

Pleasure by Timi Waters

Izonbou Diete-Spiff is determined to become CEO of Dexter petroleum. It doesn't matter that Dexter already has her elder brother Nengi as prime heir to the throne. Or that she believes her father a misogynist. All she's set to do is prove to him and the board that she's the right fit for Dexter.

Rasheed Adams is on a quest to bring his sister's killer to justice. Between his demanding job at Dexter and his endless search for a killer who rapes and burns women with acid, he believes he has no room for love and romance.

Still, looks linger, touches burn, and both their desires spiral to becoming their worst nightmare.

Ecstasy by L. Leigh

Melody is ready to begin a new chapter in her life, so when a colleague pulls out as the keynote speaker at a prestigious medical conference. She jumps at the opportunity to take over. The organizers grateful for bailing them out, throw in an all-expense paid vacation at the luxurious Twin Bliss Resort.

Femi an award-winning screenwriter and author is looking forward to his time alone at Twin Bliss—securing finance for his next blockbuster project and reflecting on his past. An email arrives which makes him question what he wants, as the trouble and drama he ran from follows him to Twin Bliss.

Acknowledgement

A bear hug with loads of kisses to The Dream for riding with me through the trials of writing this story. The endless calls and sporadic talk of Onahi and Lola, you endured it all, always fueling my thoughts with ideas. This is one of many, and I'm excited to have you with me on this journey.

Special thanks to my Beta reading team—Nelly, Bawa, Princess, Temitope, Charis, and Ruth—who helped fine tune this beautiful story.

To the pioneering authors of the Twin Bliss Resort Novels, I'm ecstatic and grateful that you believed and worked with me on this project. Cheers to many more bestsellers.

L. Leigh, I specially reserved this spot for you and your constant support and belief in me. We're going on girls only vacation soon!

To my growing loyal fan base and supporters, I am immensely grateful for giving me a reason to continually shut the world out and let the voices in my head roam free.

To my family and friends who steadfastly believe in me and where I am headed, I love you!!!

And to you, thanks for being the awesome individual who read this part.

An Excerpt from Gaga Crazy, Lagos Lovin' #1

"Good morning Mr. Benedict," she started as she breezed into the conference room. "Apologies for the delay."

That was a good start. She sounded professional and calculated.

She had not taken her time to process the man before her. If she had enough time, she would have looked closely at him before she moved close to stretch for a handshake.

He looked way younger than she had expected him to be. He looked yummy in a suit and carried himself with polished grace. She was charmed.

The expression on his face was passive as he stood to receive her outstretched hand. She could swear she saw his eyes smiling while he held a bored disinterested look on his face.

Okay, he was a little amused. For the life of her she couldn't fathom why the man would look like he was having fun.

Was it her gown? She casted a quick look down but didn't see anything untoward.

His hands touched hers and she could swear neurons from her head ran down to the spot between her legs.

The sides of his mouth twitched.

He had felt it too. His eyes and hand held hers until she shook herself mentally and pulled away.

"Good morning...?" he asked as she placed her laptop and documents on the table.

"Zoya—Ehizoya Ainabe." She said with a tight smile as she sat on a chair, keeping her distance from the man with one chair between them.

He was dangerous but didn't' look anything like it. She could stare at his face all day, trying to read all the mini expressions. He was too busy to spare unfortunate ones like her macro expressions. He had probably visited the seven world wonders, and nothing fazed him anymore. She wouldn't be fazed by anyone if she had too. But she didn't know if he had and didn't care. Yes, she didn't care. This was business and so would it be.

Next time she might probably discuss this would be with Manir and they would *lol* about it. He probably had experienced something like this before. He was the most sexually experienced human she had as a friend.

He lifted an eyebrow that protected bedroom eyes, "Zoya? Or Ehizoya?"

What had gotten into her? Bedroom eyes? When did she start thinking about body features like that?

She cleared her throat, "Ehizoya, you can call me Zoya."

Available Spring 2022 follow linktr.ee/camaa_pearlwrites for early access and information.

Made in United States
North Haven, CT
06 November 2021